"The Young Entrepreneur's Guide provides the two thing[s] ... need the most to succeed: inspiration and the tools to ach[...]"

—[...] Abney
National Minority Manufacturer of the Year

"The Young Entrepreneur's Guide provides a first-class education for anyone interested in starting a business. It brings to life the excitement of going out on your own in a vivid and practical way."

—William Bygrave
director of the Center for Entrepreneurial Studies at Babson College

"Steve Mariotti has heart—and it shows by the way he understands and communicates business principles to young people in this exciting new startup guide."

—Bonnie Drew
author, *Fast Cash for Kids*

"Without question, Steve Mariotti and NFTE are pioneers and major leaders in the field of youth entrepreneurship education. Reading Steve's insightful and practical book will show you why!"

—Verne C. Harnish
founder of the Young Entrepreneur's Organization

"The best book for young entrepreneurs—the whole process of starting and running a business—from deciding on what kind of business you want to run to creating a successful business plan."

—George C. Hescock
executive vice president, Direct Selling Association

"The Young Entrepreneur's Guide is the bible of self-help. It not only tells the story of many young people who have made the journey to success and self-respect, it shows step-by-step how you can do the same."

—Jack Kemp
former secretary of Housing and Urban Development and
founder of Empower America

"The entrepreneurial spirit is part of what made America great. *The Young Entrepreneur's Guide* is an excellent source for the next generation of young people who want to continue that tradition."

—Bennie L. Thayer
president and CEO, The National Association for the Self-Employed

"No one in America is more experienced working with aspiring entrepreneurs than Steve Mariotti. *The Young Entrepreneur's Guide* is loaded with practical advice and know-how that will benefit young people in pursuit of the entrepreneurial dream."

—Jeffrey A. Timmons
Franklin W. Olin Distinguished Professor of Entrepreneurship, Babson College

The Young Entrepreneur's Guide

To Starting and Running a

Business

The Young Entrepreneur's Guide

Guide

To Starting and Running a

Business

Steve Mariotti

with **Tony Towle** and **Debra DeSalvo**

TIMES BUSINESS

RANDOM HOUSE

To Liz, Charles, and David Koch

ISBN 0-8129-2627-7

Manufactured in the United States of America on acid-free paper

9 8 7 6 5 4 3

CONTENTS

PREFACE

This book is a hands-on, activity-packed guide on how to start and operate a small business. By the time you've finished it, you will have negotiated with a wholesale dealer, opened a bank account, registered your own small business, made flyers and business cards, and sold your product at a flea market. This book will even take you step-by-step through the creation of your own detailed business plan, which will include your projected sales, costs, and profit for an entire year.

Entrepreneurship is an art, not a science. It's the art of creating products and services that your friends and neighbors will want to buy. Like any art, it needs to be practiced and enjoyed. Above all, entrepreneurship should be fun.

The business skills you will learn from this book will greatly improve your ability to enjoy your life—to not only survive, but thrive. Did you know that most of the new jobs created last year were created by small, entrepreneurial businesses? Or that most multibillion-dollar businesses—such as Ford Motor Company and Apple Computer—began as one- or two-person operations?

There are at least three solid reasons for you to study entrepreneurship:

1. *You will be able to pursue your vision.* This book will teach you the skills to make your dream a reality. Here are some of the things you'll learn to do:

- Negotiate.
- Keep accounting records.
- Prepare an income statement.
- Calculate the return on an investment.
- Read *The Wall Street Journal.*
- Write memos and business letters.
- Make sales calls.
- Write a business plan.
- Use the phone as a business tool.

- Prepare a marketing plan.
- Raise venture capital.

2. *You will become a better employee.* Even if you don't dream of starting your own business, the business skills you will learn from this book will make you a valuable person to hire. Your employer will appreciate the fact that you understand how business works.

3. *You will become a better citizen.* You will learn how to be financially independent. You may start a business that will have a positive impact on your community.

Bear in mind as you read this book that *you* have unique knowledge that can be turned into a money-producing business. What is this unique knowledge? It is how well you know your schoolmates, your friends, and your neighbors. You know better than anyone else what they need and what they would want to buy. What problem might they have that your service business could solve? What product can't they find that you could sell to them? Start thinking this way, and you're already on your way toward becoming an entrepreneur!

This is not a hard book to read or understand, and I hope you will enjoy learning from it. The basics of business are easy to apply to starting your own small venture. Your business will also help others. As a member of the new generation of entrepreneurs, it is up to you to do well and do good. Your business can help rebuild your community.

I wrote this book, which is a distillation of every entrepreneurship course I've ever taught, so that young people everywhere can learn about the economic system and apply entrepreneurship to their lives. To keep topics clear and manageable, terminology and usage have been slightly modified on occasion. Such modifications have been made only after extensive consultation and field testing. They are in keeping with my belief that instruction in how to start and operate a small business will make a young person more independent, more employable, and a better citizen.

I firmly believe there should be a national effort to teach every child the fundamentals of starting his or her own business. I have found that inner-city children have no problem learning MBA concepts. If these young people can learn how to start and operate small businesses, so can young people from rural areas or suburbs.

One of my great concerns, however, is that our complex tax code and bewildering array of permits and licenses are dispiriting barriers to entrepreneurship. High tax rates make it very difficult for poor people to accumulate enough capital to start their own businesses. Would-be entrepreneurs are also discouraged by red tape. A streamlining of the business-licensing process and a radical overhaul of the tax code would encourage entrepreneurs to enter the marketplace. So would the establishment of special enterprise zones in impoverished areas.

If I can ever be of help to you in any way or if you are interested in purchasing additional educational products, please write to me:

Steve Mariotti
National Foundation for Teaching Entrepreneurship, Inc.
120 Wall Street, 29th Floor
New York, New York 10005

The Young Entrepreneur's Guide

To Starting and Running a

Business

PROLOGUE

MY PATH TO ENTREPRENEURSHIP

The Young Entrepreneur's Guide to Starting and Running a Business is for *any* young person who wants to start a business, no matter what his or her ethnic or economic background may be. The book's roots can be traced to the years I have spent teaching entrepreneurship to inner-city youth and, since 1987, presiding over the National Foundation for Teaching Entrepreneurship, Inc. (NFTE, pronounced "nifty"). As a public school teacher in some of New York City's meanest neighborhoods, I had discovered that even my most difficult students could successfully start and develop their own businesses. They benefited greatly from hands-on experience of the economic system and the boost it gave to their self-esteem. Entrepreneurship training seemed to foster a sense of vision and personal responsibility for their future, even in young people born into poverty and violence.

From 1982 to 1988, I worked as a business, math, and special education teacher in New York City public schools, in such notorious neighborhoods as Bedford-Stuyvesant in Brooklyn and "Fort Apache" in the South Bronx. My experiences led me—at first subtly and then increasingly more directly—to introduce entrepreneurial principles into the standard academic curriculum. I could see firsthand that, as a group, inner-city youth had no idea, or a completely distorted notion, of how our economic system worked. This was the root cause of their powerlessness to function within that system. Over time, I became more and more excited by the positive results I was having in my classes. I also realized that what I was doing could be applied in many other communities.

These perceptions led me, seven years later, to leave the public school system and found NFTE, a nonprofit organization whose mission was, and is, to bring basic business and entrepreneurial skills to disadvantaged young people. I became convinced that entrepreneurship can help these young people to achieve financial independence and that, by doing so, they can improve their lives and the economic lives of their neighborhoods. These goals are now being realized nationwide, as well as abroad.

STARTING MY OWN BUSINESS

I came to this vision by an indirect route. I graduated from the University of Michigan's School of Business in 1977 with an MBA. In graduate school, as a result of a scholarly paper published in the prestigious economics journal *Public Choice,* I won a scholarship to study Economics at The Institute for Humane Studies. I was one of twenty economists selected. Our reward was four months of pure economic theory, discussion, and research under the guidance of F. A. Hayek, the Nobel Prize winner for Economics in 1974. At the end of the summer, armed with a basic knowledge of Economics, I went to work as a financial analyst for Ford Motor Company, where my youthful enthusiasm and knack for international finance earned me the nickname "Stevie Wonder." I had a lot of responsibility, considering my age, and I got an inside look at how one of America's largest corporations operates. But I also learned that infighting and intramural politics are often part of the unofficial structure of a large business. This environment contributed to my decision that the corporate world was not for me. I moved to New York and tried the other end of the business spectrum. I started my own small sole proprietorship, an import–export firm. That was a revelation. At Ford, I was near the bottom of the corporate hierarchy. In New York, I was my own boss. It didn't matter that I didn't have high capitalization or thousands of employees. Being an independent businessperson had an immediate beneficial effect on my self-esteem and outlook.

But then I learned another of life's lessons; this one was about living in a large city. One evening in 1981, while jogging on the Lower East Side, I was approached by a group of kids who demanded ten dollars. I was wearing a jogging suit and was carrying very little money. They roughed me up and humiliated me. Afterward, the entrepreneur in me wondered why these kids would mug someone for a few dollars when they could make more money running a small business together.

Becoming another urban statistic was a traumatic experience. I had constant and painful flashbacks of the experience which soon became more painful than the experience itself. The memories took on a life of their own and I knew I had a serious problem. My strategy was to confront my fears directly. My solution was to become a public school teacher in the kinds of neighborhoods that the young people who had mugged me called home. I wanted to be assigned to the "worst" areas, to test myself, and the school administration was happy to oblige: I was assigned to Boys & Girls High School, in the Bedford-Stuyvesant area of Brooklyn. Although I had asked for it, I was a little nervous. Boys & Girls had recently been the subject of such headlines as: "Teacher's Hair Set on Fire at Troubled Boys & Girls High"; "Teacher Beaten and Dragged Down Stairs at Boys & Girls"; and "Principal Brings Calm to Chaotic City School."

Although the school had only opened in 1976 and had cost $30 million to construct, Boys & Girls had quickly established itself as the worst school in the New York City public school system, and perhaps in the country. Primarily as a result of the negative publicity, seventy-two teachers simply refused to report for duty at Boys & Girls—they preferred to be unemployed. The dropout rate at the school quickly reached 50 percent. In 1978, the New York State Board of Regents took the unprecedented step of putting the entire school on probation.

BECOMING A TEACHER

My strategy appeared to be working. Within an hour of arriving at the school, I began to view the kids with less animosity and fear. I also knew that I would like teaching; I was sure I had found a vocation. Reality set in quickly. There were fifty-nine students in my first remedial math class—a number far too high, in the best of circumstances, to teach effectively. There were only forty-two seats and thirty-nine books. If 76 percent of the class showed up, I'd be in trouble.

"Are you the new teacher?" a gigantic youth asked. At first I thought he was a security guard. He turned out to be nineteen-year-old Robert, whose math was at the seventh-grade level—and this was a class of seniors.

"Yes I am. My name is Mr. Mariotti."

"OK, Mr. Manicotti."

"Hey Robert, where did you get the midget?" yelled out the next student coming through the door.

"Sit down, please," I said, trying to keep my voice as low-pitched as possible.

"Who says?"

"I do. I'm the teacher."

"You're a shorty—what's it like being a midget?"

"Please sit down, now."

"Hey, he thinks he's a bad homeboy."

"Chill out, teach, ain't nobody hurting you."

"Please sit down."

"Bust the move, teach."

"Nice suit, homeboy. Too bad you didn't get it in the right size."

There were now forty-six students in the room, which meant that four had to stand and seven didn't have books. They were actually quiet as I gave my standard speech and wrote my class rules on the board. I closed with a plea for them to learn basic math because without it they'd be embarrassed in later life and would find it difficult not only to find a job but to function effectively in their personal lives. I then passed out the books (as far as they would go) and gave a basic diagnostic test. I found out that 20 percent of the class didn't even have pencils or paper, and I had to go in search of supplies. I gave the test to each of my five classes, with disheartening results as to the scores. For the most part, the students were relatively well behaved.

This appearance of good behavior in my remedial classes turned out to be an illusion as the days went on. When I started my lesson on fractions (only a third of the class could add ⅓ and ⅙), I soon realized everyone was talking—to everyone else. Two girls in the back of the room were showing each other new dance steps. The boys in the back rows were talking louder than I was. "Please be quiet," I said calmly. No effect. "Please be quiet!" I yelled. Still no effect. Then I just sat down, hoping I would shame them into silence. Instead, they accelerated their conversation. After a few minutes, I continued the lesson for the five or six students who were paying attention as I tried to be heard over the noise.

LOSING CONTROL OF MY CLASS

The situation got worse. I began to lose control on almost a daily basis. One student actually set fire to the back of another's coat—the student with the coat was as astonished as I was. I ordered the arsonist out of the class in a rage, and he was expelled the same day. On another occasion, I was locked out of my eighth-period class. The students would not open the door, for what seemed like an eternity. Finally, one of the girls took pity on me and opened it, just as I was going to admit total defeat and find a security guard.

In each of my three remedial classes, there was a group of six or seven kids whose behavior was so disruptive that I had to stop the class every five minutes or so to get them to quiet down. In my third-period class, I threw all the boys out. Ironically, these young men provided me with the valuable insight that set me on the road to teaching entrepreneurship. I took them out to dinner and asked them why they had acted so badly in class. They said my class was boring, that I had nothing to teach them.

Didn't anything I'd said in class interest them? I asked. One fellow spoke up: I had caught his attention when I had discussed my import–export business. He rattled off various figures I'd mentioned in class, calculated my profit margin, and concluded that my business was doing well. I was dazzled to find such business smarts in a student the public schools had labeled borderline retarded. This was my first inkling that something was wrong not only with my teaching, but also with the standard remedial curriculum.

In my eighth-period class, I was too afraid of the boys to throw them out. The most disruptive boys were Mills, Braddock, and Morrow. They seemed to really hate me, and I didn't like them much, either. They would disrupt the class by making animal noises, cursing me viciously, and treating their fellow classmates with great hostility. I would calmly threaten them with failure. I tried not to lose a joking manner, which, it turned out, they saw as a sign of weakness. One day I knew I was off to a particularly bad start when I sat in my seat and felt something stick to the back of my jacket. I got up, looked at my chair, and saw a large wad of gum. The class roared. Then, seeing the hurt and disgust on my face, they fell silent. A student named Therese came up to me and said: "You all right, Mr. Mariotti, you have gum on your back; let me help you." She pulled off as much of it as possible. I tried to make it humorous: "Judging from the amount of gum, I'd say it came from someone with a big mouth." No one laughed.

I tried to start a new subject, decimals, but asking them to learn something new at this point just made them anxious. A radio suddenly blared from the back of the room.

Me: "Please turn off the radio."

Ramon: "It's not the radio, it's the P.A."

The noise level soared, and Mills and Braddock got out of their seats and began dancing at the front of the room. The rest of the class began to clap in unison. I ran to the back of the room and threatened Ramon: "Turn it off or I'm going to fail you." By this time, Ramon was dancing too and totally ignored me. Mills got up on my desk and continued to dance.

"Turn off the goddamned radio, you twerp!" I yelled. Someone, imitating me, yelled back, "No swearing, Mr. Mariotti." I grabbed the radio and went to the front of the room. To my relief, Mills got off my desk and sat back down in his seat, cursing me as he went. I could feel my face twitching. "Look, Mariotti's having a nervous breakdown!" said another troublemaker. "You can't control this class, Mariotti, because you don't have juice," shouted Mills. "Shut up and sit!" I shouted back. "Continue with the assignment."

I was shaking as Nicole came up to my desk and asked, "Can you show me how to do this problem?" I began to show her when all of a sudden I was hit in the eye with a spitball. I felt another wave of anger. "Who threw that?" I yelled. The class was again in total chaos. Mills ran up to the front of the room, grabbed the American flag off the wall, and, holding it like a spear, started to pretend to poke me with it. He then raised it up as if to throw it. "Put the flag down," I demanded. Abbott, a Bermudian boy, came up from behind and grabbed Mills around the chest. I moved forward, took the flag, and put it back on the wall. I walked out of the class and, as I did so, was hit in the back with a wad of paper.

I didn't know how to deal with the situation. I wanted to walk out of the school and call it quits. After a minute or two, I realized that I couldn't do that. As I stepped into the hallway to regain my composure, I thought about my dinner with the young men from my third-period class. They had said I was boring—except when I talked about business, about money. After about three minutes, I walked back into the classroom and, with no introductory comments, started a mock sales pitch, hypothetically selling the class my own watch. I enumerated the benefits of the watch, explaining why the students should purchase it from me at the low price of only six dollars. I noticed immediately that as soon as I started to talk about money, and how to make money by selling something, they actually quieted down and became interested. I didn't know it at the time, but this incident, born of desperation, pointed me toward my real vocation—teaching entrepreneurship to inner-city kids.

When I had their attention, I moved from the sales talk into a conventional arithmetic lesson: if you buy a watch at three dollars and sell it for six, you make three dollars of profit, or 100 percent. Without realizing it, I was touching on the business fundamental of buy low/sell high, and on the more advanced concept of return on investment.

DEVELOPING STRENGTH

That evening, I realized I would have to start getting tough—no more Mr. Nice Guy. I even practiced my expression in the mirror. I decided

I had to come to my classes ready to be instantly angry. I knew I had to stay very alert. I had the courage and awareness of a man with his back to the wall. I couldn't let a few of these students make me lose my livelihood. I kept thinking of Samuel Johnson's remark: "Nothing focuses a man's mind so much as when he's about to be hanged." Unless I could bring my classes under control, I was of little value to students who were actually there to learn—and many of them were. Not only would I be tough, I decided, but I would begin to develop a curriculum around my students' obvious interest in business.

They noticed the difference right away.

Wanda: "What's wrong with you today?"

Tanya: "Why you busting our chops, Mr. Steve?"

Tawana: "Why you no smile, Homeboy?" The behavior of all my classes immediately improved. The noise level declined from the roar of Niagara Falls to the murmur of a fashionable café.

Finally, the eighth period arrived. This was the class whose behavior had precipitated my change. I got to the classroom early, cleaned up the debris, and straightened the chairs. By the time I'd finished, there were still no students. I stood at the door, awaiting their arrival. They sensed immediately that something was different, that I had been pushed too far. Some said a quiet "Hi," as they walked in. On the blackboard, I had written:

DO NOW: SIT DOWN.
TAKE OUT A PIECE OF PAPER. PREPARE FOR QUIZ.

The late bell rang, and I locked the door and passed out the daily assignment. About five minutes later, I heard the telltale profanity from down the hall. The students looked at me; I could sense their apprehension. The gang that had humiliated me on the previous day had arrived. They kicked at the closed door and I felt a sudden burst of adrenalin. It was them or me.

I opened the door. Mills tried to come into the room but I put my hand on his shoulder and pushed him back. Had I assaulted him? At that moment, I didn't care. I felt the elation of being right.

"Hey, man, what you doin' pushing me?"

I said nothing.

"What's wrong with you?" Braddock asked with genuine curiosity.

"We didn't mean nothing yesterday," Morrow muttered. Mills was just watching intently. I knew I was going to win.

"I want an apology. I want a *written* apology."

"We didn't do nothing to you."

Morrow tried unsuccessfully to get past me into the room. "I want an apology and it must be written," I said calmly and coldly.

Braddock's protest, "Nobody hurt you," was followed by a stream of profanity.

"You swear at me again and you'll be thrown out of this school so fast you won't even know it, you little twerp," I said, with no emotion.

"What's wrong, Mariotti? No one touched you."

I changed strategies and began to speak more forcefully. "You jerks ruined the class last Thursday. You kept your own people from learning anything. What kind of idiots are you?"

"Mariotti, chill, man," someone said. "No one wants to hurt you, man."

"Shut up, you little wimp," I continued over their noises of astonishment. "Understand this: I'm here to help you learn. If you aren't interested, don't come to class. I'm trying to teach math here. Don't get in my way."

"Mr. Mariotti, are you all right?" It was Lorraine, one of the students in the classroom. The whole class was now listening to this exchange. I ignored her.

"If you don't know basic mathematics. . . ." I caught myself; I was ruining it with syrup. "If you ever disrupt my class again, you'll never get in this room again and not in this school either. Do you understand me?"

No one spoke.

"All right," Mills said. They started to come into the room.

"No, I want a written apology from each of you. Here's paper and a pencil. Write apologies and when you're finished slide them under the door." I closed the door and walked back to my desk. The whole exchange had taken only five or six minutes. The class had obviously overhead everything. They were awaiting the outcome, just as I was. "Please get back to work," I said.

I could hardly believe it: one by one, the four pieces of paper were slipped under the door. I waited a minute and then went over to pick them up. I felt the elation of victory as I read the apologies, but by now I'd learned to show no emotion. I went to the door, opened it, and said: "Please take your seats."

The behavior of all my classes improved markedly after this episode. Mills and Braddock, particularly, showed improved conduct. I had them sit in the front of the class with me while I did problems on the blackboard. At first, they were embarrassed by the special treatment; Braddock asked me to keep my voice down as I was explaining to him what "percentage" meant. As I'd suspected, these two kids knew *no* math and their embarrassment had prompted much of their behavior.

TEACHING ENTREPRENEURSHIP

Over the next several weeks, the classes were orderly enough to give me time to think about how I might teach better, and how I could get these kids to learn basic mathematics. When I went to class one day, I had the students make change in a retailer/customer scenario. The "retailer" had to make ten correct transactions—or lose the turn if he or she made a mistake. Nobody wanted to make a mistake.

This game treated math as a practical reality rather than an abstraction. More subtly, it put the students in the position of a shopkeeper—an entrepreneur. What had begun as an intuition slowly developed into a certainty: whenever I could manage to focus a lesson on some phase of entrepreneurial business, I had the students' attention. I began to do this consciously, using all my ingenuity to get across the bedrock principles of business: buy low, sell high; keep good records. I wanted these young people to appreciate the principles of free enterprise: (1) ownership and (2) honest relations with other human beings through the rational self-interest of voluntary trade.

Next, I had the students make mock sales calls (later, when I had the funds, the sales calls were videotaped for peer review). This game taught them that, to sell something to somebody, they had to be civil and polite. They had to *convince* the customers to buy from them; they could not coerce them.

I found *The Wall Street Journal* to be an important teaching tool. When I was teaching at Boys & Girls, I had to remind myself that I was discussing the *Journal* in the most infamous high school in New York. In one class, I ended up supplying each student with a daily copy at my own expense. I held contests in which each kid would pick a stock and track it, and I offered prizes for the biggest gain. I also pointed out that the CEOs of America's largest companies, and indeed everybody who was anybody in the business world, was reading, that morning, the very same newspaper that they were.

Other teachers, and administrators, were constantly urging me to stress reading, writing, math, communications skills, and "good citizenship." I found that approach to be nonproductive, even counterproductive. When these young people got interested in starting their own businesses, they *wanted* to know how to write and add; they knew they needed these skills to conduct business effectively. They also knew that politeness and respect for the people with whom they were doing business were essential.

THE IMPACT OF
ENTREPRENEURSHIP EDUCATION

Knowledge of the principles of business modified the behavior of these kids. Entrepreneurship changed the structure of their psyches. Maurice, one of my students at Boys & Girls, although not one of the worst behaved in my classes, was still angry, belligerent, mean, and threatening. He took to salesmanship, however, which he first learned about through role-playing games in class. He became so good that I encouraged him to make actual sales. He invested a small sum in a dozen pairs of sunglasses, which I helped him to buy wholesale. As he began to make a small profit through selling the glasses, his whole facial demeanor changed. Instead of being angry, he was conversational and polite. He had learned to assert himself nonaggressively through the selling process. He had a unique knowledge of his own community, and his familiarity with his local "market" led him to pick those styles of sunglasses his peers would want to buy. By the end of the school year, he was making about $60 a week in his spare time through sales. The increase in his confidence and self-esteem was incalculable.

It became apparent to me that many of these young people had a natural aptitude for entrepreneurship. Their challenging lives encouraged independence of spirit, toughness, unselfconsciousness, and a natural ability in salesmanship. They were comfortable with risk and ambiguity. These same qualities—along with difficulty in doing well in a traditional, structured environment—characterized many great American entrepreneurs such as Henry Ford and Conrad Hilton. I found that the negative characteristics of my students, when channeled into entrepreneurial activities, became positives. The benefits they reaped went far beyond the areas of education and business and academic subjects.

Tawana, for example, had incredibly low self-esteem—until she started her own manicuring business at home after school. She was a little half-hearted about it at first, but as she began giving out the flyers and business cards we had made in class, she could see that she had a real business. She did manicures in her home for seven dollars a session. As her business increased, seemingly unrelated, her behavior changed. Previously, Tawana had rarely changed her clothes. Now, she showed a marked improvement in personal hygiene and in her ability to make friends. Her school attendance rose from an average of one and a half days a week to the whole week. School was where her potential clients were, but she also became a better student.

Tawana went from being a social outcast to having a strong and healthy ego. For Tawana, entrepreneurship was an avenue, a linkage to other human beings. Like Maurice, she knew her local market intimately. She knew which girls would be likely customers. The $40 or so a week she earned was her lifeline to interacting with other human beings in a mutual bond of self-interest. For Tawana and Maurice, business skills had also, imperceptibly, become social skills.

Other social behavior could change, too. I eventually observed that of the girls in my classes who became interested in entrepreneurship, fewer became pregnant or got married and dropped out of school. When the female students became economically literate, they were not so quick to tie themselves down with children at an early age. I gave the girls in one of my classes a pre- and post-test on their estimates of the yearly cost of being a mother. Pre-test, they thought, on average, that a baby cost $142 a year. Post-test, the average estimate was $5,600. One of my students, Sonya, seemed to have *only* sexual relationships with other human beings, particularly the boys in the school. When she developed her own little business doing her classmates' hair (both boys and girls), it enabled her to communicate in a nonsexual way. She had something else to talk about, something that permitted her to have relationships without necessarily becoming sexually involved.

Running their own businesses helped my students make better decisions in their personal lives because it taught them about delayed gratification. The primary act of business—buy low, sell high—takes place over time, with money as a reward. As a result, people seem to make better decisions in general after starting a business. Many times I saw a student's time preference (i.e., how he or she looked at the future) expand right before my eyes.

I was eager to test my entrepreneurial theories in a new environment, so even though I had survived my baptism by fire, so to speak, at Boys & Girls (which is a much better school these days, led by Principal Frank Mickens), I put in for an end-of-term transfer. I wanted to experience other schools in the system. I also wanted to test out my entrepreneurial theories in a new environment. My eighth-period class and I had been through hell together—an experience I would never forget. Yet, when I made the announcement that I would be leaving soon, there was no noticeable reaction.

But when I walked into my last class, there was food waiting for me in the front of the room, including a basket of fried chicken. On my desk were two wrapped gifts: a bottle of cologne and a record, *The Best of the Temptations*. Covering the entire blackboard in huge chalk letters was the message:

GOODBYE HOMEBOY.
FROM THE ENTREPRENEURS OF BOYS AND GIRLS HIGH SCHOOL.

Underneath were the signatures of my students.

My last day at Boys & Girls was more affecting than I would have thought possible just a short time before. I was touched by the outpouring of emotion. My class gave me a card saying I was the best teacher they'd ever had. In my business math class, they applauded and made so much noise that my supervisor came in, thinking there was a fight. Three more students came up and said that I was the best teacher they had ever had. I was particularly gratified when Braddock told me: "I've decided to start my own business."

SPREADING THE MESSAGE

In the series of schools I was subsequently assigned to, spreading my "entrepreneurial message" began to require more and more subterfuge. I was teaching the kids the subjects I was supposed to teach, but it took all my ingenuity to use an entrepreneurial or business context—which was the only way to keep up their interest. It wasn't until I was assigned to Jane Addams Vocational High School, in the "Fort Apache" section of the South Bronx, that a principal, Pat Black, understood the potential value of what I was talking about. She gave me permission to teach a class in entrepreneurship. It was an immediate success and soon became the South Bronx Entrepreneurial Project. This allowed me to be out in the open. Instead of disguising entrepreneurial principles, I could offer what I considered to be a crash course in capitalism and free enterprise to young people who didn't even know that the United States operated in a free-market economic system. One-third of the kids in my class at Jane Addams did not know that the United States was a capitalist society; they thought it was communist!

Such concepts as the free-market system aside, what my students could see clearly was that if they had their own businesses, the amount of money they could make would depend on their own hard work and how they conducted themselves. In other words, they realized that information they might have formerly considered irrelevant (reading and math), abstract (economics), or facile (advice on how to dress or behave) could profoundly affect their lives.

Entrepreneurship gave them a sense of importance and a seriousness of purpose—after all, they were the presidents of their own companies, however modest. I found that there were virtually no business concepts that could not be made comprehensible to my students.

Even such "dry" business topics as the balance sheet provided unexpected insights. My students seemed to think that the local retailers, who were mostly Asian, made somewhere between fifty and ninety cents profit on every dollar. This notion contributed greatly to a resentment based on race. When they discovered that these retailers, who worked long hours, made closer to four or five cents per sale, my students looked at such businesses, and the people who ran them, very differently.

THE CORE CURRICULUM

Eventually, my core curriculum came to include such subjects as: supply and demand; entrepreneurship as the fulfilling of consumer needs; the invention process, including patents, copyrights, and trademarks; cost/benefit analysis; business ethics; record keeping; the present and future value of money; business communication, with an emphasis on concise memo writing and speaking on the phone; debt-versus-equity financing; venture capital; balance sheets and income statements; franchising; the advantages and disadvantages of sole proprietorships, partnerships, and corporations; the production/distribution chain; how to register one's business; time management and goal setting; quality and customer service; negotiation strategies; advertising and marketing; and, of course, how to make a sales call.

I approached basic writing skills through the business memo. My students were put at ease because I was teaching them simple business communication, not literary or academic writing. I would assign memos that were due the next day, on a wide variety of topics. The main thrust was conciseness. I refused to accept any memo that had more than 300 words, and I announced that I would give an A or F grade after only one reading. The memo had to be clear. If I didn't understand it, it got the F.

Several years later, three of my students were in the wrong place at the wrong time (near a youth who was shooting off a gun) and were picked up by the police. While being held in a detention cell together, out of desperation, they composed a memo that was so simple and so convincing that they were released! I was both proud and horrified.

The incident reminded me of what my pupils were exposed to when they weren't in school. However, if they had dealt with the police in their previous verbal style of grunts, monosyllables, and profanity, the unfortunate event would not have had a happy ending.

Class trips and outside activities were important. Field trips helped demystify the world outside their neighborhoods. When I took my eighth-period students to a flea market in Greenwich Village, a new world opened up. The trip inspired them to want to sell their own merchandise. This led me to develop a two-part activity: my classes negotiated for inexpensive merchandise with wholesalers, and resold it a day or two later at a local flea market. Careful records were kept, the students designed their own posters for the flea market, and I made sure that everyone got business cards.

Later, I took my classes to the New York Stock Exchange, a trip made more meaningful by their familiarity with *The Wall Street Journal*. I found a willing banker and took classes to the bank, where every student opened an account. We toured local businesses owned by entrepreneurs from the same ethnic background as that of the majority of the class, and we registered the students' businesses at the County Clerk's office.

I discovered another important inspirational tool: emphasis on inventions as a route to entrepreneurial financial independence. I was able to tell the students about many overlooked inventions by African Americans, such as the automatic shoe-lasting machine, the gas mask, and the toggle harpoon. Invention contests set their imagination free and were a lot of fun.

A few years ago, one of our students, age 13, designed a device to protect the ears from being burned when using curling irons. Her invention was presented in conjunction with a contest held during an NFTE entrepreneurship course she was taking at the Boys' and Girls' Clubs of Newark. She had a patent pending for several years. At Jane Addams Vocational High School, another student came up with a less-than-practical idea for a kind of metal detector that could be worn while walking on the street and provide a warning that someone might be carrying a gun. Inventions are often conceptualized to solve real problems. He was trying to devise a way to survive in the ghetto, but his idea didn't work. Years later, I heard he had been shot.

The culmination of the curriculum was the writing of a brief but realistic business plan for a real business. I had each student present his or her plan before the rest of the class. Later, I learned that by bringing in outside judges—a local businessperson, an academic, someone from the media—I could get great publicity for the program and our mission.

This coverage gave the kids a further sense that what they were doing could matter to the outside world.

By 1986, even though the principal at Jane Addams was amenable to my programs, I had realized that public school systems are fundamentally bureaucratic and anti-entrepreneurial. This attitude was underscored one day when an evaluator came to observe my class of eighteen dropouts. The fact that, a week before the end of the school year, I had a class of sixteen students—and one of the absentees was legitimately out sick—was unusual in itself. The evaluation focused, however, on "excessive role playing." The evaluator said the class had "too much emphasis" on entrepreneurship, and class discussions were "too money-oriented."

With each passing year, it became clearer to me that my vocation and mission were not just to teach in the inner cities, but to teach entrepreneurship there. I came to believe, very strongly, that entrepreneurship was a more promising way out of the economic dead end of these neighborhoods than entry-level jobs, or more welfare, or other wasteful and unproductive government spending. Although I had reached about 1,800 inner-city kids between 1982 and 1986 in a number of schools in Brooklyn, Manhattan, and the Bronx, it seemed that to continue this work on the scale these programs deserved, I would have to become an entrepreneur again. My "product" would be entrepreneurship itself.

FOUNDING NFTE

I left the public school system in 1988 and founded NFTE. We operate programs in fourteen American cities, and have licensed a program in Scotland to Scottish Enterprises. We are planning to start programs elsewhere in Europe and in Africa. Based on our empirical observations, we believe our students have, on average, a business formation rate of about 5–10 percent and weekly sales of $60. The adult African American business-formation rate is 1.5 percent, the Hispanic average is 1.0 percent, and the Caucasian American rate is 6 percent. The empirical results of our programs—improved self-esteem, less teen pregnancy, lower dropout rate, business formation—are presently the subject of a long-term study by Dr. Andrew Hahn of Brandeis University. We have run a combination business camp for youth/training camp for teachers for two summers now, called NFTE University at Babson College, the nation's leading entrepreneurship education institution, in Babson Park, Massachusetts. We also run business camps at Wharton School of Business, Columbia University, and other colleges.

I'm very proud of NFTE's leadership role in creating a national movement that is teaching entrepreneurship to at-risk youth. Dozens of nationally known foundations and hundreds of major corporations and entrepreneurs are now funding youth entrepreneurship programs based on our paradigm. I am more convinced than ever that the way to turn around the economic decay of America's inner cities is through teaching its young people entrepreneurship. I think we should recognize that a significant portion of the standard curriculum as it is taught in most public school systems does not work for inner-city children. Not all entrepreneurship students will end up owning their own businesses as a lifelong vocation, but one of our most significant findings over the years is that graduates of our programs do make better employees. They are better qualified for anything they eventually do because they have a broad understanding and knowledge of business in general. They understand how the economic system works. They are better able to join the mainstream because they know how to be participants in our society instead of feeling they are merely some of its victims.

There are *many* NFTE success stories, some of which you'll read in this book, but I have also been cheered by the success of some of my students from my first year of teaching. I kept in touch with Maurice until about 1990. The last I heard, he was a sales representative for a computer company and was moving to the Midwest. Tawana, who was probably on her way to having children out of wedlock and going on welfare before she learned about entrepreneurship, was still operating her hairstyling business in 1989. Mills and I stayed in contact. He was able to graduate from high school and credited this to his interest in entrepreneurship. He had become very good at math and could do spreadsheets better than I could. After graduation, he got a job as an assistant manager at a flea market, married, and was raising a family. His personal hygiene, which had been outrageously bad, was now very good and he had excellent self-esteem.

Around 1991, I also ran into Therese. I was on my way to the subway. Therese, now twenty-four, was vending on the street (she had a city license) clothes that she had purchased wholesale. She said that when she had enough money she was going to rent a storefront and would eventually own several stores. She was attending Bronx Community College at night and had even gotten her mother interested in business. She had kept the handouts I used to distribute in my classes and used these to help her run her business. "Thanks to you, Mr. Mariotti," she said, "I have always been able to take care of myself and make a living." I have never received a higher compliment.

EVERYONE LIVES BY SELLING SOMETHING

1

WHY AMERICA NEEDS ENTREPRENEURS

> Everyone lives by selling something.
> —Robert Louis Stevenson (1850–1894)
> Scottish author

THE DIFFERENCE BETWEEN AN ENTREPRENEUR AND AN EMPLOYEE

Many people dream of owning their own business and being their own boss, with the prospect of unlimited earnings. Entrepreneurship *is* the American dream. But most people hesitate to take the plunge. Like them, you may worry that you don't have enough money, time, or experience to start and operate your own small business.

Michelle* insists that there is always time to start your own business, even if you're a single mother *and* a full-time college student. Michelle should know, because at 19 she started her own business while attending college and caring for her daughters, Angela, 3, and Erica, 18 months, and her newborn son, Kristian. Before she started her clothing resale company, À La Mode, Michelle knew nothing about running a business and had very little money. When I met Michelle, I thought she had tremendous natural elegance and poise, but it was clear that she was living a difficult life as a single mother of three children. Today, she's a successful **entrepreneur.**

---

*All stories are the experiences of actual NFTE students.

Like Michelle, most Americans earn money by working in business. **Business** is the buying and selling of products and services in order to make money. Someone who earns a living by working for someone else's business is an **employee** of that business.

There are many different kinds of employees. At Ford Motor Company, for instance, some employees build the cars, some sell the cars, and some manage the company. But they all have one thing in common—they do not *own* the business, they *work* for others who do.

Entrepreneurs, in contrast, are both owners and employees. An entrepreneur is responsible for the success or failure of his or her business.

Buy Low, Sell High—
The Key to Business Success

Michelle loved fashionable clothes, but she lived in New Bedford, Massachusetts. The stores in New Bedford didn't always sell the latest fashions, and, when they did, they charged high prices. During an entrepreneurship class conducted by the National Foundation for Teaching Entrepreneurship, Inc. (NFTE), Michelle took a trip to Manhattan's wholesale clothing district. This visit gave Michelle her business idea. A **wholesaler** is a business that purchases products in bulk from the manufacturer and sells smaller quantities to **retailers.** Retailers buy small quantities from wholesalers and sell single items to customers. At each step along the road from the manufacturer to the customer, the price of the product increases.

Michelle was surprised that wholesale prices were *much* lower than the prices of clothing in stores. Michelle knew there were, in her hometown, many young women like herself who would love to buy the latest fashions at reasonable prices. During her visit to the wholesale district, Michelle learned that all she needed to do to be able to buy from a wholesaler was to apply for a sales tax identification number. Anyone can apply for a sales tax number by calling the state sales tax office and requesting an application for a sales tax number. After the application is filled out and returned, the number will be assigned.

Michelle decided to buy clothes wholesale and mark them up for resale to her neighbors. She invited a dozen friends to her house for a clothes-buying party. If she sold them out of her home, Michelle reasoned, she could offer the latest styles at lower prices than the stores in her town were charging. Michelle had stumbled on the key to business success: Buy low, sell high. Before she visited the wholesale district again, she collected size information from her twelve friends and asked them whether they had any special requests.

Today, Michelle visits the wholesale district once a month and buys several hundred dollars' worth of clothes. There are many wholesalers in Manhattan, but Michelle has developed good relationships with a few whose products she really likes.

Michelle was afraid she would have to buy bulk quantities in order to get the wholesalers to sell to her, but she found that most of them are comfortable selling her as few as two or three items. They like dealing with Michelle because she doesn't ask for credit. She pays in full when she makes her purchases.

Michelle resells the clothes for around twice the wholesale price she paid. Sales are made from her home or on visits to customers' houses. Michelle's friends and neighbors are delighted to have a less expensive alternative to the local mall. Her customers also enjoy shopping in a more intimate setting.

As Michelle says, "Who would ever think a teenage mother with three children could ever own her own business and graduate from college?" After she finishes college, Michelle plans to open her own clothing boutique. She hopes her success will spark a revival of small businesses in her community.

Chart 1 shows three basic principles that are key to your business success.

KEYSTONING

In her entrepreneurship class, Michelle learned about **keystoning**—buying a product wholesale and then selling it for double the wholesale price. Most entrepreneurs try to keystone. It's a good rule of

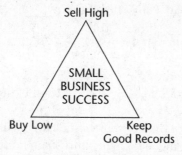

Chart 1   Buy Low, Sell High, Keep Good Records

thumb for covering your costs and making a nice profit. Like Michelle, many young entrepreneurs buy products such as lingerie, cologne, or watches from a wholesaler. You might buy T-shirts from a wholesaler for $3 each, for example, and sell each shirt to your customers for $6.

HECTOR'S SMALL BUSINESS

Hector, a high school student living in the South Bronx, needed to earn money to help support his mother and sister. He tried several fast-food restaurant jobs, but his right leg had been injured in an accident and he had trouble standing up for hours at a time.

During an NFTE entrepreneurship class, Hector learned about wholesalers and keystoning. On a visit to the wholesale district, he noticed a new type of portable cassette player. He bought ten and, in a brilliant move, *gave* five of them to the "cool" kids in school. Within days, he had sold the other five. The wholesale unit price had been $15; Hector's price to his classmates and friends was $30. That was still less than the store price, which was $45. Hector eventually sold eighty of these cassette players! Then he moved on to other products. Not only was selling easier on his leg than restaurant work, he was making much more money than the minimum wage paid at the fast-food restaurants. To figure Hector's profit on his sales, do the calculations below.

1. How much money did Hector receive from his sales of 80 cassette players?

   80 (Number of Units Sold) × _____ (Selling Price of One Unit) = _____ (Total Sales)

2. How much did he spend to buy the cassette players?

   80 (Number of Units Bought) × _____ (Wholesale Cost per Unit) = _____ (Total Cost)

3. Profit equals total sales minus total cost. What is Hector's profit?

   _____ (Total Sales) − _____ (Total Cost) = _____ (Profit)

Another good question to ask yourself is: How many hours would Hector have had to work, at a job paying him $5 an hour, to earn as much as his profit from selling 80 cassette players?

Hector buys wholesale, keystones, and keeps careful track of his money. You will make a profit in business if you do the same, as long as you are selling something people want to buy.

EVERY BIG BUSINESS STARTED SMALL

The public often thinks of business only in terms of "big" business—companies such as Ford, General Motors, IBM, McDonald's, and Nike. A "big" business is typically defined as having more than one hundred employees and selling more than a million dollars of products or services in a year. A "small" business employs fewer than one hundred employees and has yearly sales of less than a million dollars.

Surprisingly, the principles involved in running General Motors or owning a corner hot-dog stand are very similar. In fact, most of the big corporations in this country started out as small entrepreneurial businesses, or **ventures.** Each venture began as an idea thought up by an entrepreneur.

YOU HAVE UNIQUE KNOWLEDGE OF YOUR MARKET[1]

The people a business serves are its **market.** Your market, for example, might be your friends, neighbors, classmates at school, or colleagues at your current job. What might these people want to buy? No one knows the answer better than you do.

The beauty of business is that you already have the most important knowledge that you need to succeed. You know your market better than anyone else. Some successful entrepreneurs did not do well in school; some never even had a chance to go to school. Others were born into poverty. But they all used their unique market knowledge to create successful businesses.

HOW BERRY GORDY TURNED HIS UNIQUE KNOWLEDGE INTO MOTOWN RECORDS

Berry Gordy, Jr.'s Motown Record Company is one of the music industry's greatest success stories. Among the artists Gordy discovered or promoted are Michael Jackson, Lionel Richie, the Supremes, Marvin

Gaye, Stevie Wonder, and the Temptations. By recording the artists he liked and believed his market would like, Gordy created "the Motown Sound." He eventually recorded an astonishing 110 number-one hits. Gordy's market initially was the black urban community. He has described many of his first hit artists as "kids off the street."

Gordy was a kid off the street himself. He was born and raised in the tough Detroit ghetto of the 1930s and '40s. Determined to escape the grinding poverty around him, Gordy turned to professional boxing. Although he won 10 out of 14 fights as a featherweight, he realized he was not big enough to have a great boxing career.

Gordy loved pop and jazz music, so his next career move was to open a jazz record shop. The shop soon went bankrupt, however, so Gordy took a job on the assembly line at Ford Motor Company. During his spare time, he wrote songs and went to nightclubs.

As his passion for music grew, Gordy became determined to break into the recording industry. He traveled to New York to make contacts with producers and publishers. After a series of rejections, he finally sold a few songs in the mid-1950s. When Gordy was twenty-eight, Jackie Wilson recorded his song "Reet Petite." This was followed by another hit, "Lonely Teardrops," which sold a million copies. Gordy's share of the proceeds of these sales, however, was so paltry that he was forced to return to Detroit to work at Ford again. The experience made him determined to start his own production company and record label. He was tired of trying to get his foot in the door at someone else's operation.

To pursue his dream, Gordy borrowed $700 from his sister Anna and built a makeshift recording studio in the basement of a rundown house in Detroit in 1958. He began to audition performers. One of the kids who came in off the street was Smokey Robinson. Gordy signed him and a group of teenagers who called themselves the Miracles. Within a year, Smokey and the Miracles had two major hits. Gordy used the profits from their hits to sign more great newcomers such as the Supremes and Marvin Gaye.

Motown's Universal Appeal

Although Gordy started off making records for his market—black urban soul—he had an instinct for polishing his performers' sound and image to make them appealing to white middle America. The Supremes, for example, always had to be impeccably dressed and made-up, and their records were sweetened with string arrangements to make their songs sound more like the mainstream hits already playing on the radio. Producer Michael Gentile, who wrote the "Tears of a Clown" arrangement recorded by Smokey Robinson, has said that Gordy told him to write arrangements that would bring Motown artists "into the living rooms of white America on a Sunday afternoon."

Gordy devoted himself to developing his artists. He listened to every track they cut. If he didn't feel a song was perfect, it was recorded again. Soon, Motown's appeal was universal. Gordy once estimated that for one of the Miracles' hits, "Shop Around," African Americans bought only half as many recordings of it as white teenagers did.

By the early 1970s, Motown sales exceeded $10 million per year. Gordy branched into film with the movie *Lady Sings the Blues*, starring Diana Ross. By 1983, Motown was the largest black-owned company in America, with revenues of $104 million. In mid-1988, Gordy sold his company to MCA Records. He was then free to enjoy the tremendous wealth he had earned by using his unique knowledge to start a successful business.

DEVELOP YOUR UNIQUE KNOWLEDGE

You can develop your own unique market knowledge by applying your creativity and intelligence to your market. What do people in your market need? Want? Enjoy? You know your neighborhood better than someone from another neighborhood ever could. You have had life experiences that no one else has had.

These experiences make up your knowledge of the world. You can use that knowledge to become a successful entrepreneur. Entrepreneurship is about connecting your business ideas to the needs of your market.

The great thing about entrepreneurship is that your success is not limited by your abilities or education. You should never feel that you are not good enough, or creative enough, or smart enough to succeed. In fact, recent research indicates that your creativity and intelligence are limitless, as long as you use them.

It's not how smart you are, but how you are smart.

Rule of Thumb

BUSINESS IS AN ADVENTURE

Entrepreneurs are constantly discovering new markets and trying to figure out how to supply those markets efficiently and make a **profit.** A business makes a profit when money from sales is more than money spent paying the bills. Business is very unpredictable—entrepreneurs never know ahead of time how people are going to react to any of their decisions. That's what makes entrepreneurship such an adventure.

I worked in the international financial department of Ford Motor Company before I became an entrepreneur. People sometimes ask me whether it's scary to leave the security of a corporate job and start your own business. Personally, when I started my first little business, I felt nothing but exhilaration. The day I founded my business my self-esteem soared. I went from being unemployed to being a professional entrepreneur.

WHERE OTHERS SEE PROBLEMS, ENTREPRENEURS SEE OPPORTUNITY

After I left Ford, I began working as a consultant. My first contract was for a foundation, which paid me to go to the Caribbean and interview entrepreneurs about the problems they were having exporting their products to the United States. During those interviews, I realized that there was a huge opportunity to solve their problems by starting an import–export business. When I returned to New York, I began advertising my services as a manufacturer's representative in Chamber of Commerce newsletters. I had found out that an ad could be placed in the newsletters for free. I started to get 800 to 900 letters a month from developing countries. Soon, I was representing manufacturers from West Africa, Pakistan, Bangladesh, and other countries.

BUSINESS IS A PROCESS OF DISCOVERY

Business is a process of discovery. A big part of the entrepreneurial experience is trying to forecast the future of consumer needs. Some famous entrepreneurs have gone bankrupt and then succeeded later with a different business. Henry Ford went bankrupt twice before the Ford Motor Company succeeded. It's important to learn from failure or disappointments. Don't let them get you down.

Most successful entrepreneurs open and close many businesses during their lifetimes. A new business usually takes some time to turn a profit. If a new business continues to lose money, however, the entrepreneur may close it. A business that is losing money is **insolvent.** Closing a business is nothing to be ashamed of; it may be the best decision that can be made.

Some entrepreneurs will try very hard to keep a business open even when it is losing money. If money from sales is still not enough to pay bills, however, the business will eventually go **bankrupt.**

A bankrupt business is declared legally unable to pay its bills. A court can force the owner to sell items of value owned by the business, or **assets,** to raise money to pay bills. Sometimes, even the personal possessions of the owner are sold and the proceeds are given to **creditors.** Creditors are people to whom the business owes money.

Failure is the chance to begin again more intelligently.
—Henry Ford

Rule of Thumb

THE ENGINE OF THE ECONOMY: ENTREPRENEURSHIP[2]

Entrepreneurship is sometimes called the engine of our economy. Most of the new jobs created in this country in the past decade have been in small, not big, businesses. Because starting a business does not require large amounts of time, money, or experience, entrepreneurship has proven to be an effective way for minorities and women to enter the business world. The U.S. Small Business Administration (SBA) reports that 70 percent of all African-American owned start-ups, or new ventures, are funded from personal savings or by family and friends. Most are started with less than $5,000.

During the 1990–1991 recession, many people who lost their jobs made new careers for themselves by starting their own businesses. As a result, while big businesses continued to lose jobs, the small business sector was creating them. According to the latest U.S. Census, in 1990, 4 million new jobs were created by new small business ventures. In contrast, big business lost 1.7 million jobs in 1990.

Even though the economy has reportedly recovered from the recession, layoffs are continuing as corporations restructure and downsize, according to *The Wall Street Journal* ("Amid Record Profits, Companies Continue to Lay Off Employees," May 4, 1995). In this uncertain employment climate, entrepreneurship is an attractive option for people who had previously depended on corporations for lifetime employment. Presently, almost half of all new products are created by small, entrepreneurial companies. Almost half of the workforce in the United States is employed by small businesses. In 1992, for example, businesses owned by women were employing more of the U.S. population than all the Fortune 500 companies combined.

A SUCCESSFUL ENTREPRENEUR CREATES JOBS AND WEALTH

Entrepreneurs have a powerful impact on society. A successful entrepreneur can create jobs, products, services, and wealth. These come about when the entrepreneur makes good choices about how to use scarce **resources.** Resources are things such as oil, wood, cotton, **capital,** labor, or land that are used by businesspeople to create products and services. Capital is money used as a business resource. Most resources are scarce; that is, the available supply is limited.

As an entrepreneur, your goal will be to add value to scarce resources. Let's say you are selling homemade cookies. You buy butter, eggs, flour, sugar, and other ingredients to make your cookies. These ingredients are your resources. You hope that people will like your cookies so much that they will be willing to buy them for a price that covers the cost of the ingredients *and* provides you with a profit. If customers buy your cookies for that price, you can be said to have added value to your resources. They are worth more when you use them to bake cookies. If your cookies taste bad, however, and customers don't want to buy them, you have wasted those resources.

I believe that every person should learn how to start and operate a business. Imagine how a hundred new entrepreneurs could revitalize an impoverished community.

PROFIT TELLS YOU IF YOU'VE MADE THE RIGHT CHOICES

Entrepreneurs are constantly making choices about how to use scarce resources. Those choices directly affect how much profit a business makes. You might decide this week, for instance, to buy margarine instead of butter because margarine is cheaper, even though your cookies may not taste as good made with margarine. This type of choice is called a **tradeoff.** You are giving up one thing (taste) for another (money).

If your customers don't notice the change and continue to buy your cookies, you have made a good choice. You have conserved a resource (money) and increased your profit by lowering your costs. The increase in profit confirms that you have made the right choice.

If your customers notice the change and stop buying your cookies, your profit will decrease. The decrease in profit signals that you have made a bad choice. Next week, you'll probably buy butter again. The tradeoff wasn't worth it. Every choice an entrepreneur makes is a tradeoff.

THE PROS AND CONS OF BEING AN ENTREPRENEUR[3]

Being an entrepreneur can be a 24-hour-a-day obsession. It can be extremely rewarding or very painful. Being your own boss can be exhilarating one minute and terrifying the next. So can being financially responsible for the success or failure of your enterprise. As you read the pros and cons listed below, think about what you want out of life. What are your priorities? If being independent, working hard, and building your own fortune are goals of yours, and you aren't afraid of taking risks and possibly failing, entrepreneurship may be for you. If you value financial security and the support of colleagues, you'll probably do better as an employee rather than an entrepreneur.

Pros of Entrepreneurship

- **Independence:** Business owners do not have to follow orders or observe working hours set by someone else. Entrepreneurship can even provide an opportunity for someone to prove to society what he or she can accomplish. In the 1960s, Thomas Burrell came to believe that, because he was African American, no matter how good he was at his advertising job, he wasn't going to be promoted any further by the ad agency that employed him. He quit and started his own company, Burrell Communications Group. Today, with annual sales of over $60 million, it is the largest black-owned ad agency in the United States.

- **Satisfaction:** Turning a skill, hobby, or other interest into your own business can be very satisfying. Edwin Land, founder of Polaroid, turned his love of photography into a multimillion-dollar business when he developed and marketed the instant-print camera.

- **Financial Reward:** Through hard work, the sky can be the limit. Most of the great fortunes in this country were built by entrepreneurs. Countless small businesses have grown into large companies that have produced fortunes for their owners. Many entrepreneurs also create wealth by building businesses and selling them once they are profitable. A successful business can sometimes be sold for a tremendous sum. At the age of 48, for example, Jeno Paulucci sold his Chinese food business, Chun King, to R.J. Reynolds for $63 million in cash.

- **Self-Esteem:** Knowing you created something valuable can give you a strong sense of accomplishment. Oil tycoon Jake Simmons, Jr.'s first job was as a porter on a train. When a white passenger told him, "Boy, come here and get my bags!" Simmons told the man that he resented being called "boy." The man's response was, "Young man, if you don't want to be called a boy, then don't do a boy's work, because boys carry bags for men." Simmons was so shaken that he left the job as soon as he could and swore to himself that he would be his own boss. He went on to create the world's most successful minority-owned oil conglomerate.

Cons of Entrepreneurship

- **Business Failure:** Many small businesses fail. You risk losing not only your money but also the money invested in your business by others. Henry Ford, the founder of Ford Motor Company, had several small business failures before making it big. He once said, "Failure is a chance to begin again more intelligently. It is just a resting place." He also said, "We learn more from our failures than our successes."

- **Obstacles:** You will run into problems that you will have to solve by yourself. You may face discouragement from family and friends. Liz Claiborne's family was dead set against her becoming a fashion designer and starting her own business. Her father was afraid the business world would be too rough on her. Claiborne proved him wrong by building Liz Claiborne, Inc. into a billion-dollar corporation.

- **Loneliness:** It can be lonely and even a little scary to be completely responsible for the success or failure of your business. In the early 1900s, Madame C. J. Walker traveled all over the United States by herself for two years, promoting her hair care products—a brave move in those days for a widowed African American woman with little education.

- **Financial Insecurity:** You are not guaranteed a set salary or any benefits. You may not always have enough money to pay yourself. King C. Gillette invented the disposable razor and started the Gillette Company, which is a billion-dollar business today. In 1901, though, Gillette's fledgling company was $12,500 in debt—a lot of money, back then. As Gillette recalled, "We were backed up to the wall with our creditors lined up in front waiting for the signal to fire." Gillette managed to secure financing from a Boston millionaire and save the company. An entrepreneur may face equally intense financial challenges many times.

- **Long Hours/Hard Work:** You will have to work long hours to get your business off the ground. Some entrepreneurs work six or seven days a week. During the early years of establishing McDonald's restaurants around the country, Ray Kroc worked about eighty hours a week. His simple motto was, "Press on."

As you may have realized while reading these pros and cons, they often represent two sides of the same coin. The hard work of establishing and running your own business can reap great financial rewards and build your self-esteem. Although you may face loneliness, financial insecurity, and other setbacks, as you overcome these obstacles you will become a much stronger person. Even if your business fails, you will have gained valuable business experience. Your next business will be more likely to succeed.

When I was self-employed in the import–export business, for example, I worried more about money than I did when I was working for Ford, but I felt much less stress in my interpersonal relationships. I really enjoyed not being dependent on anyone but myself for my job security.

At the end of each chapter of this book, you will find discussion of a business that is ideal for a young or beginning entrepreneur who has limited time, money, and experience. All of the types of businesses described have been successfully run by young people.

Business for the Young Entrepreneur

CASE STUDY: T-SHIRTS

Herbert and Koung were in one of the first entrepreneurship classes I taught at Wharton School of Business. They sat next to each other and were two of the quietest pupils I'd ever had. I was concerned that they wouldn't do well because they were so quiet. I also thought they probably wouldn't become friends because Herbert is African American and Koung is Cambodian. Within a few days, however, I noticed that they always had their heads together. Next thing I knew, they had decided to go into business together.

Herbert and Koung realized that between the two of them they owned dozens of T-shirts imprinted with various logos or designs. Like them, their friends practically lived in T-shirts, so Herbert and Koung started a T-shirt screening business called T-Shirt Designers, in Minneapolis. They began by hand-screening shirts for a local restaurant. Eventually, they saved up enough money to purchase a silkscreening machine. They can now print up to one hundred shirts an hour and use up to four colors per shirt. This has enabled them to take on much larger T-shirt printing jobs and earn more money. One of their clients is the National Foundation for Teaching Entrepreneurship, Inc. Their story shows that business often crosses ethnic and cultural lines and can lower friction between different groups of people.

How many T-shirts do you own with something printed or painted on them? How many do your friends own? Decorated T-shirts are very popular. It's easy to make colorful T-shirts that other people will want to buy from you.

Silkscreening and fabric painting are two easy ways to turn a plain T-shirt into a profitable creation without investing much money.

Silkscreening

Silkscreening is a stencil method of printing. Place the silkscreen, which has your design cut into it, on top of the T-shirt. Next, use a wedge to push the ink through the screen onto the T-shirt. The ink only comes through the screen where your design has been cut into it.

Supplies	Where to Find
Silkscreen	Arts & crafts store
Wedge	Arts & crafts store
Ink	Arts & crafts store
Plain T-shirts	Wholesaler

Fabric Painting

Fabric painting is a good method to use if you want each of your T-shirts to have a unique design. You paint directly onto each shirt. Experiment with gluing decorative jewelry to shirts, too.

Supplies	Where to Find
Fabric paints	Arts & crafts store
Plain T-shirts	Wholesaler

Market Research

Before making your T-shirts, conduct some market research. Ask your friends and other potential customers what size T-shirts they buy. Ask them what designs they might like. Ask what price they might be willing to pay for your shirts.

Tips

- Wear one of your creations to promote your business.
- Offer to silkscreen T-shirts for a school sports team or a local rock band to sell. They supply the design, you translate it onto the T-shirts.
- NFTE graduates have sold just about anything one can buy from a wholesaler. Typical products purchased for resale have included watches, lingerie, earrings, combs, pens, calculators, and hats.

ANSWERS: HECTOR'S SMALL BUSINESS

1. How much money did Hector receive from his sales of 80 cassette players?

   80 (Number of Units Sold) × \$30 (Selling Price of One Unit) = \$2,400 (Total Sales)

2. How much did he spend to buy the cassette players?

   80 (Number of Units Bought) × \$15 (Wholesale Cost per Unit) = \$1,200 (Total Cost)

3. Profit equals total sales minus total cost. What is Hector's cost?

   \$2,400 (Total Sales) − \$1,200 (Total Cost) = \$1,200 (Total Profit)

4. How many hours would Hector have to work at a job paying him $5 per hour to earn as much as his profit from selling 80 cassette players?

$1,200 (Total Profit) ÷ $5 per hour = 240 hours

RESOURCES

Books

A *Teen's Guide to Business: The Secrets to a Successful Enterprise* by Linda Menzies, Oren S. Jenkins, and Rickell R. Fisher (New York: MasterMedia Limited, 1992).

The authors are successful teen entrepreneurs. The book covers everything from how to dress for different business situations to how to run different types of youth enterprises.

Magazines for Entrepreneurs

Inc. magazine, founded by my friend Bernard Goldhirsh, is the magazine most widely read by entrepreneurs. If you want to know what's happening in entrepreneurship in America, read *Inc.* It's available at newsstands and bookstores and by subscription.

Inc.: The Magazine for Growing Companies
38 Commercial Wharf
Boston, MA 02110
(800) 842-1343

Another excellent publication for entrepreneurs is *Success* magazine.

Success
230 Park Avenue
New York, NY 10169
(800) 234-7324

As entrepreneurship has taken hold among women and minorities, several magazines have sprung up to serve those markets. The best are:

Black Enterprise Magazine
130 5th Avenue
New York, NY
(212) 242-8000

Hispanic Magazine
331 Madison Avenue
New York, NY
(212) 986-4425

Working Woman
230 Park Avenue
New York, NY
(212) 551-9500

Other Resources

The Small Business Administration (SBA) is a government agency created to support and promote entrepreneurs. The SBA offers free and inexpensive pamphlets on a variety of business subjects. Some local offices offer counseling to small business owners. Contact the SBA at:

Small Business Administration
409 Third Street, S.W.
Washington, DC 20416
(800) 827-5722

Call this toll-free number to reach the Small Business Answer Desk, which assists entrepreneurs with their questions and can help you locate an SBA office near you: (800) 368-5855.

The Service Core of Retired Executives (SCORE) is a group of retired businesspeople who volunteer as counselors and mentors to entrepreneurs. To locate an office near you; contact:

Service Core of Retired Executives
26 Federal Plaza
New York, NY 10021
(212) 264-4507

The National Association of Women Business Owners helps female entrepreneurs network.

National Association of Women Business Owners
1413 K St., NW, Suite 637
Washington, DC 20005
(301) 608-2590
Fax (301) 608-2596

2 A SUCCESSFUL VENTURE SATISFIES A CONSUMER NEED

AND *YOU* KNOW WHAT THE CONSUMERS IN *YOUR* MARKET NEED

No nation was ever ruined by trade.
—Benjamin Franklin (1706–1790)
American statesman, writer, and inventor

SATISFYING A CONSUMER NEED

The goal of an entrepreneur is to figure out what he or she can sell that consumers need to buy. The most important thing an entrepreneur needs for success is a vision of what consumers need. Some entrepreneurs recognize a consumer need that consumers themselves don't see immediately.

Henry Ford imagined an automobile in front of every home long before most consumers ever thought of owning their own cars. Stephen Wozniak envisioned a computer inside every home at a time when computers were used only by universities, labs, and corporations. With his close friend, Steve Jobs, Wozniak founded Apple Computer. Apple became a leader in the development of personal home and office computers. Bill Gates, inspired by Apple's success with selling computer hardware, started Microsoft, a company that would become the world leader in computer software.

How Apple Developed
the Personal Computer

Apple Computer was founded by Wozniak and Jobs in a garage in 1975, when the two friends were only in their early twenties.

Wozniak had a natural aptitude for electronics. His father was an outstanding engineer who worked for the Lockheed Corporation in California. Wozniak started reading his father's technical literature when he was only nine years old. He built his own radio receiver and transmitter and got into ham radio operation when he was only eleven. "The Woz," as he was nicknamed, became fascinated with computers as an eighth-grader. His room was filled with pictures of them. He designed and built a computer that won first prize at the Bay Area Science Fair.

Wozniak had a playful side, as well. He loved to play baseball and was big on practical jokes. In fact, he spent most of his first year at the University of Colorado playing practical jokes on his dorm mates. That summer, he met Steve Jobs, a high-strung, enterprising young man. He and Jobs became best friends.

Jobs encouraged Wozniak to go into the business of selling to college students a "blue box" he had built. The blue box was an illegal electronic device that could be used to make free long-distance telephone calls. The boxes cost $60 to make. Jobs and Wozniak sold them wholesale for $80. After selling about 200 boxes in 1973, they decided the business was too risky and closed shop.

Wozniak dropped out of college and landed a job with Hewlett-Packard, a major computer company. Jobs dropped out too, and traveled to India. He shaved his head and made a determined effort to study Buddhism. He soon tired of meditating and returned to Cupertino, California, where he got a job with Atari and hooked up again with Wozniak.

Wozniak was a member of the Homebrew Club, a group of computer enthusiasts. He was determined to build a small "personal" computer to show the Club.

When Wozniak finally succeeded, Jobs saw its market potential. They agreed to go into business together. First, however, Wozniak offered Hewlett-Packard a chance to develop his small computer. Hewlett-Packard failed to see the potential of the personal computer and turned him down. So, with $1,300, Jobs and Wozniak started Apple Computer in Wozniak's parents' garage in Cupertino, California.

At first, business was very slow. Jobs and Wozniak knew they needed to build a better computer. Wozniak worked on his design until he created the Apple II, which is considered one of the great achievements of the computer industry.

Jobs, meanwhile, searched for someone willing to invest in the company. After being turned down by friends and family, he found Mike Markklula. Markklula invested $91,000 in the company in return for a share of the profits. Within three years, Apple's sales grew to over $100 million.

In 1994, Apple set a record with net sales of $9.19 billion, up 15 percent over 1993. Apple was successful because Jobs and Wozniak filled a consumer need that the giants of the computer industry had failed to notice. The company continues to succeed by producing new products, such as small portable computers, that consumers want.

FIVE WAYS TO SATISFY A CONSUMER NEED

For a business to be successful, it must satisfy a need of enough **consumers** to generate a profit. There are five basic ways an entrepreneur can satisfy a consumer need:[1]

1. Develop a new **product** or **service.**
2. Uncover new resources or technologies.
3. Apply existing resources or technologies in new ways.
4. Find new markets for an existing product or service.
5. Improve an existing business.

Filling a consumer need generates **revenue,** or money from sales.

APPLE'S SUCCESS AND NEW CONSUMER NEEDS: BILL GATES FOUNDS MICROSOFT

Because consumer needs constantly change, new business opportunities are always developing. Bill Gates, the founder of Microsoft, was, like Wozniak, supersmart and obsessed with computers. A few years younger than Wozniak and Jobs, Gates grew up hearing about Apple's efforts to place a computer on every office desk and in every home. Gates quickly realized that because Apple had developed a new product and was applying existing resources or technologies in new ways, new consumer needs were developing.

Owners of Apple computers needed software to run them. Gates decided that he would fill that consumer need by applying the resources and technologies he knew and uncovering new resources and technologies. He was also determined to find new markets by making his software so easy and so much fun to use that people who had never dreamed they could operate a computer would realize that they could.

Jobs and Wozniak were the hardware kings, so Gates resolved to be the software king. In those days, software—the programs that made computers *do* things—was not considered an important business. Software was boring. It was more often given away or traded than sold.

Gates's great insight was to commercialize software. He hired brilliant young people like himself to design software that made computers do things ordinary working people wanted them to do—calculate and display budgets, edit manuscripts, add graphics. Gates made his software colorful and easy to use. He packaged it attractively. Gates made software fun, and consumers kept coming back for more. By 1992, Microsoft was worth $22 billion, and Bill Gates was worth over $7 billion. At 36, he was the richest person in America.

How Did Gates Do It?

The best entrepreneurs love risk and adventure, and they possess great vision and drive. Bill Gates has these qualities in spades. He has used them, along with his formidable brainpower, to build Microsoft Corporation into one of the most powerful players in the computer industry and to make himself the richest person in America. He even replaced his hero, Steve Jobs, as the media's designated personal computer visionary.

In 1976, Gates and his friend Paul Allen hired several other talented programmers and began writing the software for two corporate customers' hardware. National Cash Register and General Electric were the customers.

By the end of 1982, however, the age of the personal computer had arrived, and millions of people wanted software to run their new gadgets. Revenues at Microsoft were up to $34 million; over 200 people were working for the company. Gates developed a reputation for hiring the best and the brightest and running them ragged. The press called his employees "Micro-kids." The youthful employees, dressed in jeans and sneakers, conducted plastic sword fights in the hallways. Stressed-out programmers eased the tension of their eighty-hour workweeks by exploding homemade bombs.

Gates himself was developing a reputation as intense, driven, and work-addicted. He had bought a high-performance Porsche that enabled him to speed between his home and Microsoft. Despite his hectic schedule, Gates kept his vision in mind: People want easy-to-use software. This vision led to the development of Windows, a software program whose graphics were so easy to understand that someone with no experience on a computer could figure out how to use it by trial and error.

GATES ROLLS OUT WINDOWS

Gates rolled out Microsoft Windows on May 22, 1990, before a throng of reporters, analysts, and industry watchers. He was just 34, and a multibillionaire. He was also taking on IBM, one of the world's most powerful corporations. Gates had tried to sell Windows to IBM, with whom he had a partnership, but IBM had turned him down and was developing its own competitive software, an operating system called OS/2.

Like many of Gates's pet projects, Windows was enormously risky, but the reward was great. Gates used his company's power to try to gobble up his competition and make Windows the industry standard. His competitors responded with a price war. As profits on software sales fell, Gates expanded into other computer-related developments, such as faxing and the information highway. Microsoft programmers continue to hack out new or improved programs to help consumers use the latest advances in the fast-moving digital universe. The 1995 version of Windows, for example, includes software for running a modem and getting on-line.

Today, Gates recognizes the impact entrepreneurship education can have on young people. Microsoft is sponsoring a NFTE program in Seattle, as well as a high-tech center for young entrepreneurs in Boston. One of my goals is to get successful entrepreneurs more involved with entrepreneurship education so that more young people can gain a basic knowledge of how to create wealth.

PRODUCTS AND SERVICES

Along with their products, both Apple and Microsoft provide their consumers with services, such as consulting and technological assistance.

Products (also called "goods") are *tangible*—they can be seen and touched. Some examples of products a young entrepreneur might sell are ties, candy, baked goods, T-shirts, or watches.

Services are *intangible*—they can't be touched. Some examples of services a young entrepreneur might sell are baby-sitting, pet care, house painting, or word processing. Gates made his megafortune by anticipating the needs of consumers as computer technology developed. Today, many people are using their computers to go "on-line" and gain access to the information highway. Where there are consumers, entrepreneurs follow.

RIDING THE INFORMATION HIGHWAY

As more people invest in fax machines and use modems to get on-line, the opportunities to promote your business are expanding. Instead of mailing ads or coupons to prospective customers, for instance, why not fax them? If you have a modem hooked up to your computer and fax machine, you can save time by programming your computer to fax your flyer to a list of fax numbers. The computer will automatically send your promotional piece to the numbers on the list, leaving you free to do something else.

At one time, an account at a university or government agency and a working knowledge of a difficult programming language were needed to hook into the information highway. Now, all you need is a modem and an account with America Online, CompuServe, or any of the Internet access providers around the country. Microsoft and IBM are building Internet software into the latest versions of Windows and OS/2. Numerous books are available to guide you. Two of the best are *The Whole Internet User's Guide and Catalog* (O'Reilly & Associates, Sebastopol, California, 1992) and *New Riders Official Internet Yellow Pages* (New Riders, Indianapolis, 1994).

Your access provider will give you software that your computer will use to browse the Internet (the Net) and to send and receive electronic mail (e-mail). Once you're on the Net, you can send and receive e-mail from an estimated 30 million users. You can use e-mail to communicate with suppliers and customers.

You can also keep in touch with thousands of special-interest newsgroups. No matter what your business, your potential customers will be talking about their needs in a Net newsgroup. Once you are exploring the Net, you will be able to find lists of newsgroups that discuss every subject imaginable. Newsgroups are excellent sources of information about markets for your business, too.

THE WORLD WIDE WEB

When you're comfortable with being on-line via your server, you'll be ready to explore deeper levels of the Internet. The World Wide Web (the Web) is a subsection of the Internet. Documents on the Web can include images and sound. These documents are also called home pages. Establishing a home page on the Web is the most exciting approach to making your presence known.

Designing a Web page for your business isn't simple, but where there's a consumer need, there's usually an entrepreneur. You should be able to find someone offering a Web page design service. Try the computer department of a local college. One of the students might be the entrepreneur you need.

The Internet Business Center offers many business resources, including examples of commercial Web pages, or sites. Another source of information about putting your business on the Web is a site called Commercial Use.

VOLUNTARY EXCHANGE

All business, whether conducted on-line or off-line, is made up of **voluntary exchange.** Voluntary exchange is a trade between two people who agree to trade money for a product or service. When you buy new software for your computer, no one is forcing you to trade. You and the seller of the software agree to the exchange because you both benefit from the trade.

The opposite of voluntary exchange is **involuntary exchange.** A mugging is an involuntary exchange. One person forces the other person to give up something and get nothing of value in return. Involuntary exchange requires force. Only one person benefits from an involuntary exchange. To start a successful business, you will need to sell a product or service for which someone will *want* to exchange money.

THE DESIRE FOR MONEY IS NOT A STRONG ENOUGH REASON TO START A BUSINESS

Any business, large or small, needs to make money to survive and grow. Some of the most successful entrepreneurs in the world, however, have said that the desire to make money is not a good enough reason to start one's own business.

I heard Steve Jobs make that point during a speech he gave in the mid-1980s. He talked about how important it is to follow your heart and do something that you love. Focusing on the money, he said, does not get you very far. An entrepreneur needs a vision.

The financial rewards of owning your own business may not appear until after many years of very hard work. The desire to make money may not be enough to keep you going through the difficult early period of your business.

Most successful companies are founded by someone who has a dream. Henry Ford dreamed of a "horseless carriage" that the average American could afford. Jobs and Wozniak imagined a computer on every desk. Gates imagined his software in every computer. A vision provides the motivation to succeed.

When Wozniak and Jobs envisioned a computer in every home, computers were very large, expensive appliances. They were available only to universities, scientists, and large companies. What product or service that is available today to only a few select consumers can you envision meeting a need for many consumers in the future? Let your imagination run wild. You just might come up with the vision for a successful business.

SUCCESS STARTS WITH IDEAS— NEW OR REPACKAGED

Profitable businesses are all based on good ideas, but don't be discouraged if you haven't come up with a brand new idea for a business that has never been imagined before. Very few ideas are actually new. Most new companies are started by repackaging old ideas and concepts or combining them with new technology. Computer dating, for example, combined existing computer technology and personal dating services.

To be an entrepreneur, you don't have to come up with a new invention or product. *It is necessary, though, to provide a product or service that fills a consumer need.*

Business for the Young Entrepreneur

CASE STUDY: BABY-SITTING SERVICE

Providing baby-sitting service is the first business of many young people. Most baby-sitters go to the home of the children, but Tanya had a different idea. She decided to offer a baby-sitting service based in her own home, for four children in her South Bronx neighborhood. In that way, the children could play together.

Like many NFTE students, Tanya had grown up under the tremendous stress of living in a harsh urban environment. I constantly told her that because she had overcome all the things she had faced already, she was certainly strong enough to run a small business. That's a point I'd like to stress: Any pain or difficulty you've had in your life will actually make you a stronger, more resilient entrepreneur.

Rule of Thumb

Out of every adversity comes an equal or greater benefit.
—Napoleon Hill

On two evenings a week, the parents of the four children brought them to Tanya's house for two hours. This gave the parents time to go out to dinner or do errands. The children enjoyed going to Tanya's house because they got to play together.

Tanya charged $5.00 per child for the two-hour period. For each baby-sitting evening, therefore, she earned:

$$\$5.00 \times 4 \text{ children} = \$20.00$$

Each week, Tanya earned $40.00 from her business. Her cost per child for each week was around $.50 for juice and milk. Her total weekly costs were $2.00. Her weekly profit, therefore, was $38.00. Tanya realized that she could easily double her profit by caring for another set of four children on two other weekday evenings. She also began offering weekend baby-sitting services for the same rate.

As Tanya learned, parents of young children are always searching for responsible baby-sitters. You probably have friends who baby-sit. Think about starting a service like Tanya's, or serving as a baby-sitter *finder* for busy parents.

Each week, have the baby-sitters who work for your service call to tell you when they can work. In return for matching baby-sitters with jobs, you can charge a commission. A commission is a percentage of each sale. You could charge 10 percent, for example.

Let's say the Smith family needs a baby-sitter on Friday night for four hours. You look on your list and see that your friend Sara can work Friday night and lives near the Smiths. Mrs. Smith agrees to pay Sara $5.00 per hour. That means Sara will earn:

$$\$5.00 \text{ per hour} \times 4 \text{ hours} = \$20.00$$

Sara pays *you* 10 percent of $20.00 because you got her the job. To figure your commission, first you need to express the percentage as a decimal.

1. "Percentage" means "out of a hundred." Ten out of a hundred is stated as 10 percent, or 10%.

$$\frac{10.00}{100} = .10$$

2. Another way to express any percentage as a number is to move the decimal point two places to the left (this is the same as dividing the percentage by 100):

   20% becomes .20   45% becomes .45   10.5% becomes .105

3. To figure your commission, multiply the percentage, expressed in decimal form, by the total sale:

$$\text{Commission on Sara's job} = \$20.00 \times .10 = \$2.00$$

Your commission is $2.00. That may not sound like much, but it will add up as your service expands.

What You'll Need to Get Started

- Babysitters and parents must be able to contact you. You'll need to circulate a phone number (call-waiting service is a good idea) *where they can reach you* and an answering machine. Record a message on the machine that reassures your callers that you're a responsible person.

- Set up a simple **filing system** (a grocery box and some folders will do) to keep track of:

   parents: phone numbers, addresses, directions to their homes, number of children, ages of children, any special problems or needs

   sitters: phone numbers, times and days they can work, allergies or other special problems or needs (you can't send someone who is allergic to cats to baby-sit in a home where there are cats, for example)

jobs: when and for what family each baby-sitter worked, how much money he or she made, whether he or she paid you your commission

- A large month-by-month **calendar** with day-boxes, to mark the dates and baby-sitters you've booked. Day books and calendars are often sold at a discount in January each year.

- **Flyers** advertising your business. A flyer is a one-page advertisement of the service you're offering. From one neat, dark-inked original, you can photocopy countless copies.

- **Business cards** that give basic facts about your service and how to contact you.

- **Marketing ideas.** Place flyers on local grocery store bulletin boards, in laundromats, and in other neighborhood places that busy parents frequent. Give a flyer and a business card to any parents you meet. Make **T-shirts, headbands,** or **hats** advertising your service, and give one to each baby-sitter you sign up.

THE ENTREPRENEUR AS PROBLEM SOLVER

Where other people see problems, entrepreneurs see opportunities for creating new businesses. Countless businesses, great and small, have been started because an entrepreneur was annoyed by a problem.

Anita Roddick started The Body Shop, Inc.—a skin care and cosmetics company that uses natural ingredients—because she was tired of paying for perfume and fancy packaging when she bought makeup. Before her, Georgette Klinger founded her self-named skin care company because she had terrible acne.

I. Try thinking of three problems that annoy you and a business solution for each:

Problem	Business Solution
1. _____	1. _____
2. _____	2. _____
3. _____	3. _____

II. Now think about where you live. Are there any problems you could solve for your community? List five business opportunities in your community and the need(s) each would satisfy:

Business Opportunity	Need(s) Satisfied
1. _____	1. _____
2. _____	2. _____
3. _____	3. _____
4. _____	4. _____
5. _____	5. _____

III. One good way to start thinking like an entrepreneur is to imagine how you would respond to a challenge or an opportunity, or even to some information about consumers. Given the following hypothetical situations, what business would you consider starting?

Situation	Business Opportunities
1. A 100 percent increase in the price of gasoline is announced.	_____
2. A going-out-of-business sign is placed in the window of the local grocery store.	_____
3. A new airport is being built near your home.	_____
4. The number of women entering the workforce is dramatically increasing.	_____
5. Three new families with children are moving into your neighborhood.	_____
6. You know a lot of people who are planning to get married.	_____
7. You live near a college.	_____

SAMPLE ANSWERS:
THE ENTREPRENEUR AS PROBLEM SOLVER

I. Three problems that annoy you and a business solution for each:

Problem	Business Solution
1. Many neighborhood pet cats are having kittens.	1. Provide a "Kitten Giveaway" service.
2. Delivery people have a hard time reading addresses on houses.	2. Offer to paint addresses on curbs.
3. It snows a lot each winter where you live.	3. Start a snow removal service.

II. Think about where you live. List five business opportunities in your community and the need(s) each would satisfy:

Business Opportunity	Need(s) Satisfied
1. After-school day care	1. Need for working parents to have children cared for until parents come home.
2. Party clown service	2. Need for entertainment for children's parties and other events.
3. Garage cleaning	3. Need for someone to take care of a messy and time-consuming job.
4. Car wash and wax	4. Need to have car cleaned regularly.
5. Resell used clothing and toys	5. Families need inexpensive clothes and toys for growing children.

III. Given these hypothetical situations, what business would you consider starting? Remember, every problem is an opportunity to make a profit by solving it.

Situation	Business Opportunities
1. A 100 percent increase in the price of gasoline is announced.	1. Start a carpool service.
2. A going-out-of-business sign is placed in the window of the local grocery store.	2. Offer delivery service from a grocery store near the neighborhood.

Situation	Business Opportunities
3. A new airport is being built near your home.	3. Start a car service.
4. The number of women entering the workforce is dramatically increasing.	4. Open a day care center.
5. Three new families with children are moving into your neighborhood.	5. Start a baby-sitting service or a playgroup.
6. You know a lot of people who are planning to get married.	6. Start a bridal shower planning service.
7. You live near a college.	7. Provide word processing and research assistance for term papers.

RESOURCES

Books

Gates by Stephen Manes and Paul Andrews (New York: Touchstone, 1994) is a fast-paced biography of Bill Gates and a national bestseller.

Insanely Great by Steven Levy (New York: Viking, 1994) tells the story of how Apple grew.

Accidental Empires: How the Boys of Silicon Valley Make Their Millions, Battle Foreign Competition, and Still Can't Get a Date by Robert X. Cringely (New York: Harper Business, 1992) is a hugely entertaining story of the development of the computer industry.

Two books that will help you navigate the Internet are:

The Whole Internet User's Guide and Catalog (Sebastopol, California: O'Reilly and Associates, 1992).

New Riders Official Internet Yellow Pages (Indianapolis: New Riders, 1994).

For a thorough discussion of the role of the entrepreneur in satisfying consumer needs, see:

Master Curriculum Guide: Economics and Entrepreneurship, edited by John Clow et al. (Joint Council on Economic Education, 1991). Contact:

National Council on Economic Education
1140 Avenue of the Americas
New York, NY 10036
(212) 730-7007

Other Resources

The Young Entrepreneurs' Organization (YEO) is a nonprofit organization whose mission is to assist entrepreneurs under thirty-five. YEO was founded by my friend and NFTE board member Verne Harnish in 1987. Contact YEO at:

The Young Entrepreneurs' Organization
10101 North Glebe Road
Arlington, VA 22207
(703) 527-4500

Junior Achievement (JA) is one of the leading youth educators in the fields of economics and business. For information on a JA program near you, contact:

Junior Achievement
National Headquarters
1 Education Way
Colorado Springs, CO 80906
(719) 540-8016

THERE'S NO SUCH THING AS A FREE LUNCH

3

There's no such thing as a free lunch.
—Milton Friedman (b. 1912)
American economist

SUPPLY AND DEMAND

Choosing a business was easy for nine-year-old Darryl of Newark, New Jersey. He loved video games and electronics more than anything. More importantly, though, Darryl had a great ability to think about what people would buy. A lot of kids don't think that way; they buy what *they* want. Darryl tried to figure out what *his customers* wanted.

Darryl started selling electronic games to his family and friends. He soon realized, though, that he and his customers craved variety. Darryl noticed that video clubs were renting a variety of movies to members but no one was renting out video *games.* Darryl decided to start a video game club. His customers can rent lots of different games for the price of buying one.

Without realizing it, Darryl was responding to a demand for rental electronic games. This was a demand that the local stores had not recognized. Darryl noticed it because he—being a kid who loves video games—had unique knowledge of the market.

By renting cartridges at 25 cents per night, Darryl's Electronics boasts profits of $15 per week. Not bad, considering he is only open for business on Friday and Saturday!

Supply is the business (entrepreneurial) response to consumer demand. Supply is the amount of a product or service businesses are willing to provide at various prices.

Demand is the amount of a product or service that consumers are willing and able to buy at various prices.

HOW PRICES COMMUNICATE INFORMATION

In a **free-enterprise** (or free-market system), what is produced, the price, and the quantity bought and sold are determined by supply and demand. In a free market, anyone—even a nine-year-old!—may start a business.

Price relays information between the consumer and the entrepreneur. The entrepreneur knows quickly when the price of a product is too high because most consumers refuse to buy the product. The entrepreneur knows when the price is too low because the product sells out very quickly and consumers want more. The price of the product is being determined by the laws of supply and demand.

FILLING PRESCRIPTIONS AT A LOWER PRICE[1]

Jane C. I. Hirsh has used the power of pricing to build her business, Copley Pharmaceuticals, from a $500 loan from a friend into a billion-dollar company. Copley produces generic drugs, in response to consumer demand for cheaper prescription drugs.

Hirsh worked as a hospital pharmacist for eight years after college. She learned that many drug companies were making a substantial profit. Hirsh realized that part of the amount the consumer was paying for was the brand name of the product. She reasoned that if she produced generic versions of common drugs, she could sell her drugs at lower prices and draw consumers away from brand-name drugs.

In 1972, Copley and her husband started Copley Pharmaceuticals, Inc., in Canton, Massachusetts. Although the company initially had some close brushes with failure, as it developed the strength to get its products placed in more pharmacies, sales began increasing at a steady rate of 30 percent per year.

Today, Copley makes generic versions of fourteen over-the-counter drugs and fifty-six prescription drugs. Its biggest sellers are Miconazole Nitrate (which treats yeast infections) and Procainamide (a heart drug). Of her business, Hirsh says, "I'm not a high-finance person, I'm a pharmacist. I care about people, product development equipment, and manufacturing. It isn't sexy, but it sure is profitable."

LAW OF DEMAND[2]

Hirsh knew nothing about business or economics when she started her business, but she knew lower prices would attract customers. She was instinctively relying on the law of demand.

According to the law of demand, as price goes up, the quantity demanded by consumers goes down. As the price falls, the quantity demanded by consumers rises.

Let's say you get permission to sell soda at a Little League baseball game. During the first half of the game, you charge $2.00 per can of soda and sell two dozen cans. During the second half of the game, you try lowering your price to $1.00 per can. You sell five dozen cans.

The people attending the game have "obeyed" the **Law of Demand:** if everything else remains the same, people will demand more of something at a *lower* price than they will at a *higher* price.

LAW OF SUPPLY

On the other side of every market is a supplier. The supplier also reacts to price changes.

If your small business is baking and selling cookies, for example, how many cookies would you be willing to make if you thought that the cookies would sell for $.25 each? What if people were willing to pay $1.00 each? You would probably work harder and try to supply more cookies at that price.

The entrepreneur who acts this way is obeying the **Law of Supply:** if everything else remains the same, businesses will supply more of a product or service at a *higher* price than they will at a *lower* price.

SUPPLYING $400 CALCULATORS

William R. Hewlett was obeying the laws of supply and demand in 1972 when he had his electronics company, Hewlett-Packard, start manufacturing scientific calculators that were to sell for around $400. At the time, most scientists used slide rules to make their calculations. Slide rules cost only $20. As a supplier, Hewlett was attracted to producing the higher-priced calculators. As a brilliant engineer, Hewlett believed that other scientists were probably as sick as he was of using slide rules and would buy the expensive calculators as a substitute, despite their higher price. He was eager to start supplying the high-priced calculators.

The calculators became the hottest product in the electronics industry and quickly rendered the slide rule obsolete. Hewlett-Packard's sales tripled to $1.8 billion by 1978. In 1994, Hewlett-Packard's sales were $25 billion.

USING THE LAWS OF SUPPLY AND DEMAND TO PREDICT MARKET BEHAVIOR

Knowing the laws of supply and demand will help you make good business decisions. If you believe the demand for a product is going to rise, for instance, it would be wise to start selling that product, because the price that people are willing to pay for it is going to rise, too.

For example, what can you expect will happen to the demand for air conditioners in the summer? Why? What is likely to happen, therefore, to the price of air conditioners in the summer?

The demand for air conditioners will probably rise in the summer because more people will want air conditioners to cool their houses and offices. At first, therefore, the price of air conditioners will probably rise. Suppliers of air conditioners will be able to raise their prices because more people will be demanding air conditioners. The higher prices of air conditioners, in turn, will encourage more suppliers to supply air conditioners. Eventually, the price of air conditioners will come down again.

If you suspect that the demand for a product is going to drop, it would make sense to get out of that market and start producing something else. What do you think would happen to the price of gasoline, for example, if many people were to begin using electric cars? Why?

If everyone were to begin using electric cars, the demand for gasoline would fall. Suppliers would be forced to sell gasoline at a lower price to try to attract consumers away from electric cars. Many suppliers would probably stop selling gasoline and move into another market.

SETTING THE PRICE

Together, demand and supply determine how much will be bought and sold and what the price will be in a market. Remember, a market is a group of people buying and selling a product or service. Businesses would like to charge high prices for their products and services. Consumers seek low prices. The market price is a compromise between what the buyer wants to pay and the entrepreneur wants to charge.

There is a price at which the amount that producers want to sell equals the amount that consumers are willing to spend. This is the **market clearing price.**

SUPPLY AND DEMAND SCHEDULES

Let's say you go to a record store to check out some CDs. Whether you will purchase anything will depend on the price of CDs at the store. If there is a sale and all CDs are discounted from $16 to $14, you might buy more CDs than you would if they were $16 each.

In contrast, the owners of the store would prefer to sell the CDs at the highest price they can get. The forces of supply and demand are at work on both you (the consumer) and the owners of the store (the suppliers). You will buy more CDs if the price of a CD decreases. They will supply more CDs if the price of a CD increases.

A list of how many units of a product consumers are willing to buy at different prices is called a **demand schedule.** Here is a demand schedule for a customer at a record store. Every individual has a different demand schedule. Your demand schedule reflects how you feel about money and CDs.

Price of One CD	Number of CDs Customer Is Willing to Buy at That Price
$20	0
18	1
16	2
14	3
12	4
10	5
8	6

You can see from the demand schedule that as the price of CDs declines, the customer is willing to buy more of them.

A list of how many units of a product producers are willing to supply at different prices is called a **supply schedule.** Here is a supply schedule for the record store owner.

Price of One CD	Number of CDs Owner Is Willing to Supply at That Price
$ 8	0
10	1
12	2
14	3
16	4
18	5
20	6

You can see from the supply schedule that as the price of CDs rises, the record store owner is willing to supply more of them.

THE MARKET CLEARING PRICE

The supply and demand schedules for the CDs have been plotted on Chart 2. The point at which the supply and demand curves cross is the **market clearing price.** This is the price at which the number of CDs the customer is willing to buy and the number the record store owner is willing to supply are the same.

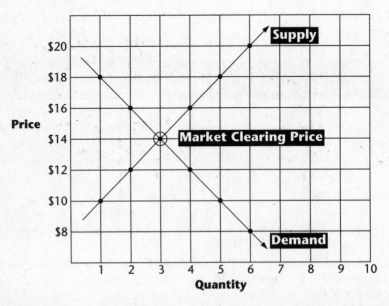

Chart 2 How Supply and Demand Affect the Market Clearing Price

According to the chart, the market clearing price is $14. For $14, the customer wants to take home three CDs. For that price, the record store owner is willing to sell three CDs.

Supply, demand, and price information are communicated quickly and clearly between consumers and entrepreneurs in the free market system. Learning to forecast supply and demand in your market is a key to success.

COMPETITION KEEPS PRICES DOWN AND QUALITY HIGH

The laws of supply and demand work best in competitive markets. When businesses are competing with each other, they try to attract consumers by lowering prices, improving quality, and developing new products and services.

Government regulations, or anything else that keeps entrepreneurs from entering a market, will make it less competitive. Less competition leads to higher prices, poorer quality, and fewer new products and services.

MONOPOLY

When a market has only one supplier of a product or service, that supplier is commonly said to have a monopoly. The word **monopoly** comes from two Greek words—*monos*, which means "single," and *polien*, which means "to sell."

If there is only one grocery store in your neighborhood, there is less incentive, or encouragement, for that store to lower its prices or improve quality to attract customers. If you are the only seller of T-shirts in your market, there is less incentive for you to create new designs.

A monopoly is the opposite of competition and has the opposite effect. In a monopoly, the supplier has no incentive to lower prices or improve quality to attract the consumer. The consumer has no choice but to go to that supplier. Monopolies generally keep prices high and quality low.

In free markets, monopolies seldom last long. Other entrepreneurs will enter the same market with the same or similar products and compete for the same customers. If you ever find yourself in a monopoly position, you should behave as if you have many competitors: offer the lowest possible price with the highest possible quality. If you don't, you will soon find yourself with many competitors and fewer customers.

The best ways to prevent monopolies are: keep markets free, make it easy for people to start businesses, and encourage as many people as possible to learn the basics of entrepreneurship.

GOVERNMENT-OWNED OR GOVERNMENT-ENCOURAGED MONOPOLIES

Most of the monopolies that exist today in the United States are owned and operated by some level of government. The United States Postal Service is one example, public schools are another.

Some people believe the government should not own and operate these monopolies but should allow postal, educational, and other services to be supplied by private businesses. These people argue that private businesses, competing with each other, would provide better and cheaper service than the government monopolies do.

Monopolies that arise in the private sector tend to be the result of government interference in the marketplace. Such monopolies tend to be destroyed by competition once the government interference is removed. One example is AT&T, which virtually monopolized long-distance phone service until certain government regulations concerning licensing for long-distance phone service providers were removed in the 1980s. Since then, MCI, Sprint, and other competitors have been able to grab shares of the market away from AT&T by offering cheaper phone service rates. AT&T has responded by lowering its rates and by improving the quality of its service with its True Voice® system. Consumers of phone service have benefited greatly from the increased competition in the market.

BREAKING AT&T'S MONOPOLY: HOW MCGOWAN STARTED MCI[3]

AT&T's monopoly of the long-distance telephone business was largely broken up by the dogged determination of one man, William McGowan. He founded MCI Communications Corporation, which destroyed AT&T's monopoly by offering an alternative service using radio microwaves. The price to consumers was as much as 50 percent cheaper.

William McGowan took on AT&T with a company he had purchased in 1968 for only $50,000. McGowan had been contacted by John Goeken, who was trying to build a microwave system between Chicago and St. Louis to expand his mobile-radio business. For five years, AT&T had used its might to prevent Goeken from receiving Federal Communications Commission (FCC) approval for his operation. Goeken was driven close to bankruptcy.

As McGowan told *Money* magazine in 1982 ("Six Who Succeeded," December 1982), he bought Goeken's company because "the fact that it [taking on AT&T's monopoly of communication] had never been done before made the idea all the more irresistible." After the FCC finally approved the Chicago–St. Louis link in 1969, McGowan went on a fund-raising crusade for his new venture. He raised over $100 million in four years and got the FCC to agree to support nationwide long-distance phone competition.

AT&T, meanwhile, fought MCI at the FCC, in Congress, and by filing numerous harassing lawsuits. Although conducting the fight was expensive for McGowan, the results were worth it many times over. In 1980, a federal jury in Chicago found AT&T guilty of antitrust violations and awarded $1.8 billion in damages to MCI. Although the award amount was reduced when AT&T appealed the case, the damage had been done. MCI was in business as a viable alternative long-distance service provider. Other competitors, such as Sprint, jumped into the market as well.

Today, MCI has over a million customers. MCI, Sprint, and AT&T still duke it out with television commercials and price wars. The biggest winner is the consumer.

COMPETITION ENCOURAGES CHANGE

Like McGowan, every entrepreneur is trying to fill a consumer need more cheaply and effectively than the competition.

Suppose you have a T-shirt business. Everybody at your school wants to wear one of your custom-made designs. They pay a relatively high price that allows you to make a large profit. Your T-shirt business is a monopoly. You are the single seller of custom T-shirts in your market.

But then a friend of yours also goes into the T-shirt business. Many of the students like her designs, too. Now you have competition. The supply of custom T-shirts in your market has just increased.

What's more, your friend decides to sell her T-shirts for three dollars less than yours. Now she's getting all your customers. To compete with her and win back your customers, you will have to lower your prices and perhaps bring out new designs as well.

You may decide that rather than compete with your friend for T-shirt customers, you are going to sell jewelry. The famous economist Joseph Schumpeter called this process of constantly changing businesses "creative destruction."[4]

COMPETITION KEEPS BUSINESS EXCITING

Entrepreneurship is never boring. The market is always changing, and competition is always around the corner. Risk and uncertainty are two elements that make small business so exciting.

Entrepreneurship is a discovery process. Each time you make any choice regarding your business, you will quickly get feedback from your market: the demand for your product or service will rise or fall. If the demand for your product or service falls, the market is telling you to move on to a different product or service. If the supply of your product or service rises, the price will start to fall. You might find that you can't sell enough of your product or service to make a profit. If you are in the marketplace as a competitor, don't be ashamed if you lose a business. The market is just telling you to move on to a new enterprise.

Business for the Young Entrepreneur

CASE STUDY: HOME AND OFFICE PLANT CARE

Do your friends say you have a green thumb? People like to have plants in their homes and offices but don't always have time to care for them. Home and office plant care is a business that is inexpensive to start and doesn't require a lot of time. Most plants need attention only once or twice a week, so plant care is a great small business for a busy student or parent.

Make a flyer and ask permission to put it up in the lobbies of office buildings near your home or school. To recognize and learn how to care for different types of plants, visit your local plant nursery or shop. Ask the owner to recommend some books you can read, or look up some titles in the book index at your library.

Supplies	Where to Find Them
Watering can (a long, narrow spout is best)	Hardware store or nursery
Plant food	Nursery or flower shop
Rag for dusting plant leaves	Make from old shirts or towels
Notebook for instructions on how to care for plants	Stationery store
Calendar to keep track of visits	Stationery store

Tips

- Ask customers for detailed instructions on how they care for each plant. Write them down!
- Offer customers a discount on your service if they refer you to a new customer.

Fresh Produce or Flowers

If you have a *really* green thumb, try a fresh produce or flower business, like James did.[5] At age ten, James grew a row of watermelons and cantaloupes. He made $150 selling the fruit his family didn't use to friends and relatives. James was so excited that he kept increasing his crop a little bit each year.

By the time he was fifteen, James was planting two-and-a-half acres and supplying three local grocery stores with produce. He named his business Fresh-Pik Produce and had business cards printed. He used custom-made stickers to label his boxes of produce.

At age sixteen, James had enough money saved to build a large greenhouse for starter plants. He rented ten acres, a tractor, a sprayer, and a plow. From that year's planting, James supplied eight local stores and several wholesalers. He plans to major in horticulture and make farming his life's work.

RESOURCES

An engaging overview of economic thinkers, from Adam Smith to present experts, is *The Worldly Philosophers*, 6th Edition, by Robert Heilbroner (New York: Simon & Schuster, 1986).

For a very readable explanation of the principles of economics, try *The Economic Way of Thinking* by Paul Heyne (Otappan, NJ: Macmillan, 1994). One of the classics on the subject is *Capitalism and Freedom* by Milton Friedman (Chicago: University of Chicago Press, 1963).

A groundbreak recent discussion is *Black Economics: Solutions for Economic and Community Empowerment* by Jawanza Kunjufu (Chicago: African American Images, 1991).

For a great discussion of supply and demand, see: *Master Curriculum Guide in Economics, Part II, Strategies for Teaching Economics*, which is available from:

National Council on Economic Education
1140 Avenue of the Americas
New York, NY 10036
(212) 730-7007

WHAT KINDS OF PEOPLE BECOME ENTREPRENEURS?

4

Entrepreneurship is personal. It is what you can do almost by yourself.
—John H. Johnson (b. 1918)
American publisher of *Ebony* and *Jet* magazines

WHAT KINDS OF PEOPLE BECOME ENTREPRENEURS?

Many successful entrepreneurs started life with very little money or education. Some came from families that had little financial wealth but were rich in their ability to turn dreams into reality.

Entrepreneurs tend to be risk takers who are good at adapting to change and developing their personal strengths. This may be why a fair share of great American entrepreneurs have been **immigrants.** Immigrants are people who move away from their homeland to settle in a new country. They face many challenges that exercise their minds, including learning a new language and new customs. In a sense, they are forced by circumstances to become entrepreneurial. Immigrants may also see market opportunities that people already living in a community have overlooked. Perhaps this is why so many immigrants to the United States have started their own small businesses.

HOW A YOUNG IMMIGRANT BECAME A SUCCESSFUL ENTREPRENEUR

A national winner of NFTE's Entrepreneurial Spirit Award in 1994 was a sixteen-year-old whose family had immigrated to California from China after living for a while in Vietnam. When Linh's family arrived in San Francisco, she quickly learned that business was an important part of American life. She never thought of herself as the entrepreneurial type, though.

Linh came from a culture that valued quiet, respectful behavior. She was somewhat suspicious of salespeople. "Acquiring the knowledge of business made me understand that salespeople are not scam artists," she says, "[and] this allowed me to be open to the concept of selling products."

Linh originally sold candy through her company, Sensational Sweets Unlimited, but when she found candy to be a slow seller, she switched to wholesale jewelry. Perhaps because she was sensitive to the negative reaction some people might have to a strong verbal sales pitch, Linh decided to create a catalog for her business. Linh took color photographs of each style of costume jewelry she was offering and combined them with descriptions, prices, and order forms to create her own product catalog. Her catalog has been a big hit and a great sales tool for her expanding business. Linh has recently added hair bands and stationery to her product line.

CHILDHOOD CHALLENGES CAN INSPIRE GREATNESS

Linh's childhood was very challenging. Her family left China because of the political repression there, but when they moved to Vietnam they found it wasn't much safer. When Linh moved to San Francisco, she faced both culture shock and the challenge of learning a new language.

Like Linh, many successful entrepreneurs have come from challenging backgrounds. Growing up in a tough environment required them to become driven and competitive just to survive.

DAVE THOMAS OF WENDY'S: OVERCOMING BEATINGS AND CHILDHOOD TRAUMA

Dave Thomas, the founder of the Wendy's restaurant chain, was only five years old when his adoptive mother died. Dave was raised by his adoptive grandmother until his adoptive father remarried. His grandmother's husband was killed working on a railroad, and she had worked very hard to support four children. Thomas says he got most of his down-to-earth family values from her.

Thomas's adoptive father often beat Dave with a strap. His father remarried three times, so Dave was bounced around a lot from home to home. In his biography, *Dave's Way*, Thomas says these childhood traumas taught him some important lessons that helped him become successful in business. These lessons were:[1]

1. Look for people who care about you, and learn from them.
2. Dream early, and build your goals on your dream.
3. Learn to rely on yourself early.
4. If there are things you don't like in the world you grow up in, make your own world different.
5. Take a step every day.
6. Be yourself.

Many other great entrepreneurs have overcome poverty, racism, and language and cultural barriers. For example:

- The most successful African American in the oil industry, Jake Simmons, Jr., was raised on a ranch in Oklahoma in the early 1900s. At that time, the state government was openly racist. Some blacks were even lynched, but Simmons and other black Oklahomans fought hard for their freedom. Simmons went on to build a great fortune from oil and land deals.

- The owner of the Chun King Chinese food company, Jeno Paulucci, was born to a very poor Italian family in Minnesota. His father was a coal miner. To make extra money, the Paulucci family ran a grocery store out of their home. Paulucci had a knack for making different kinds of food attractive to the consumer. He sensed the American consumer would buy canned versions of popular Chinese foods, like chow mein. He used funny commercials to make Chun King foods very popular.

- Shipping tycoon Aristotle Onassis was one of the richest people in the world in the 1960s. As a youngster, Onassis had immigrated to Argentina from Greece. He learned Spanish at night and sold tobacco by day. When he was only fifteen, he landed a big tobacco order and used his earnings to invest in more tobacco to sell. As he accumulated more money, he started the small businesses that he eventually built into his great financial empire. Onassis married Jacqueline Kennedy after her husband, President John F. Kennedy, was assassinated.

TOM MONAGHAN:
BUILDING DOMINO'S PIZZA WITH $900

Tom Monaghan, the founder of Domino's Pizza, had a tough childhood. He was raised in orphanages and foster homes; his father had died when he was four. He lived with his mother for a couple of years, but she sent him to a foster home when they could not get along. Monaghan struggled in school—he graduated last in his high school class and was expelled from a Catholic seminary. He tried college six times but never got past his freshman year.

In 1960, Monaghan and his brother Jim borrowed $900 and bought a foundering pizzeria in Ypsilanti, Michigan. Jim left within the year, but Tom hung on, surviving two near-bankruptcies and a fire. Slowly, he opened new stores. In 1979, he was sued by the Amstar Corporation for infringing on the name of Domino sugar. Amstar won the first round, but Monaghan won on appeal. Through entrepreneurship, Monaghan—who had never succeeded at anything—discovered that he had perseverance and drive. He enjoyed making pizza and was committed wholeheartedly to making Domino's Pizza a household name.

During these years, Monaghan worked eighteen hours a day, seven days a week. He traveled all over the Midwest visiting other pizzerias to check out their operations. By the time the lawsuit with Amstar was settled, Domino's had grown to 290 stores. Only a year later, Monaghan opened his 500th store. Today, Domino's has almost 5,000 stores in the United States and about 300 in other countries.

In 1983, Monaghan realized a boyhood dream when he purchased the Detroit Tigers baseball club for $54 million. A year later, the Tigers won the World Series.

CHARACTERISTICS OF THE
SUCCESSFUL ENTREPRENEUR[2]

No one is born with all the characteristics needed for success. Think about the traits represented in Chart 3. Which of these characteristics do you already possess?

If you are lacking some characteristics but have energy and motivation, the other traits can be developed. Listed below are a dozen of the traits generally considered most important for an entrepreneur to develop. Which ones do you think you could develop with a little effort?

Adaptability

Persuasiveness

Risk Taking

Honesty

Confidence

Vision

Competitiveness

Perseverance

**Chart 3   Do You Have What It Takes to Be a Successful
Entrepreneur? (Artist: Al Stern)**

1. Adaptability—the ability to cope with new situations and find creative solutions to problems.
2. Competitiveness—the willingness to compete with and test oneself against others.
3. Confidence—the belief that you can do what you set out to do.
4. Discipline—the ability to stay focused and stick to a schedule and deadlines.
5. Drive—the desire to work hard to accomplish one's goals.
6. Honesty—the commitment to tell the truth and deal with people fairly.
7. Organization—the ability to structure one's life and keep tasks and information in order.
8. Perseverance—the refusal to quit; the willingness to keep goals in sight and work toward them despite obstacles.
9. Persuasiveness—the knack for convincing people to see your point of view and to get them interested in your ideas.
10. Risk Taking—the courage to expose oneself to possible losses.
11. Understanding—the ability to listen to and empathize with other people.
12. Vision—the ability to see the end results of your goals while working to achieve them.

From the list above, list four traits that you think you have:

1. _____

2. _____

3. _____

4. _____

Now list four traits that you think you could develop:

1. _____

2. _____

3. _____

4. _____

THE POWER OF A POSITIVE MENTAL ATTITUDE

No matter how many entrepreneurial characteristics you have or develop, they won't do you any good unless you combine them with a positive attitude. Numerous entrepreneurs have cited "a positive attitude" as a key to their success ever since Napoleon Hill coined the phrase in his inspirational books.

A man who knew the meaning of "the power of positive thinking" was W. Clement Stone. He turned a positive attitude into a $500 million fortune by building one of the largest insurance companies in America, Combined Insurance Company.

When he was only fifteen, Stone began selling insurance policies to help his mother pay the bills. His first assignment was a large office building. He was so afraid to even enter the building that, to get up his courage, he made up optimistic phrases like "When there's nothing to lose and much to gain by trying, try." Once inside the building, he actually *ran* from office to office trying to sell his policies before his fear of rejection could overwhelm him.

Stone discovered that people responded to his positive attitude by buying insurance policies. While still in high school, Stone was selling forty insurance policies a day. He went on to revolutionize the sales profession with the idea that it was the attitude of the salesperson that sold the product.

Entrepreneurs are optimists—they *have* to be, in order to see opportunities where others see only problems. At NFTE, we've learned to think of the brain as hardware and thoughts as software. Essentially, your thoughts program your brain.

MADAME C. J. WALKER: THE ENTREPRENEUR AS A FORCE FOR SOCIAL GOOD

When I was still teaching, I took some students on a field trip in Harlem. We went into a beauty shop and asked the woman who owned it how she got started in business. She said she would ask her mother. Her mother, who was a wonderful elderly lady, said she had gotten her start in the business through Madame C. J. Walker. That's how I first heard of this influential African American entrepreneur.

Some people don't realize they have what it takes to be entrepreneurs until later in life. Madame C. J. Walker didn't start her own business until she was thirty-eight. She became one of the first African

American millionaires. Her success had a tremendous positive impact on her community. Not only did she employ many black women, she set them up in business for themselves.

Madame Walker was orphaned in early childhood and raised by her married sister in Louisiana farm country. When Madame Walker was age twenty her husband died. She moved to St. Louis where she worked as a washerwoman for eighteen years to support herself and her daughter.

Walker Starts Her Business at Age 38

When she was thirty-eight, Walker developed a formula for a new hair product for African American women. In addition, she created a compound specially suited to the complexion needs of black women. In 1906, Walker remarried and moved to Denver, Colorado. She began selling her products door-to-door. This sales method allowed her to demonstrate their benefits. Soon, Walker was training other women to sell her products. She also set up a thriving mail-order business.

At the peak of her career, Walker employed over 3,000 people. Most of her employees were women who sold the products door-to-door as "Walker Agents," much like today's Avon Ladies sell makeup and personal care products.

Walker organized her agents into clubs that promoted not only their business, but also social and charitable causes. Walker gave cash prizes to the clubs that did the most charitable and educational work for African Americans.

The attention drawn to the Madame C. J. Walker Manufacturing Company by the charitable work of Walker and her agents was considerable. Walker became one of the most famous women in America. She made large contributions to the National Association for the Advancement of Colored People (NAACP), as well as to homes for the aged and needy, and to scholarships for African American students.

When Walker died in 1919, she left two-thirds of her fortune to educational institutions and charities. She also left behind many Walker Agents who started their own businesses. Her legacy of African American women owning small businesses is still strong in many urban areas today.

ENTREPRENEURS AND PHILANTHROPY

Like Madame Walker, many entrepreneurs have been drawn to philanthropy, which is a desire to help humanity expressed through gifts to charities or foundations. Most philanthropic foundations in this country were created by entrepreneurs. Some examples are The Rockefeller Foundation, The Ford Foundation, The Coleman Foundation, Inc., The Charles G. Koch Foundation, and The Carnegie Foundation.

Ironically, some of the most aggressive entrepreneurs in American history, such as Andrew Carnegie, have also been the most generous.

In 1901, after a long and sometimes ruthless business career, Carnegie sold his steel company to J. P. Morgan for $420 million. Overnight, Carnegie became one of the richest men in the world. After his retirement, Carnegie spent most of his time giving away his wealth to libraries, colleges, museums, and other worthwhile institutions that still benefit people today. He often said that a rich man dies disgraced. By the time of his death from pneumonia, in Lenox, Massachusetts, on August 11, 1919, the 84-year-old Carnegie had given away $350 million.

ENLIGHTENED CAPITALISM: THE BODY SHOP, INC.

Today, some entrepreneurs practice what Anita Roddick has dubbed "enlightened capitalism." Roddick treats her company, The Body Shop, as a force for social change. Each Body Shop store is expected to get involved with a local community project. The store staff is encouraged to do volunteer work at the project on company time. "I pay my staff to be active citizens," Roddick has said.

Roddick had never expected to be wealthy; she opened the first Body Shop to support herself and her children while her husband was away in South America on an expedition. In 1984, however, The Body Shop stock went on sale and quickly rose in price until the company was worth £8 million (British pounds). The Roddicks were millionaires.

Anita and her husband Gordon discussed their future. Suddenly they had power and wealth, which they wanted to use wisely. Anita had already been campaigning against animal testing of cosmetics; now she had the clout to make her voice heard.

She and Gordon decided to use their shops to educate people about social and environmental issues. In 1985, they paid for Greenpeace, an environmental group, to put up posters protesting the dumping of hazardous waste into the North Sea. Customers could join Greenpeace at Body Shop stores. The next year, The Body Shop protested the slaughter of sperm whales for their oil. The Body Shop uses jojoba oil, a desert plant wax, instead of sperm oil in its products. Greenpeace designed posters and leaflets for the stores.

The Body Shop worked next with Friends of the Earth on campaigns against acid rain and to foster awareness of the dangers to the ozone layer from aerosol sprays. During these campaigns, the Roddicks learned to keep the message clear and provide plenty of easy-to-understand information to Body Shop employees and customers.

THE REACH OF BODY SHOP CAMPAIGNS

The environmental campaigning attracted media attention as well as customers. Roddick has estimated that the publicity generated by Body Shop campaigns has been worth millions in free advertising. The campaigns have also made Body Shop employees happier and more motivated. Their jobs have offered them an opportunity to learn about new things and change the world.

Some campaigns have been highly successful. In 1989, the European Community proposed that all cosmetics be tested on animals. More than five million people signed The Body Shop's petition against this testing, and the proposal was withdrawn. More recently, a campaign for Amnesty International resulted in the release of fifteen political prisoners due to letters from Body Shop customers. As Anita said in a speech in New York in 1993: "That is the relevancy of what business should be doing in the marketplace."

Another important campaign was "Stop the Burning," which focused public attention on the destruction of the Brazilian rainforest. Anita traveled to Brazil to meet with tribal leaders as part of The Body Shop's "Trade Not Aid" program. She lived with Brazil's Kayapo Indians, exploring how she could trade without destroying their culture. The Body Shop now buys brazil nut oil and vegetable dye beads from the tribe and is committed to helping them survive.

"Trade Not Aid" stemmed from the Roddicks' belief—which I share—that the best way to help people in poor areas is to help them establish their own small businesses. "We avoid governments and go straight to the people in the countries," Anita says.

Although the Roddicks are deeply committed to using their business to help people and protect the environment, Anita says, "I am not rushing around the world as some kind of loony do-gooder; first and foremost, I am a trader looking for trade."

Anita and I both belong to the Social Venture Network, an organization for business leaders seeking solutions to social problems. Although I have my differences with organizations such as Greenpeace, because they consider government ownership one possible solution to environmental problems, I think Anita's emphasis on helping to solve social and environmental problems through entrepreneurship is a real breakthrough.

HOW MUCH OF AN ENTREPRENEUR ARE YOU?[3]

This survey, developed by The National Federation of Independent Business, is a great way to assess your character. Read each of the qualities and explanations listed. Rate the degree to which you believe you possess that quality by circling a number from 1 to 10. After six months, you can mark the survey again, using a different color pen or pencil, and see how you've grown.

Quality	Explanation	Range
Drive	Highly motivated	1 2 3 4 5 6 7 8 9 (10)
Perseverance	Sticking to task or goal	1 2 3 4 5 6 (7) 8 9 10
Risk taking	Willing to take chances	1 2 3 4 5 6 7 8 9 (10)
Organization	Life and work in order	1 2 3 4 5 6 (7) 8 9 10
Confidence	Sure of yourself	1 2 3 4 5 6 7 8 9 (10)
Persuasiveness	Able to convince others	1 2 3 4 5 6 7 8 (9) 10
Honesty	Open, truthful	1 2 3 4 5 6 7 (8) 9 10
Competitiveness	Eager to win	1 2 3 4 5 6 7 8 (9) 10
Adaptability	Coping with new situations	1 2 3 4 5 6 7 8 (9) 10
Understanding	Empathy with others	1 2 3 4 (5) 6 7 8 9 10
Discipline	Able to stick to schedule	1 2 3 4 5 (6) 7 8 9 10
Vision	Able to think of long-term goals	1 2 3 4 5 6 7 8 9 (10)

(low ⟶ high)

Date of first self-rating _____ Total Score _____

Date of second self-rating _____ Total Score _____

CASE STUDY: HOUSE CLEANING

When Maria's husband was sentenced to four years in prison for selling drugs, she didn't know how she was going to support herself and her two young children. Fortunately, she had taken a NFTE course in high school, so she decided to start her own business.

Business for the Young Entrepreneur

Today, Maria has an apartment-cleaning business in Manhattan. She cleans for four customers per week. Maria charges $64.00 per cleaning job, so her gross income per week is $256.00 (4 clients × $64.00 per client).

Maria's only expense is travel, which costs her around $15.00 per week. All the cleaning supplies are provided by the customers, and Maria does no advertising of her business. Instead, she asks each satisfied customer to recommend her to a friend. Maria's net income is $241.00 per week ($256.00 gross income per week − $15.00 weekly expenses).

It's hard for working mothers and fathers to keep up with housework. This could be a great money-making opportunity for you.

You probably have already had some "on-the-job training" if you've done chores at home. Make flyers to advertise your services. A flyer is a one-page advertisement that you hand out to potential customers and post on bulletin boards. You can draw a flyer by hand or design it on a computer. It can be simple or fancy, but should be eye-catching and include your name, the name of your business, and your phone number. List on your flyer the following jobs that you can do: sweeping, mopping, dusting, emptying garbage, doing dishes, cleaning bathrooms, doing laundry.

Put up your flyers in grocery stores and laundromats, and on community bulletin boards. You could offer your customers the choice of having you use their cleaning supplies at their house, or, for a higher fee, having you bring your own supplies.

Tips

- Do a great job so you can build a base of repeat customers.
- Write on an index card the name, address, and phone number of each customer, and list the exact chores you did for them. Review the list if you're called back for additional cleaning sessions.
- Offer a discount to any customer who hooks you up with a new customer.
- If the service grows, think about expanding into office cleaning.

RESOURCES

Here are some books about how to develop success characteristics, including the W. Clement Stone classic and an update of Napoleon Hill's famous *Think and Grow Rich* by an African-American author.

Have You Got What It Takes? How To Tell If You Should Start Your Own Business by Joseph Mancuso (New York: Prentice-Hall Press, 1982). This book is short and funny, and is still a bestseller today.

Success Through a Positive Mental Attitude by W. Clement Stone (Englewood Cliffs, NJ: Prentice-Hall, 1962).

Think and Grow Rich by Napoleon Hill (New York: Harper & Row, 1989).

Think and Grow Rich by Dennis Paul Kimbro (New York: Fawcett Columbine, 1991).

Another business that is very active on the environmental and social front is Ben & Jerry's Homemade, Inc. The former CEO of Ben & Jerry's describes the company's remarkable history in *Ben & Jerry's: The Inside Scoop: How Two Real Guys Built a Business with a Social Conscience and a Sense of Humor* by Fred "Chico" Lager (New York: Crown Publishers, Inc., 1994).

Anita Roddick tells the story of The Body Shop, Inc. in *Body & Soul* (Crown Publishers, Inc., New York: 1991).

My own self-published book, *Homeboys,* is an account of my teaching days in the New York City public schools and how I came to realize that many of my students possessed entrepreneurial characteristics as a result of their urban experiences. For a copy, write to me at:

Steve Mariotti
NFTE
120 Wall Street, 29th Floor
New York, NY 10005

5 You Get What You Negotiate

MAKING WIN–WIN AGREEMENTS

> You don't get what you deserve, you get what you negotiate.
> —Chester L. Karrass
> American negotiation expert and author

NEGOTIATION IS ABOUT COMPROMISE, NOT WINNING

Negotiation is the process of achieving one's goals through discussion and give-and-take. An example of negotiation is a buyer and a seller discussing the price of an item until an agreement is reached.

A big part of my job at NFTE is negotiating with our funders. Even though I'm running a nonprofit organization, I do as much negotiating as I would if I were the president of a for-profit corporation. In your personal life, you are probably continually involved with negotiations. The better you get at negotiating, the better you will become at getting what you want by helping the other person to get what he or she wants.

In his best-selling book, *You Can Negotiate Anything*, Herb Cohen tells the story of a brother and sister squabbling over how to divide the last quarter of a pie. Just as the boy gains control of the knife, their mother arrives on the scene. "Hold it!" she says. "I don't care who cuts the pie, but whoever does cut it has to give the *other* person the right to select the piece they want."

To protect himself, the boy cuts the pie into two pieces of equal size. The moral of the story is that if fighting parties shift their focus *from defeating each other to defeating the problem,* everyone benefits.

Negotiation is about **compromise,** not about winning. Compromise is sacrificing something you want so that an agreement can be reached that is acceptable to you *and* the person with whom you are negotiating. In the example above, the brother and sister were more interested in beating each other to the biggest slice of pie than they were in satisfying their appetites.

The siblings forgot the most important principle of negotiation: The other person is not your enemy! The best negotiations are those in which both parties are satisfied—they have reached a "win–win" agreement. Conduct your negotiations as if you will be dealing with that person again very soon.

BEFORE NEGOTIATIONS

In 1980, when Bill Gates was only twenty-four, he conducted one of the most important negotiations of his life with one of the most powerful companies in the world, IBM.[1] IBM was interested in having Microsoft work with it on IBM's top-secret effort to develop a personal computer. No doubt, "Big Blue," as IBM was known, expected little Microsoft, which was a $7 million company with fewer than forty employees at the time, to be a pushover. After all, IBM's annual revenues were hitting $30 billion.

Before his negotiations with IBM, however, Gates had set his goals and organized his thoughts. He knew exactly what he wanted to achieve and just what his boundaries were. IBM offered to pay Microsoft $175,000 for an operating system, called MS DOS, for IBM's new personal computers. Gates wasn't willing to sell his company's program code for that price, however, because he knew IBM would want to use the code on a variety of future machines. Gates decided he would hold out for royalties and retain ownership of MS DOS. He also wanted to retain the right to license copies of the program's code to other parties. Later, IBM was to regret its failure to purchase MS DOS outright. The licensing deal ended up costing Big Blue a lot of money.

The principles of negotiation that Gates used before entering this important negotiation with IBM were the same ones you should use before any negotiation. They are:

1. Set your goals and organize your thoughts. What do you want to achieve in the negotiation? Write down your goals and thoughts on note cards, and keep them with you during the discussion.

2. Decide what your boundaries are. Think about what the best deal for you would be. Then think about what the worst deal would be. What is the minimum you would be willing to accept? What is the maximum you are seeking? Knowing these limits ahead of time will prevent you from getting carried away and giving up too much of one thing in order to get something else.

3. Put yourself in the other person's shoes. What does he or she want from the negotiation? What is his or her minimum? Maximum? Things that aren't very important to you could be very important to the other person. You could give up these to get what you want.

DURING NEGOTIATIONS

During the negotiations with IBM, Gates stuck to his plan. Despite the nervousness he felt inside about negotiating with IBM, Gates gave clear, calm presentations to IBM executives regarding the operating system that Microsoft proposed to supply IBM. In the past, Gates had jeopardized deals with customers and suppliers by being too intense and too eager to win. This time, he knew he would have to make a worthwhile offer for the deal with IBM to succeed.

IBM's representative, Sandy Meade, was surprised by Gates's boldness on the royalty issue. Meade recalled, in the book *Gates* by Stephen Manes and Paul Andrews (Touchstone, 1994), that, unlike other software companies with which IBM had negotiated, "I never felt they [Microsoft] needed the money."

Meade's negotiating tactic was to remind Gates that his relationship with IBM was a "long-term relationship with the potential for big business." Gates had guessed correctly that IBM would be willing to pay royalties to use Microsoft's program code in IBM's personal computers. In return for IBM's agreement to pay royalties, Microsoft committed to a brutal delivery schedule. Gates was in the habit of having dinner at his parents' home on Sunday nights. After he signed the deal with IBM, Gates told his mother not to expect him for at least six months.

During negotiations, Gates and his team used all of the tactics listed below. Memorize them and practice using them during your negotiations.

1. Let the other person name a price first. When discussing a price, try to let the other person make an offer first. This will reveal his or her position.

2. Try extremes. If the person won't reveal his or her position, throw out an extreme figure—very high or very low. This will force the other person to come forward with some type of response that will guide you.

3. Show a willingness to bargain. As negotiations proceed, respond to each counteroffer by giving up something you already decided in advance that you could afford to give up.

4. Use silence as a tool. After you have initially stated your case, don't say anything for a few moments. Your silence can prompt the other person to say something that you can turn to your advantage.

5. Always ask for more than you are offered. When the other person wants you to pay back a loan in ten days, for instance, ask for fifteen. You may have to settle for twelve, but that's better than the original demand.

As a small business owner, you will have to negotiate frequently—with suppliers, with customers, and with employees. How well you negotiate will greatly affect the success of your business.

NEGOTIATION IN ACTION

Here's an example of how the techniques listed above can be used in a simple negotiation. A young entrepreneur who wants to sell his product at a flea market is ready to negotiate with the flea market manager. Before the negotiation, the entrepreneur has determined his goals:

1. To be excused from paying the entrance fee.
2. To be allowed to set up early.

He has also thought about the flea market manager's needs. The key to a successful negotiation is similar to the key to a successful business: figure out the other person's needs and how you can satisfy them.

As you read the dialogue below, notice that the entrepreneur is careful to make sure the manager understands how the negotiation can benefit him and the flea market. See if you can spot the negotiation techniques in action.

ENTREPRENEUR: Hi, I'm Steve, and I'd like to sell here on Saturday. I was wondering if I could talk to you about it.

MANAGER: Sure, go ahead.

ENTREPRENEUR: I think there are three good reasons for having young people like me get involved with the flea market. It's good for community relations, you can probably get some publicity out of it, and it will attract more young people to the flea market as customers.

MANAGER: Well, that sounds great, do you want to sign up now?

ENTREPRENEUR: I do, but as a young entrepreneur I don't have the money to cover the fee. As I develop my business here, though, I could begin to pay you.

MANAGER: I don't know if I'm willing to waive the fee.

ENTREPRENEUR: (Doesn't say anything.)

MANAGER: How about $50 instead of $100?

ENTREPRENEUR: (Doesn't say anything.)

MANAGER: How about $25?

ENTREPRENEUR: I understand what you do here, I think it has value. But my position is that I would be bringing a lot of value to the flea market, and I need to put my initial capital into building my business, which will benefit you in the long run.

MANAGER: All right, I'll waive the fee.

ENTREPRENEUR: I have something else that would really help me. Could I come in an hour early to set up?

MANAGER: No. No way.

ENTREPRENEUR: I need to do this because I feel I'm at a disadvantage with the more experienced vendors.

MANAGER: (Doesn't say anything.)

ENTREPRENEUR: When do you get here?

MANAGER: This Saturday I won't get here until a half hour before we open.

ENTREPRENEUR: That would be great. Could I meet you here and come in with you? That way I won't inconvenience you.

MANAGER: OK.

NEGOTIATION IN ACTION II

Here's a negotiation between Jack, who's selling a used stereo, and Sara, who wants to buy it. Before the negotiation, Sara determines her goals:

1. To be able to return the stereo if it stops working within two months.

2. To pay one-third what it would cost in the store.

The essence of negotiation is figuring out how to meet the other person's needs, so Sara thinks about what she has to offer in return. The stereo has been advertised in the paper for a couple of weeks, so she figures that the seller would like to get rid of it and not have to worry about selling it anymore. She can offer:

1. To pay immediately in cash.

2. To take the stereo away that day.

Next, she sets her boundaries:

1. Not to spend more than $250.

2. Not to accept less than one month for return if the stereo stops working.

SARA: Are you still interested in selling the stereo?

JACK: Yes, I am.

SARA: What price were you looking for?

JACK: I'd like $500.

SARA: (Doesn't say anything and shows frustration on her face)

JACK: Well, I'm willing to negotiate down to $400 but that's my final offer.

SARA: I know you've had the ad in for a couple of weeks. I'm willing to pay cash and take the stereo today. I feel $150 would be fair.

JACK: $150 is ridiculous. I'm willing to go down to $300.

SARA: (After remaining silent for a few moments) I'm willing to go up to $200 but I want two months to return it if something goes wrong, and I'd like to try it today.

JACK: All right, you can try it. Here it is.

SARA: I still want to be covered in case it breaks in two months.

JACK: Two months is unreasonable.

SARA: I'm willing to negotiate on that. What can you offer as a price and money-back guarantee?

JACK: (After a moment of silence) I'll go $250 and give you one month.

SARA: OK. How about $225 and a month and a half.

JACK: You've got a deal.

DON'T LET "MAYBE" WASTE YOUR TIME[2]

The most frustrating negotiations are not the ones that end in a firm No but those that end with a Maybe.

Maybes feel encouraging, but they waste your time and keep you from pursuing other options. When someone can't seem to give you an answer, say something like, "I know you can't say Yes right away, but I think it's fair for me to ask you to give me a No by the end of the week."

If he or she says No at the end of the week, fine; now you can move on to a new person. Don't forget to ask the person who says No: "If you can't do it, whom can you recommend who might?"

Business for the Young Entrepreneur

CASE STUDY: SOUND AND LIGHTING COMPANY

When Harold was sixteen, he started spinning records for parties in his Philadelphia neighborhood. His first gig was at an aunt's wedding reception, for which he was paid $125 for five hours. Harold recalls, "It would have taken me a full week of working at my fast-food restaurant job to make that kind of money."

As a student in the University Community Outreach Program's (UCOP/NFTE) entrepreneurship course at the Wharton School of Business, Harold had learned how to use flyers and business cards to promote a business. He used his initial earnings to buy business cards, and he posted flyers around town. Soon, Harold was taking home as much as $400 after spinning records all weekend. In 1991, when Harold was twenty-two, he formed the Nu X-Perience Sound and Lighting Company with a friend, Jeffrey. Jeffrey invested the $50,000 he had inherited from his father's estate in the business.

Jeffrey's investment put the company in the big leagues. After a year of doing sound and lights for fraternity parties, the partners began to attract major clients, including the United Negro College Fund and the Philadelphia Labor Day parade. The company now earns as much as $2,000 on weekends.

Eventually, Harold hopes to provide sound and lights for concert headliners. "That's where the money is," Harold says, adding, "there are few African American companies doing that."

Harold started his business because he enjoyed playing music for people. If you're the kind of person who keeps up with the latest musical trends, you'd probably make a great DJ, too. People hire DJs for a variety of events, including parties, weddings, and sales. This is a more expensive business to start than some—unless you already own one or two turntables and lots of records.

Some DJs join or form record pools. These are clubs that let DJs rotate or share records, so they always have new records to play at parties. Ask at your local record store about DJ clubs. DJs also get records by getting on mailing lists for record labels. Do you know of any local record labels trying to get more attention for their artists? Call them and ask about getting free records in return for exposing the artists to a wider audience by playing the records at parties.

What You'll Need to Get Started

- One or two turntables. If you use two turntables, you'll also need a mixer.
- Speakers and amplifier.
- Records.
- Flyers. Advertise your service by handing out flyers at parties and school events.

RESOURCES

Books

The following books are among the best written on negotiating. Cohen's book is filled with humorous anecdotes and is easy to read. Karrass's book is a classic by the father of negotiation theory, and Jandt's book provides an in-depth look at the win–win philosophy.

You Can Negotiate Anything by Herb Cohen (New York: Bantam Books, 1993).

The Negotiating Game: How to Get What You Want by Chester L. Karrass (New York: Harper Business, 1992).

Win–Win Negotiation: Turning Conflict into Agreement by Fred Jandt (New York: John Wiley & Sons, Inc., 1987).

Field Guide to Negotiation by Gavin Kennedy (Cambridge, MA: Harvard Business School Press, 1994).

6

How to Set Up Financial Records That Will Help Your Business Grow

The second half of a man's life is made up of nothing but the habits he has acquired during the first half.

—Feodor Dostoevski (1821–1881)
Russian novelist

A Necessary Habit

Nothing you will learn as an entrepreneur will be more important than the habit of keeping accurate records. John D. Rockefeller reportedly kept track of every penny he spent from age sixteen until his death in 1937 at the age of ninety-eight. His children said that he never paid a bill without examining it and making sure he understood each item. His ledgers became an important source of information about him to his biographers.

Most entrepreneurs aren't as enamored of keeping good records as Rockefeller was. I've personally had a hard time paying attention to my own record keeping. I finally made a deal with NFTE's financial manager. When I'm late turning in my personal expense accounts to him, I pay him twenty dollars! This motivates me to do it on time. I've found that being up-to-date with my personal financial records gives me a great feeling of organization and self-confidence.

NFTE students are required to keep daily records of their personal spending while they are taking our course. Getting in the habit of keeping good records helps them run their businesses more effectively.

After graduating from high school, Tokunbo took a summer entrepreneurship course with the UCOP program run by NFTE at Columbia University. During the course, she learned how to keep good records. "Bookkeeping and record keeping became major priorities," she says.

Tokunbo has her own nail-care business. She uses nail enamel and paste-on gems to create elaborate custom fingernail designs for her customers. Her prices range from $6.50 for regular manicures to $25 for a full set of tips and wraps.

At first, Tokunbo didn't think she needed to worry about accounting. After a while, though, she realized that "Keeping good records enables you to be smart about money."

"With basic accounting skills," she adds, "I have been able to expand my business and gradually able to see a profit." Tokunbo has even shown other people in her family how to start their own businesses.

How to Set Up Your Financial Records

Start keeping a record of all your income and expenses on ledger sheets or in an accounting journal. These are sold at stationery stores or office supply stores. Set up your records to look like Chart 4A–4D (pages 86–89).

Income is recorded as a **credit** entry. Income is money received from the sale of products or services, or from your job or an allowance. **Expenses** are recorded as **debit** entries. Expenses are the costs of doing business.

Record Cash Transactions on the Left Page of Your Ledger

Income is recorded on this page as cash received. Expenses are recorded as cash disbursed. Label each column of the page as follows:

1. Date
2. Explanation
3. (Paid) To/(Received) From
4. Cash Received
5. Cash Disbursed
6. Cash Balance

BUSINESS LEDGER					
Date	Explanation	To/From	Cash Received	Cash Disbursed	Cash Bal.

Chart 4A   Business Ledger, Left Page

BUSINESS LEDGER				
Startup/Invest.	Revenue (1)	C.O.G.S. (2)*	Op. Costs (3)**	
				Income Statement
				Revenue (1): $
				Less C.O.G.S. (2): $
				Gross Profit: $
				Less Op. Costs (3): $
				Profit: $
				Taxes: $
				Net Profit: $
				Return on Investment
				Net Profit ÷ Startup/Inv.

*Cost of Goods Sold
**Operating Costs

Chart 4B Business Ledger, Right Page

PERSONAL LEDGER					
Date	Explanation	To/From	Cash Received	Cash Disbursed	Cash Bal.

Chart 4C   Personal Ledger, Left Page

PERSONAL LEDGER						
Revenue		Cost				
Business/Work	Allowance/Gift	Food	Clothing	Travel	Entertainment	Other

Chart 4D   Personal Ledger, Right Page

When you sell your product or service to a customer, always give the customer a bill **(invoice).** You will need to purchase a receipt/invoice book with two-part, carbon-copy receipts/invoices. When you make a sale, give the top copy to the customer as his or her receipt (or record of expense). Keep the second copy as your invoice (or record of income).

When your customer has paid the bill, mark the invoice "paid." It represents your customer's receipt. Keep a record of each invoice, usually in numbered order or organized by customer name. Each invoice that is prepared and sent (or given) to a customer is recorded as a credit entry when the invoice is paid by the customer.

EXPLAIN THE TYPE OF INCOME OR EXPENSE ON THE RIGHT PAGE OF YOUR JOURNAL

This kind of bookkeeping is called "double-entry bookkeeping" because each transaction is entered twice—once on the left page, and once on the right. If you receive cash from making a sale, for example, you enter the amount of the sale under "Cash Received" on the left page. You *also* enter it under "Revenue" on the right page. If you spend money on an operating cost like making flyers, you enter the amount of the cost under "Cash Disbursed" on the left page. You also enter it under "Operating Costs" on the right page. Label the right page as follows:

1. Start-up (Costs)/Investment
2. Revenue
3. Cost of Goods Sold
4. Operating Costs

Always get a **receipt** for every purchase you make. A receipt is a slip of paper with the date and amount of your purchase printed on it. You can refer to the receipt to fill out your journal.

Save your receipts until tax time, when they will literally be worth money. The U.S. tax laws allow business owners to deduct many of their expenses from their taxable income. These **deductions** can save you money, but you must keep the receipts to prove that you actually had the expenses.

Keep your receipts in a shoebox or file. In another shoebox or file, keep all your invoices.

Using Your Journal

If you start with a balance of zero, the journal **balance** is determined by subtracting total cash disbursed from total cash receipts. The actual physical amount of money you have in your hand after a day of business will match the balance in your ledger if you have been keeping good records.

Keeping good records is really very simple, as long as you do it every business day. If you start skipping days, or trying to keep numbers in your head, maintaining a journal will be hard. There will be times when you will be too busy to record a credit or debit in your journal at the moment it occurs. But if you follow the rules below, you will always have a written record that you can use to fill in your journal later.

Keeping track of the flow of money in and out of your business will teach you how to adjust your efforts to make your business successful. The journal shows you how you are spending your money. You can try to improve your balance by lowering certain expenses or increasing income.

As you can see from Chart 4D, your income statement falls out of your accounting journal. Simply total each column and put the totals from the columns labeled (1), (2), and (3) in the appropriate places in the income statement. When you know your Net Profit, shown on your Income Statement, you can determine your business's Return on Investment: divide your Start-Up Costs or Investment into your Net Profit.

Cash Flow

Start using your journal to keep track of the money your business earns and spends each business day. Keeping receipts for every purchase you make will help you get in the habit of keeping track of your **cash flow.** Cash flow is the cash receipts less the cash disbursements for a business over a period of time. One measure of your cash flow at a point in time is the cash balance in your journal.

You can be running a profitable business but still be insolvent if your cash balance becomes negative. To avoid getting caught without enough cash to pay your bills, follow these three rules:

1. Collect cash as soon as possible. When you make a sale, try to get paid in cash at the time of the sale.

2. Delay paying bills as long as possible without irritating the supplier. Most bills come with a due date. The phone bill, for instance, is typically due within thirty days. That means you can take up to thirty days to pay it without irritating the phone company and having them come after you for the money. *Never* pay a bill after the due date, however, without getting permission from the supplier first.

3. Always know your cash balance.

Rule of Thumb

> **Collect your cash and postpone your bills!**

KEEPING GOOD RECORDS

Jason has a T-shirt silkscreening business. Listed below are his transactions for the month of July. Study how Jason recorded each transaction on his ledger pages (Chart 5A and 5B), and how he calculated his income and return on investment for the month. Assume an opening cash balance of $1,000.

1. To start his business, Jason buys a silkscreen frame, ink, a wedge, and other basic supplies on July 1. These cost him $250.

2. On July 2, he buys four dozen T-shirts from a wholesaler for $240.

3. On July 6, Jason registers to sell his T-shirts each weekend in July at a local flea market. Registration costs him $100. He then goes to a print shop and spends $20 on business cards and $10 on flyers.

4. On July 7, Jason goes to the flea market. He sells all his T-shirts at $12 each.

5. On July 10, Jason goes back to the wholesaler and buys five dozen T-shirts for $300.

6. On July 14, he sells four dozen T-shirts at $12. To get rid of the last dozen, he drops his price to $10 each.

JASON'S BUSINESS LEDGER					
Date	**Explanation**	**To/From**	**Cash Received**	**Cash Disbursed**	**Cash Bal.**
6/30/95					$1,000
7/1/95	Silkscreen start-up supplies	Ace Arts		$250	750
7/2/95	4 dozen T-shirts	Joe Wholesale		240	510
7/6/95	Monthly registration fee	Flea market		100	410
7/6/95	Business cards	Print shop		20	390
7/6/95	Flyers	Print shop		10	380
7/7/95	Sold 4 dozen T-shirts @ $12	Flea market	$576		956
7/10/95	5 dozen T-shirts	Joe Wholesale		300	656
7/14/95	Sold 4 doz. @ $12, 1 doz. @ $10	Flea market	696		1,352
7/16/95	5 dozen T-shirts	Joe Wholesale		300	1,052
7/16/95	Silkscreen ink	Print shop		50	1,002
7/16/95	Flyers	Print shop		10	992
7/21/95	Sold 3 doz. @ $12 (rained)	Flea market	432		1,424
7/25/95	2 dozen T-shirts	Joe Wholesale		120	1,304
7/26/95			576		1,880
Totals			$2,280	$1,400	

Chart 5A   Jason's Business Ledger, Left Page

Startup/Invest.	Revenue (1)	C.O.G.S. (2)*	Op. Costs (3)**	
				JASON'S BUSINESS LEDGER
$250				
		$240		
			$100	Income Statement
			20	
			10	Revenue (1): $2,280
	$576			Less C.O.G.S. (2): $960
		300		Gross Profit: $1,320
	696			Less Op. Costs (3): $190
		300		Profit: $1,130
			50	Taxes: $282.50
			10	Net Profit: $847.50
	432			
		120		
	576			Return on Investment
				Net Profit ÷ Startup/Inv.
$250	$2,280	$960	$190	$847.50 ÷ $250 = 339%
				Instructions
				1. Record transactions as
				they occur.
				2. Keep all receipts and invoices.
				3. Estimate taxes as 25%, or
				profit × .25. In this case,
				$1,130 × .25.

*Cost of Goods Sold
**Operating Costs

Chart 5B   Jason's Business Ledger, Right Page

7. On July 16, Jason buys five dozen T-shirts for $300. He spends $50 on ink and prints another $10 worth of flyers.

8. Jason is back at the flea market on July 21, but it rains in the afternoon and he sells only three dozen shirts at $12 each.

9. On July 25, he buys and screens two dozen more shirts for $120. During the final flea market on July 28, Jason sells all his remaining shirts (four dozen) for $12 each.

Using Jason's records as a model, make ledger entries of separate transactions—purchases and sales—on at least eight business days for the business you would like to start (or have started) as an entrepreneur. Be sure to track your cash balance carefully.

CASE STUDY: PERSONAL GROOMING SERVICE

Business for the Young Entrepreneur

Tokunbo took her high school business with her to college. At school, she does the nails of about four customers a week. Her costs are minimal, since she conducts her service either in her room or in her customers' rooms. Tokunbo advertises her business through flyers.

Monique is another young woman who started a personal grooming business—African hair braiding. Unfortunately, the state of Kansas shut the fifteen-year-old down for operating without a cosmetology license. Ironically, Monique was forced to close her business because an official at the Kansas Cosmetology Board read about an entrepreneurship award she had won.

Monique's business, A Touch of Class, had been earning her a profit of about $100.00 a month. The Board informed her that she could not braid hair for profit without taking a year of classes at a cosmetology school. Monique says few schools even teach braiding and none will take her until she turns seventeen.

Monique's plight caught the interest of *The Wall Street Journal,* which published an article critical of the Kansas Board. "The Board won't let me earn my own money," Monique says in the article, "and won't let kids like me learn how to take care of ourselves."

Monique's story illustrates the importance of researching all state and local laws before starting your own small business. To learn what licenses you may need, contact your local Chamber of Commerce. You should also check with your state or local Board of Health.

Tips

- When providing personal grooming services, always keep your equipment very clean. Many states require manicurists to sterilize all nail-care instruments.

- Be friendly to your customers. Getting one's hair or nails "done" should be relaxing and enjoyable.

RESOURCES

Books

The Complete Guide to Money and Your Business by Robert E. Butler and Donald Rappaport (Englewood Cliffs, NJ: Prentice-Hall, Inc., 1989).

Accounting the Easy Way, 3rd Edition, by Peter J. Eisen (New York: Barron's Educational Series, Inc., 1995).

Other Resources

Kid's Business Software
Homeland Publications
2615 Calder Road
League City, TX 77573
(713) 332-9764

Send a self-addressed stamped envelope to receive more information on computer software Bonnie Drew has developed to help you print business cards, keep track of appointments, and manage money for your business. The software is for IBM PCs and costs $14.95. (Site licenses are available for schools.)

UNDERSTANDING YOUR COSTS

7

Keeping good records helps you keep track of the costs of running your business. Finding creative ways to cut costs often means the difference between having a struggling business and a thriving one. Anyone can spend unlimited amounts of money and create a great product, but then he or she has used up more resources than the product is worth. The entrepreneur's goal is to create a product for *less* than the consumer is willing to pay for it.

When Henry Ford was trying to make his vision of an automobile in front of every house in America a reality, the cost of building a "horseless carriage" stood in his way. The automobile had just been invented and was very expensive to produce. It was considered a plaything for rich people. But Ford was determined to build an automobile that many consumers could afford.

In those days, cars were manufactured one at a time. It was a slow, expensive process. To cut manufacturing costs, Ford invented the assembly line. The cars were assembled, or built, as they rolled past the workers on a conveyer belt. The concept of the assembly line was adopted by many companies and helped develop many industries.

Ford's idea cut costs enough to be able to sell an affordable automobile to the average American and still make a profit. His Ford Motor Company became one of the biggest car manufacturers in the world. He also revolutionized industry by introducing the concept of mass production on a grand scale.

At NFTE, we've lowered our programs' cost per child by 30 percent in the past two years. Keeping careful records showed us that one cost we could attempt to reduce was the cost of our BizBag™. The BizBag™ is a book bag filled with our books and with receipt books, calculators, and other items students need to run their businesses. We've been able to lower the cost of the BizBag,™ while still improving its contents, by finding cheaper suppliers and ordering in bulk.

COSTS

The costs of starting and operating a business are divided into the following categories:

1. Start-up costs.
2. Cost of goods sold.
3. Operating costs, including fixed costs and variable costs.

Start-up costs are the one-time expenses of starting a business. Start-up costs are also called the "original investment" or "seed money." In a restaurant, for example, start-up costs would include stoves, food processors, tables, chairs, silverware, and other items that are not replaced on a regular basis. Also included might be the one-time cost of buying land and constructing a building.

For a hot-dog stand, start-up costs might look like this:

Hot-dog cart	$1,500.00
License from the city	200.00
Starting supply of hot dogs, buns, mustard	300.00
Business cards and flyers	50.00
Telephone answering machine	100.00
Total start-up costs	$2,150.00

OPERATING COSTS

The **operating costs** of a business are those costs that are necessary to operate the business, not including the cost of goods sold. Operating costs can almost always be divided into six categories. An easy way to remember the six operating costs that most businesses will have is to memorize the code word USAIIR. It stands for:

1. **U**tilities (gas, electric, telephone).
2. **S**alaries.
3. **A**dvertising.
4. **I**nsurance.
5. **I**nterest.
6. **R**ent.

Operating costs are also called **overhead**.

OVERHEAD IS DIVIDED INTO FIXED COSTS AND VARIABLE COSTS

Operating costs are divided into two types of costs: fixed costs and variable costs. **Fixed costs** are operating costs that stay the same, regardless of the range of sales the business is making. Rent can be an example of a fixed cost. Whether a shoe store sells 200 or 300 pairs of shoes in a month, it still pays the same rent on the store, so the rent is considered a fixed cost.

Variable costs are operating costs that change depending on the volume of sales, but cannot be assigned directly to the unit of sale. If a cost can be assigned directly to a unit of sale, it should be viewed as part of the cost of goods sold.

An example of a variable cost might be electricity. A flower shop, for example, stores many more flowers in its refrigerators around Easter or Mother's Day. The refrigerators require more electricity to cool all the flowers. Electricity, therefore, is an operating cost that is higher when the store is selling more flowers. In a small business, those operating costs that stay constant are fixed costs. Those that fluctuate with sales, but cannot be assigned to a specific unit of sale, should be viewed as variable costs.

JACOBY AND MEYERS: AFFORDABLE LAWYERS[1]

Cutting overhead costs can make the difference between a profitable and an insolvent business. Cutting costs can also help a company break into a new market by enabling it to offer its products or services at a lower price than the competition. In 1976, entrepreneur and lawyer Gail Koff teamed with lawyers Leonard Jacoby and Stephen Meyers to use this strategy to develop an untapped market for legal services.

Koff and her partners realized that wealthy people could afford to pay for lawyers, and poor people had access to legal aid. Middle- and working-class people were left in the lurch. Indeed, the American Bar Association had estimated that nearly 70 percent of the population did not have adequate access to the legal system.

Jacoby & Meyers' solution was the retail legal clinic—a neighborhood law office that would provide quality legal services to average-income people at a reasonable cost.

Instead of the lush suite of law offices visitors to a law firm typically encounter, customers of Jacoby & Meyers can visit any one of 110 small storefront offices around the country. Koff and her partners developed an office management system to be followed by all their branch offices. Improving office efficiency was another way to cut costs.

To keep fees low, though, would also require a high volume of cases, so Jacoby & Meyers became the first law firm to advertise. In its television commercials, Jacoby & Meyers offers very inexpensive consultations and guarantees that customers will receive a written estimate of potential fees.

Today, Jacoby & Meyers serves over 10,000 people a month. The Federal Trade Commission has noted that legal clinics have stimulated the legal services industry to become more competitive, leading to lower prices and better service for consumers.

COST OF GOODS OR SERVICES SOLD

The **cost of goods sold** can be thought of as the cost of selling *one additional unit* of a product. The **cost of services sold** is the cost of serving one additional customer. For Jacoby & Meyers, the cost of goods sold is the cost of providing legal services for one customer. The cost of goods sold in a restaurant is the cost of the food served to a customer. The *total* cost of goods sold increases as the number of customers served increases.

An example of the cost of goods sold of a turkey sandwich is shown in the following table.

Item	Analysis	Cost per Sandwich
Turkey (4 oz.)	$ 2.60 per pound ÷ 4	$0.65
Bread (large roll)	.32 per roll × 1/2	0.16
Mayonnaise (1 oz.)	1.60 per 32-oz. jar ÷ 32	0.05
Lettuce (1 oz.)	0.80 per pound ÷ 16	0.05
Tomato (4 oz.)	2.20 per pound ÷ 1/8	0.28
Pickle (1/4)	0.20 per pickle ÷ 4	0.05
Wrapper	10.00 per 1,000 ÷ 1,000	0.01
Cost of goods sold		$1.25

GROSS PROFIT PER UNIT

Once you know your cost of goods sold and have defined your unit, you can calculate your gross profit per unit.

The cost of goods sold of the sandwich, subtracted from the price customers pay for the sandwich, equals the **gross profit per unit** for the sandwich.

Selling Price − Cost of Goods Sold = Gross Profit per Unit

In this case:

Price of sandwich	$4.00
Cost of goods sold	−1.25
Gross profit per sandwich	$2.75

As an entrepreneur, you must keep the cost of goods sold secret. If customers learn your cost of goods sold, they'll use that information to try to negotiate a lower selling price. If someone tries to sell you a sandwich for $4.00 and you know it costs only $2.75 to make it, would you be willing to but it? Or would you try to negotiate the seller down to $3.00? What if you knew it cost $1.25 to make it?

Rule of Thumb

Never reveal your cost of goods sold. If you do, customers will try to negotiate a lower selling price.

Gross profit can be figured per unit, as in the turkey sandwich example. To get an idea of how a business is doing as a whole, however, you'll need to figure total gross profit. This is done by subtracting total cost of goods sold from total revenue, as in the following example.

Yolanda has a business selling designer watches. She buys the watches from a wholesaler for $15.00 each. Her cost of goods sold for each watch, therefore, is $15.00. She sells them for $30.00 each. What is her gross profit when she sells ten watches?

$$\text{Total Revenue} = 10 \text{ watches} \times \underset{\text{Selling Price}}{\$30.00} = \$300.00$$

$$\text{Total Cost of Goods Sold} = 10 \text{ watches} \times \$15.00 = \$150.00$$

$$\text{Total Gross Profit} = \underset{\text{Revenue}}{\$300.00} - \underset{\text{Cost of Goods Sold}}{\$150.00} = \$150.00$$

Total Revenue − Total Cost of Goods Sold = Total Gross Profit

PROFIT

Gross profit only subtracts cost of goods sold (for a "product" business) from revenue. It does not take into account the operating costs of running a business. To figure profit, the entrepreneur must subtract operating costs from gross profit. In other words, Yolanda does not actually keep $150.00 from the sale of ten watches. She still has operating costs to cover.

Yolanda spends $25.00 per week on flyers that she puts up all over town to let people know what styles of watches she has available and how to contact her. Her profit, therefore, is:

$$\underset{\text{Gross Profit}}{\$150.00} - \underset{\text{Operating Costs}}{\$25.00} = \underset{\text{Profit}}{\$125.00}$$

Gross Profit − Operating Costs = Profit

PROFIT PER UNIT

Sometimes, an entrepreneur wants to know how much of the sale of each unit is profit. An easy way to calculate profit per unit is to divide total units sold into profit. If Yolanda wants to know how much profit she makes each time she sells a watch, she would divide the number of watches she sells into the profit.

Profit per Unit = $125.00 ÷ 10 watches = $12.50 per watch

For every watch she sells, Yolanda is earning a profit of $12.50.

> **Profit ÷ Units Sold = Profit per Unit**

PRACTICE SESSIONS

The principles covered in this chapter are super-important for your knowledge and control of your business. Spend the time needed to work out and *understand* the practice questions on the next few pages. Compare your figures with the answers that begin on page 106.

Cost of Goods Sold

Cost of goods sold is the cost of producing one additional unit. Let's break apart a sandwich and find its cost of goods sold.

Item	Analysis	Cost per Sandwich
Ham (4 oz.)	$ 2.60 per pound ÷ 4	$0.65
Bread (2 slices)	1.20 per 12-slice loaf = $.10 × 2	0.20
Cheese (1 oz.)	3.20 per pound ÷ 16	0.20
Lettuce (1 oz.)	0.80 per pound ÷ 16	0.05
Tomato (2 oz.)	2.20 per pound ÷ 8	0.28
Mustard (1 oz.)	1.60 per 32 oz. jar ÷ 32	0.05
Wrapper	10.00 per 1,000 ÷ 1,000	0.01
Cost of goods sold:		$____

Price of sandwich: $ 4.25
Less cost of goods sold: _____
Gross profit per sandwich: $_____

From Total Revenue to Profit per Unit

1. What is the Total Revenue for the following items?

Units Sold (A) × Selling Price (B) = Total Revenue (C)

A × B = C

	A Units Sold	B Selling Price	C Total Revenue
1.	25	$ 4.00	$100.00
2.	30	10.00	_____
3.	12	2.50	_____
4.	75	2.00	_____
5.	20	45.00	_____

2. What is the Total Cost of Goods Sold for the units listed in question 1?

Units Sold (A) × Cost of Goods Sold per Unit (B) = Total Cost of Goods Sold (C)

A × B = C

	A Units Sold	B Cost of Goods Sold per Unit	C Total Cost of Goods Sold
1.	25	$ 2.00	$50.00
2.	30	5.00	_____
3.	12	1.00	_____
4.	75	1.00	_____
5.	20	20.00	_____

3. What is the Total Gross Profit for the items in questions 1 and 2?

Total Revenue (A) − Total Cost of Goods Sold (B) = Total Gross Profit (C)

$$A - B = C$$

	A Total Revenue	B Total Cost of Goods Sold	C Total Gross Profit
1.	$100.00	$50.00	$50.00
2.	_____	_____	_____
3.	_____	_____	_____
4.	_____	_____	_____
5.	_____	_____	_____

Hint: Get Total Revenue from Column C of question 1, and Total Cost of Goods Sold from Column C of question 2.

4. What is the Total Profit for the units in the previous questions?

Total Gross Profit (A) − Total Operating (B) = Total Profit (C)

$$A - B = C$$

	A Total Gross Profit	B Total Operating Costs	C Total Profit
1.	$50.00	$ 25.00	$25.00
2.	_____	60.00	_____
3.	_____	8.00	_____
4.	_____	25.00	_____
5.	_____	300.00	_____

Hint: Get Total Gross Profit from Column C of question 3.

5. What is the Profit per Unit for the units sold?

Total Profit (B) ÷ Units Sold (A) = Profit per Unit (C)

$$B \div A = C$$

	A Units Sold	B Total Profit	C Profit per Unit
1.	25	$25.00	$1.00
2.	30	_____	_____
3.	12	_____	_____
4.	75	_____	_____
5.	20	_____	_____

ANSWERS: COST OF GOODS SOLD

Cost of goods sold is the cost of producing one additional unit.
Let's break apart a sandwich and find its cost of goods sold.

Item	Analysis	Cost per Sandwich
Ham (4 oz.)	$02.60 per pound ÷ 4	$0.65
Bread (2 slices)	1.20 per 12-slice loaf 5 $.10 3 2	0.20
Cheese (1 oz.)	3.20 per pound ÷ 16	0.20
Lettuce (1 oz.)	0.80 per pound ÷ 16	0.05
Tomato (2 oz.)	2.20 per pound ÷ 8	0.28
Mustard (1 oz.)	1.60 per 32 oz. jar ÷ 32	0.05
Wrapper	10.00 per 1,000 ÷ 1,000	$0.01
Cost of goods sold		$1.44

Price of sandwich:	$4.25
Less cost of goods sold:	1.44
Gross profit per sandwich:	$2.81

ANSWERS:
FROM TOTAL REVENUE TO PROFIT PER UNIT

1. What is the Total Revenue for the following items?

Units Sold (A) × Selling Price (B) = Total Revenue (C)

A × B = C

	A Units Sold	B Selling Price	C Total Revenue
1.	25	$ 4.00	$100.00
2.	30	10.00	300.00
3.	12	2.50	30.00
4.	75	2.00	150.00
5.	20	45.00	900.00

2. What is the Total Cost of Goods Sold for the units listed in question 1?

Units Sold (A) × Cost of Goods Sold per Unit (B) = Total Cost of Goods Sold (C)

A × B = C

	A Units Sold	B Cost of Goods Sold per Unit	C Total Cost of Goods Sold
1.	25	$ 2.00	$ 50.00
2.	30	5.00	150.00
3.	12	1.00	12.00
4.	75	1.00	75.00
5.	20	20.00	400.00

3. What is the Total Gross Profit for the items in questions 1 and 2?

Total Revenue (A) − Total Cost of Goods Sold (B) = Total Gross Profit (C)

A − B = C

	A Total Revenue	B Total Cost of Goods Sold	C Total Gross Profit
1.	$100.00	$ 50.00	$ 50.00
2.	$300.00	150.00	150.00
3.	$ 30.00	12.00	18.00
4.	$150.00	75.00	75.00
5.	$900.00	400.00	500.00

4. What is the Total Profit for the units in the previous questions?

Total Gross Profit (A) − Total Operating (B) = Total Profit (C)

A − B = C

	A Total Gross Profit	B Total Operating Costs	C Total Profit
1.	$ 50.00	$ 25.00	$ 25.00
2.	$150.00	60.00	90.00
3.	$ 18.00	6.00	12.00
4.	$ 75.00	25.00	50.00
5.	$500.00	300.00	200.00

5. What is the Profit per Unit for the units sold?

$$\text{Total Profit (B)} \div \text{Units Sold (A)} = \text{Profit per Unit (C)}$$
$$B \div A = C$$

	A Units Sold	B Total Profit	C Profit per Unit
1.	25	$ 25.00	$ 1.00
2.	30	90.00	3.00
3.	12	12.00	1.00
4.	75	50.00	0.66
5.	20	200.00	10.00

CASE STUDY: HANDMADE CRAFTS

Do you like to work with wood? Or sew? If making things comes easy to you, consider making a simple product to sell. People enjoy buying handmade products. Some products you could make include: decorative pillows, stuffed animals, puppets, bird cages, jewelry, and candles.

Business for the Young Entrepreneur

Think of something that you will enjoy making *and* that people in your market will want to buy!

A great place to sell handmade crafts is at a flea market. You can obtain a list of flea markets from the Chamber of Commerce in your town or city. Contact the flea market management office to find out how to rent a booth or table.

Some of our students have sold their handmade items in unusual places—like hospitals. One of our most successful students, Kathleen, spent 90 percent of the last year of her life in a hospital, but that didn't stop her from running a successful business from her bed.

Kathleen made jewelry. Her cost of goods sold was roughly $1.50 per unit. Her selling price was $5 or $6. Kathleen's market was the doctors, nurses, and administrators in the hospital, as well as parents of other hospitalized children. Parents who were visiting their children in the ward loved to buy Kathleen's jewelry as presents. Kathleen's average sales were around $300 per week. She even started a NFTE course in the hospital for other terminally ill young people. The course was very helpful in counteracting the depression that some of them felt.

Another NFTE student, Susan, was very ill with lupus, but started a business selling handmade dolls. Her start-up cost was $200 and the cost of goods sold for each doll was $7.50. Susan put four hours of labor into each doll and valued her time at $5 per hour. Her total cost for each doll, therefore, was $27.50. She sold the dolls for $45 each, and sold about eight per week. Susan made the dolls at home and sold them at local flea markets. Several stores in the area also sold her beautiful dolls.

Before starting any business in your home, call your local Chamber of Commerce and look into zoning laws and licensing requirements. For example, some towns prohibit manufacturing operations in residential areas.

What to Bring to the Flea Market

- Colorful flyers.
- Business cards to give to customers.
- A receipt book; give each customer a receipt.
- Lots of change.

RESOURCES

Books

For a thorough treatment of costs, see Chapter 2, "Cost, Volume and Profit Analysis," in *The Portable MBA in Finance and Accounting*, edited by John Leslie Livingstone (New York: John Wiley & Sons, Inc., 1992).

Another great reference is *The Complete Guide to Financial Management for Small and Medium-Sized Companies* by Donald Brightly (Englewood Cliffs, NJ: Prentice-Hall, 1995).

Other Resources

A *Handbook of Small Business Finance* is available from the Small Business Administration for a small fee. To order it, call your local SBA office or contact:

Small Business Administration
409 Third Street, N.W.
Washington, DC 20416
(800) 827-5722

THE INCOME STATEMENT

8

THE ENTREPRENEUR'S MONTHLY SCORECARD

> Money is better than poverty, if only for financial reasons.
> —Woody Allen (b. 1935)
> American filmmaker

THE INCOME STATEMENT IS A SCORECARD FOR THE BUSINESS OWNER

Now that you are familiar with costs, you can learn to prepare a monthly **income statement**. Monthly income statements show the financial condition of your business at the end of each month. They show your sales and your costs during the month. If sales are greater than costs, your income statement balance will be positive, showing that your business earned a profit. If sales are less than costs, your income statement balance will be negative, showing a loss. The income statement is also called a **profit and loss statement**.

An income statement is a scorecard for any business owner. If the business is not making a profit, examining the income statement can tell the business owner what may be causing the loss. The owner can take steps to correct problems before net losses make the business insolvent.

Please, don't skip this chapter because you think learning to prepare an income statement is going to be complicated or difficult. My special ed students have learned to prepare income statements. You can too. I've discovered through years of teaching that if you are convinced that something is important to know and that you are going to apply it to your life, it's much easier to learn. The income statement you will learn in this chapter is very simple and will be a valuable business tool for you.

A Car Stereo Installation Business

One of my proudest moments as a teacher was when I watched one of my students, Daniel Harris, give a speech at the 1993 *Inc.* magazine convention in Des Moines, Iowa, honoring owners of the fastest growing private ventures in the nation. Daniel received a standing ovation after he told these business owners how entrepreneurship has helped him overcome the obstacles in his life and create a dream for his future.

Before Daniel started his car stereo installation business, he was doing poorly in high school and was unsure what he would do with his future. Participating in an entrepreneurship program run by the Wichita, Kansas, division of NFTE turned his life around, Daniel says. "I learned that you could make something you really like into a business," he says.

What Daniel really likes are stereos. Today, he installs about six or seven stereo systems a month. He handles sales and some installations, and has another installer working for him. His slogan is: "Trust Your Sound to Underground." Daniel is keeping his business going while he pursues a degree in entrepreneurship from Wichita State University.

Daniel uses monthly income statements to track revenue, costs, and profit for his car stereo installation business, Underground Sound. Daniel never thought he would actually enjoy doing something that required math, but "keeping good records and doing monthly income statements help me figure out how to improve my business all the time."

Daniel believes many young people don't seem to have much of a work ethic because "they get tired of fast-food places, working for nothing." In contrast, Daniel says, entrepreneurship has enabled him to "make in a day what someone makes at a fast-food place in two weeks," and this inspired him to master simple accounting.

Remember, though, that any job experience—even at the bottom of the rung—will teach you a great deal about operating a business. Fast-food employers such as McDonald's expose thousands of young people to business. Some even go on to become restaurant owners through franchising. I'll discuss franchising in Chapter 21.

Work Experience Can Inspire You

Work experience can also inspire you to start a business in a particular area. Entertainment mogul David Geffen started out working in the mailroom of a record company. Today he owns record companies and is involved in all aspects of producing entertainment.

THE SEVEN PARTS OF AN INCOME STATEMENT*

Income statements will encourage you to keep your ledger up-to-date and accurate. You will use the ledger to prepare your income statement at the end of each month.

Income statements are made up of the following parts, labeled A through G. We'll be using their call letters when we place these parts in equations.

A. Sales: how much money the company receives for selling a product.

B. Total cost of goods sold: the cost of goods sold for one unit times the number of units sold. *Never disclose your cost of goods sold.* You want to keep secret how much you are paying for your product so you can sell it for a profit.

C. Gross profit: sales minus cost of goods sold.

D. Operating costs: items that must be paid to operate a business, including fixed (D1) and variable (D2) costs. These items include Utilities, Salaries, Advertising, Insurance, Interest, and Rent (referred to as USAIIR).

E. Profit before taxes: a business's profit before paying taxes and after all costs have been paid.

F. Taxes: payments required by federal, state, and local governments, based on a business's profit. A business must pay sales, income, and other business taxes.

G. Net profit or loss: a business's profit or loss after taxes have been paid.

The power of the income statement is that it tells you whether you are succeeding at buying low, selling high, and meeting customer needs. Remember Hector's small business, described in Chapter 1? Let's say

*This income statement is simplified, but effective for a simple small business.

Hector finds a wholesaler looking to unload some ties. Hector buys twenty-five ties at $2.00 each and sells them all at $4.00 each. His revenue is $100.00. He spent $24.00 on flyers to advertise his ties. The income statement quickly shows whether Hector is making a profit.

Hector's Income Statement		The Math
A. Sales	$100.00	25 ties × $4.00/tie = $100
B. Less: Total Cost of Goods Sold	50.00	25 ties × $2.00/tie = $50
C. Gross Profit	$ 50.00	A − B = C
		$100.00 − $50.00 = $50.00
D. Less: Operating Costs (flyers)		$24.00 for flyers
D1. Fixed Costs $24		
D2. Variable Costs + 2	$ 26.00	
E. Profit before Taxes	$ 24.00	C − D = E
F. Taxes	6.00	Taxes = $6.00
G. Net Profit/(Loss)	$ 18.00	E − F = G
		$24.00 − $6.00 = $18.00

Hector's business is profitable.

FINANCIAL RATIO ANALYSIS

To analyze an income statement, divide sales into each line item. You can then express each item as a **percentage**, or share, of sales. We said earlier that "percentage" literally means "out of a hundred." Percentages express numbers as part of a whole, with the whole represented as 100 percent.

Relating each element of the income statement to sales by stating the element as a percentage will help you notice changes in your costs from month to month.

You probably know that half (½) of something can be expressed as 50 percent, but here's how that percentage is actually figured:

1. Divide the numerator (top number) by the denominator (bottom number) of the fraction. To do that, add two decimal places to each number:

$$½ = 1.00 \div 2.00 = .50$$

2. Multiply that result by 100 to express it as a percentage:

$$.50 \times 100 = 50 \text{ percent } (50\%)$$

By expressing each item on the income statement as a percentage of sales, you'll find it easier to see the relationships between the items. A dollar is made up of 100 pennies, so a percentage also helps you express each item as part of a dollar. In the example in Chart 6, for every dollar of sales, 40 cents (40 percent of that dollar) was spent on cost of goods sold. The gross profit per dollar of sales was 60 cents (60 percent). The net profit, after 30 cents were spent on operating costs and 10 cents on taxes, was 20 cents (20 percent). These percentages are referred to as a business's **financial ratios**.

It's amazing how much you can learn about a business by looking at its financial ratios. Analyzing income statement items as percentages of sales makes clear how costs are affecting net profit. Apple Computer, Inc. noted in its financial overview for 1994, for example, that it reduced operating costs that year to 21.2% of net sales, down from 28.8% in 1993. Net profit rose 15% in 1994, and a portion of that increase was probably due to a 7.6% reduction in operating costs.

	Dollars	Math	Financial Analysis (% of Sales)
Sales	$10	$\frac{\$10}{\$10} = 1 \times 100 = 100\%$	100%
Less Total Cost of Goods Sold	4	$\frac{\$4}{\$10} = .40 \times 100 = 40\%$	40
Gross Profit	6	$\frac{\$6}{\$10} = .60 \times 100 = 60\%$	60
Less Operating Costs	3	$\frac{\$3}{\$10} = .30 \times 100 = 30\%$	30
Fixed Costs	3	$\frac{\$3}{\$10} = .30 \times 100 = 30\%$	30
Variable Costs	0	0	0
Profit	3	$\frac{\$3}{\$10} = .30 \times 100 = 30\%$	30
Taxes	1	$\frac{\$1}{\$10} = .10 \times 100 = 10\%$	10
Net Profit/(Loss)	2	$\frac{\$2}{\$10} = .20 \times 100 = 20\%$	20

Chart 6   Financial Ratio Analysis

A FAST-FOOD RESTAURANT'S INCOME STATEMENT

Given below are income statements for a month and a year, for a fast-food restaurant in New York City. Successful entrepreneurs know it's important to keep track of costs *each month* in order to make sure profits aren't getting eaten up. For a real challenge, try doing a financial ratio analysis of this income statement.

		1 Year	The Math
Sales		$2,600,000	_____
Cost of Goods Sold:			
Food	$792,000		_____
Paper	108,000		_____
Less: Total Cost of Goods Sold		900,000	_____
Gross Profit		$2,700,000	_____
Less: Operating Costs		2,000,000	_____
Profit		$ 700,000	_____
Less: Taxes		233,000	_____
Net Profit/(Loss)		$ 467,000	_____

CREATING WEALTH BY SELLING A PROFITABLE BUSINESS

We've called the income statement the scorecard of your business. If your business is successful, your income statements will prove it by showing net profits. A successful small business can usually be sold for between three and five times its yearly net profit. If your net profit for one year is $10,000, for example, you might be able to sell your business for at least $30,000 (3 × $10,000).

Charles Schwab opened his own brokerage firm in 1971, when he was thirty-four.[1] Like Jacoby & Meyers, Schwab uncovered a market niche when he began offering discount pricing for informed investors who were tired of paying hefty commissions to stockbrokers. Investors who didn't need someone else to do their research and make their decisions flocked to Charles Schwab & Company. By 1981, the company's earnings were $5 million. In 1982, BankAmerica Corporation bought Charles Schwab & Company for $53 million but left Schwab in place as CEO. Today, Schwab has offices across the United States and is expanding overseas.

We tend to think that only companies involved with social activism or progressive politics are "doing good," but, in fact, most successful entrepreneurs are improving society simply by finding a more efficient way to use scarce resources. Charles Schwab, for instance, offers stock trading at commissions that are 30 to 40 percent below average. On a $1,000 trade, therefore, the consumer saves $30 to $40 that he or she can spend elsewhere. Schwab's company has also created 1,500 jobs.

ANDRE MEYER: ACQUISITION PIONEER

Some businesspeople have made the acquisition and sale of businesses the focus of their career. One such wheeler-dealer was Andre Meyer, a Frenchman. Meyer pioneered the art of purchasing a foundering business, getting it back on track, and then selling it for a substantial profit.

In his twenties, Meyer had developed habits that he kept for a lifetime. He rose at 4 A.M. every morning and planned his financial strategy for the day. He kept a telephone on the table while his family was eating. As he ate dinner, he discussed business.

By 1939, Meyer's future in the French banking world looked limitless. Then came World War II and the German invasion of France. Andre Meyer had no illusions about the future of Jews in France under the German occupation. He fled with his family to the United States in July 1940.

At age forty-two, Meyer found himself in a new country where he could not even speak the language. Nevertheless, he showed up at the New York offices of the Lazard Frères Investment bank. Meyer, who had worked for Lazard Frères in France, was taken under the wing of the president, Frank Altschul. Altschul was a powerful financial force on Wall Street, and he generously showed Meyer the ropes. Altschul had underestimated Meyer's ruthlessness, however. Within two years, Altschul was out and Meyer was in.

During the next thirty-five years, Meyer ruled Lazard Frères with an iron hand. It wasn't until the late 1950s and early '60s, though, that Meyer found the niche that made his company hundreds of millions of dollars: mergers and acquisitions.

The first company acquired was Avis Car Rental. By the late 1950s, Avis was being clobbered by Hertz Rent-A-Car. Sensing that the company was salvageable, Meyer had Lazard buy 600,000 of the 1.5 million outstanding Avis shares for $7 million.

To turn Avis into a profitable company, Meyer slashed overhead and brought in new personnel. The new president, Robert Townsend, had the company $3 million in the black by 1964. The following year, Meyer sold Avis to the ITT conglomerate for $52 million, earning a profit of about $45 million in just a few years.

Using the Avis deal as a guide, Meyer made hundreds of similar acquisitions, many for ITT. He pioneered this method of creating wealth, which is now taken for granted. In addition, Meyer made an estimated $70 million by financing the career of the real estate magnate William Zeckendorf. He also sat on dozens of corporate boards, including Fiat, Chase International Investment Corporation, Radio Corporation of America, and Newport Mining Corp. He gave extensively to charity and was a trustee of New York University, Sloan-Kettering Institute, and Mount Sinai Hospital.

PRACTICE SESSION

Reading about how to do something isn't as helpful as actually doing it. Apply what you've read in this chapter to the next few sections to be sure you understand what the chapter covers.

Preparing an Income Statement

David and Robbie are NFTE grads who make a product they've called Floppy Hats. They buy fabric and decorations in the local wholesale district. The hats have become very popular in their Minneapolis neighborhood. They've named their company Floppy Hats USA.

David and Robbie sell each Floppy Hat for $10.00. Each hat costs $5.00 for them to make. The hats are decorated with a variety of sports logos, stripes, or ethnic prints. The partners sell Floppy Hats at local festivals and flea markets. Their operating costs include printing of flyers and business cards. Every customer who buys a hat gets a business card. This makes it easier for their customers to refer other customers to them, David and Robbie say.

In a typical month, David and Robbie make and sell 12 hats. They spend $30 on posters and business cards and pay $12 in taxes. Prepare the Floppy Hats USA income statement for one month of business.

Total Sales are: $_____

Total Cost of Goods Sold is: $_____

Gross Profit is: $_____

Operating Costs (USAIIR) are:

(Fixed 1 Variable)

    Fixed Costs are $_____

    Variable Costs are   + $_____ = $_____

Profit before Taxes is: $_____

Taxes are: $_____

Net Profit/(Loss) is: $_____

Analyzing an Income Statement

Now prepare a financial analysis of the income statement for Floppy Hats USA.

Line Items	Dollars	Math	Financial Analysis (% of Sales)
Sales	_____	_____	_____
Total Cost of Goods Sold	_____	_____	_____
Gross Profit	_____	_____	_____
Operating Costs	_____	_____	_____
Profit	_____	_____	_____
Taxes	_____	_____	_____
Net Profit/(Loss)	_____	_____	_____

Creation of Wealth

Assuming each of the businesses listed below could be sold for three times its annual net profit, what is the sale price for each?

	Annual Net Profit	Sale Price
Business A	$ 20,000	$60,000*
Business B	32,000	_____
Business C	1,500,000	_____
Business D	300,000	_____
Business E	12,000	_____

*$20,000 × 3 = $60,000

Preparing Your Own Income Statement

Using the information you wrote up on ledger sheets in Chapter 6, prepare an income statement. If you are an active entrepreneur, use your ledger for your most recent business day.

Sales	_____
Less Total Cost of Goods Sold	_____
Gross Profit	_____
Less Operating Costs (USAIIR)	
(Fixed + Variable)	
Fixed _____	
Variable + _____ =	_____
Profit before Taxes	_____
Less Taxes	_____
Net Profit/(Loss)	_____

ANSWERS: FINANCIAL ANALYSIS OF A FAST-FOOD RESTAURANT'S INCOME STATEMENT

	1 Month (as % of Sales)	1 Year (as % of Sales)
Sales	100 %	100 %
Cost of Goods Sold:		
Food	22	22
Paper	3	3
Less: Total Cost of Goods Sold	25	25
Gross Profit	75	75
Less: Operating Costs	58	55
Profit	16.66	19.44
Less Taxes	5	6.47
Net Profit/(Loss)	11.66	12.97

ANSWERS: PREPARING AN INCOME STATEMENT

In a typical month, David and Robbie make and sell 12 hats. They spend $30 on posters and business cards and pay $12 in taxes. Prepare the Floppy Hats USA income statement for one month of business.

Total Sales are:		$120.00
Total Cost of Goods Sold is:	60.00	
Gross Profit is:		$ 60.00
Operating Costs (USAIIR) are:		
(Fixed 1 Variable)		
Fixed Costs are	$30.00	
Variable Costs are	+0.00 =	30.00
Profit before Taxes is:		$ 30.00
Taxes are:		12.00
Net Profit/(Loss) is:		$ 18.00

ANSWERS: ANALYZING AN INCOME STATEMENT

Now prepare a financial analysis of the income statement for Floppy Hats USA.

Line Items	Dollars	Financial Analysis (% of Sales)
Sales	$120.00	100 %
Total Cost of Goods Sold	60.00	50
Gross Profit	60.00	50
Operating Costs	30.00	25
Profit	30.00	25
Taxes	5.00	4.1
Net Profit/(Loss)	25.00	20.8

ANSWERS: CREATION OF WEALTH

Assuming each of the businesses listed below could be sold for three times its annual net profit, what is the sale price for each?

	Annual Net Profit	Sale Price
Business A	$ 20,000	$ 60,000
Business B	32,000	96,000
Business C	1,500,000	4,500,000
Business D	300,000	900,000
Business E	12,000	36,000

Business for the Young Entrepreneur

CASE STUDY: TRANSCRIPTION SERVICE

Barbara, who has multiple sclerosis, was transcribing documents for years as a home worker for companies that provide transcription. She took a NFTE course at Queensborough College, where physically challenged people were being trained to start businesses in their homes. Barbara became convinced that she could make more money and be more independent working for herself. Her company, Barrett Unlimited, now earns revenues of around $2,500 a month providing legal and medical transcriptions.

Not only is Barbara pleased with her success and independence, she believes starting a home business "will be an important part of the future for disabled workers."

According to a January 26, 1993, article in *The Wall Street Journal*, more and more physically challenged people like Barbara are turning to entrepreneurship. Gregory, who is paralyzed below the neck and breathes with the aid of a respirator, started Jireh Medical Supply Company from his St. Louis home. He supplies medical equipment to the disabled via mail order. Gregory says his market niche is disabled people who are overcharged by medical equipment suppliers.

Other home-based businesses started by disabled entrepreneurs include phone services such as tarot-card readings, and handmade merchandise. Zully started making shoes for people who, like herself, suffer from misshapen or odd-sized feet due to polio or other illness. She originally sold the shoes from her Chicago home, but the demand for them became so great that she opened a store called "Zully's." Her store's annual revenue was $55,000 in 1993, according to the *Journal*.

Tips

- Disabled people who receive federal disability assistance of any kind should investigate whether earnings from a home-based business could jeopardize their payments. Inquiries should be addressed to the local office of the Social Security Administration.

RESOURCES

Books

For a very clear, entrepreneur-oriented discussion of the income statement, see Chapter 10, "Accounting and Management Decision Making," in

The New Portable MBA, edited by Eliza G. C. Collins and Mary Anne Devanna (New York: John Wiley & Sons, Inc., 1995).

How to Start, Expand & Sell a Business by James C. Comiskey is a guide to the creation of wealth through entrepreneurship (Santa Barbara, CA: Venture Perspective Press, 1985).

Other Resources

The *Small Business Reporter* is a series of over 100 pamphlets on entrepreneurial subjects, including financial statements. Each pamphlet is available for a small postage and handling charge. For a free index, write to:

Small Business Reporter
Bank of America
P.O. Box 3700, Dept. 36361
San Francisco, CA 94317

9

RETURN ON INVESTMENT

A GREAT DECISION-MAKING TOOL

All our records had to be hits because we couldn't afford any flops.
—Berry Gordy (b. 1929)
American founder of Motown Record Company

INVESTMENT

"To invest" means to put money, time, and energy into something from which you expect to gain financial profit or personal satisfaction in return. Starting your own business requires an **investment** of your time, energy, and money.

The decision to attend college is also an investment. You stay in school instead of going to work because you believe the investment in college will pay off later. You believe college will help you obtain better career opportunities and achieve financial profit and personal satisfaction.

RATE OF RETURN

When you start your own business, you commit to an investment of time, energy, and money. You do this because you believe that someday your business will return more than the value of the time, energy, and money you put into it. Without realizing it, you have calculated the **rate of return** on your investment and have found it to be acceptable.

Businesspeople need to know what the rate of return will be on their investments. Rate of return is often called **return on investment** (ROI). It is expressed as a percentage of the original investment.

I have found that any young person can learn to calculate rate of return. In my own business, I discovered that rate of return is an invaluable decision-making aid for a new entrepreneur. I started my business with $32,000. For every cent I spent, I did a mental calculation of return on my original investment. I asked myself: Will this expenditure increase my ROI or not? That constant analysis really helped me.

How to Calculate ROI

In business formulas, "on" means "divided by" and "return" means "profit." Here's how to calculate return on investment.

1. Start with the amount of money you possess at the close of a business period. Call this your end-of-period wealth (A).
2. Subtract the amount of your original investment. Call this investment your beginning-of-period wealth (B).
3. Divide the resulting number by your beginning-of-period wealth.
4. Multiply by 100 to express your return as a percentage.

$$\text{Formula: } \frac{A - B}{B} \times 100 = ROI$$

Let's say you find out that your church is planning an arts-and-crafts event for local children. Fifty silkscreened shirts are needed for the children. You go down to the wholesale district and spend $200 for fifty shirts at $4 each:

$$50 \text{ shirts} \times \$4 \text{ per shirt} = \$200$$

You then sell the shirts to the church for $400. Using the four steps above, what is your return on investment?

$$\frac{\$400 - \$200}{\$200} = \frac{\$200}{\$200} = 1 \times 100 = 100\%$$

The return on your investment is 100%.

Here's an easy way to remember this formula:[1]

Rule of Thumb

ROI = What you made over what you paid, times a hundred.

$$\frac{\text{What you made}}{\text{What you paid}} \times 100 = \text{ROI}$$

PRACTICE SESSION

Take a few minutes here to practice ROI calculations. The return you'll realize in your own business will be critical to its success.

Return on Investment (ROI)

$$\frac{\text{End-of-period wealth} - \text{Beginning-of-period wealth}}{\text{Beginning-of-period wealth}} \times 100 = \text{ROI}$$

Assume a one-year investment period and calculate the ROI for the figures below. (Leave off the two decimal places (for cents) to make the math easier.)

End-of-Period Wealth	Beginning-of-Period Wealth	Rate of Return
$ 2	$ 1	100%*
40	10	_____
15	5	_____
20	5	_____
6	3	_____
350	175	_____
80	60	_____
1,500	1,000	_____
9	3	_____
75	25	_____

$*\dfrac{2-1}{1} = \dfrac{1}{1} = 1 \times 100 = 100\%.$

ANSWERS: RETURN ON INVESTMENT (ROI)

$$\frac{\text{End-of-period wealth} - \text{Beginning-of-period wealth}}{\text{Beginning-of-period wealth}} \times 100 = \text{ROI}$$

Assume a one-year investment period and calculate the ROI for the figures below. (Leave off the two decimal places (for cents) to make the math easier.)

End-of-Period Wealth	Beginning-of-Period Wealth	Rate of Return
$ 2	$ 1	100%
40	10	300
15	5	200
20	5	300
6	3	100
350	175	100
80	60	33
1,500	1,000	50
9	3	200
75	25	200

ROI is a decision-making tool I use every day. You can apply this concept not only to business but also to personal decisions that you make. Remember, whenever you spend your time, money, or effort on something, you are making an investment. If you can't decide whether to do something, look at the ROI.

In business formulas, "on" means "divided by" and "return" means "profit." Return On Investment means Return (A − B) divided by Investment (B).

Rule of Thumb

ROI IS AFFECTED BY RISK

The return demanded by an investor depends on how risky he or she thinks an investment is. If the investment is very risky, the investor will want a high rate of return.

Risk factors include time and liquidity. The more **time** an investment is tied up, the greater the rate of return should be. The longer someone has your money, the greater the chance that it could be lost in some unforeseen way. You, as an investor, will want to be compensated for that risk.

As an investor, you also have to consider **liquidity.** Liquidity refers to the ease of getting cash in and out of an investment. How "liquid" is the investment? Can you call the business in which you have invested and get your money back if you suddenly have need for it? If so, the investment is "liquid," or easily converted into cash.

In general, the longer you have to wait for the payback on your investment, the greater the return should be. The easier your money is to retrieve, the lower your return will probably be.

SMALL BUSINESS RISK AND RETURN ARE HIGH

The rate of return on a small business can be very high. The risk of failure for most types of small businesses is also very high. The Small Business Administration has estimated that only one in seven small businesses survive. On the other hand, many entrepreneurs have survived business failures and gone on to become millionaires or billionaires with new ventures. As long as your basic reserves are not depleted by a business failure, it can be a great learning experience.

Always have a plan for failure. Sit down and imagine what could happen if you are not able to provide your product or service at a cost that is attractive to consumers. Will you go back to work for someone, or start another business? Do you have enough money put aside to cover your basic living expenses until you can start generating income again?

Rule of Thumb

The higher the risk of the investment, the higher the demanded rate of return.

RUPERT MURDOCH: GETTING A KICK— AND MILLIONS—OUT OF RISK

Some entrepreneurs really thrive on risk. One risk-loving entrepreneur is Rupert Murdoch. He even started his own television channel—Fox

TV—when most industry observers said it couldn't be done. But Fox's outlandish—some say, tasteless—programming, including such popular shows as "Married With Children" and "The Simpsons," has been a huge hit.

The Fox TV channel is just one piece of Murdoch's media empire. Murdoch is the owner of News Corporation, a deceptively simple name for one of the largest publishing companies in the world. Its rapid growth is the result of Murdoch's impulsive buying and willingness to take risks.

Murdoch's company owned a dozen newspapers in Australia before he moved to England in 1969 to buy the Sunday publication, *News of the World.* Most of his papers had been bought cheaply, with borrowed money. He made them profitable by turning them into scandal-loving tabloids and by running bingo contests and girlie pictures in the papers.

Murdoch was thirty-eight and relatively unknown when he made the riskiest purchase of his life (up to that time). He bought the *Sun* of London for the British equivalent of a million dollars. In 1970, the *Sun* was a dull socialist paper. After buying it, Murdoch quickly applied his tried-and-true formula. Then he swung its editorials to the political right. The *Sun* became the most profitable of Murdoch's holdings, earning him over $50 million.

MURDOCH CROSSES THE ATLANTIC: THE U.S. EXPANSION

In 1973, Murdoch quietly came to the United States and bought two papers in San Antonio, Texas, for $18 million. He then launched the *Star,* a sensational national weekly modeled after the well-known *National Enquirer.* After that, he bought some very well-known American publications. Among them were the *New York Post,* the *Village Voice, New York Magazine,* and the *Boston Herald.* In 1984, Murdoch bought the Chicago *Sun-Times* for $96.5 million and applied his "brighteners," as he calls his tabloid formula.

Overseas, Murdoch acquired the London *Times,* perhaps the most historically prestigious newspaper in the world, and took a half-interest in Ansett Transport Industries, an Australian airline. Many of Murdoch's purchases look reckless when he makes them. But in most cases he turns a profit.

Murdoch operates with a phenomenal amount of debt, because he refuses to dilute his 46 percent stake in his company. He keeps a tight lid on expenses; after every acquisition, the first change he makes is to slash costs significantly by letting go of all nonessential employees and installing cost-cutting equipment.

Murdoch's latest foray is into satellite broadcasting. His plan is for a nationwide pay-TV network beamed directly into American households via satellite. This venture has so far cost $20 million and has been unsuccessful. But Rupert Murdoch is not one to give up on a risky venture.

INTERGALACTIC VENDING: A SMALL BUSINESS WITH A BIG RETURN

Most businesses that young people start face a lower risk of failure than the small businesses started by adults. The young entrepreneur usually has fewer fixed costs, such as rent or insurance. For this reason, businesses started by young people can have a high rate of return despite the lower risk.

Landon, a graduate of NFTE's Twin Cities program, bought a vending machine for $500.00 and installed it at his school in Minneapolis. He knew that if he could sell soda for a lower price than the stores and vending machines in and around the school, students would buy from his machine. Landon searched for the best wholesale dealer for soda. Because he found a low wholesale price, he was able to afford to resell his soda for ten cents less than the average vendor at his school.

Soon, Landon was making a 300 percent return per *day* on his investment. He used his profit to buy a car and purchase more inventory. He named his business Intergalactic Vending.

After reading about Landon in the paper, Midwest Vending Company donated a candy vending machine and a change machine to his enterprise. Midwest was switching to computerized machines and didn't need the older machines anymore. Midwest also gave Landon a year of free machine servicing. Landon has hired someone to run his vending machine business while he looks for new business opportunities.

LOWER RISK = LOWER RATE OF RETURN

The lower the risk of the investment, the lower the demanded rate of return. Savings banks typically offer a low return of, say, 4 percent over a year because the risk of losing your money is very low. Compare the rates of return for a typical savings account and a young person's after-school business:

	A (End of Period*)	B (Beginning of Period)	Rate of Return
Savings account	$104	$100	4%
After-school business	$500	$100	400%

*Period = one year

INVESTING IN STOCK

Financial investments such as stocks and bonds also offer a return on investment. When Andrew Carnegie was persuaded by Tom Scott to buy ten shares in Adams Express for $600, he received a $10 dividend within a short time. Carnegie said, "I shall remember that check as long as I live; it gave the first penny of revenue from capital—Eureka!"

Another entrepreneur who became very excited about the prospects of using money to make more money was John D. Rockefeller. As a teen, he loaned a neighboring farmer $50. When the farmer paid him back, he added $3.50 as interest. At the time, Rockefeller had just earned only $1.12 for a full thirty hours of back-breaking work hoeing potatoes for another neighbor. As Rockefeller said in his autobiography, *Random Reminiscences,* "From that time on, I was determined to make money work for me."

One very popular investment is stock. A share of stock represents a share of ownership of a corporation. The stockholder literally owns a piece of the company.

Once a corporation sells shares, it has no control over them. The shares are bought and sold on the stock market by investors looking for return on their investment. Before we discuss this further, however, you'll need to learn to read stock tables.

READING STOCK TABLES

Reading stock tables is a great lesson in cause and effect. There's always a reason behind every stock price move. Stock prices are influenced by economic and political news, trends, and many other factors.

At first glance, stock tables appear to be written in a foreign language, but they are not hard to interpret. To prove it, study this part of a typical stock table and then answer the questions below.

| 52 WKS | | STOCK | SYM | DIV | YLD | PE | VOL 100S | HI | LO | CLOSE | NET CHG |
HI	LO										
$8\frac{3}{8}$	5	ChockFull	CHF	1.00	—	28	132	$6\frac{3}{8}$	$6\frac{1}{8}$	$6\frac{1}{4}$	—
$58\frac{7}{8}$	$38\frac{3}{8}$	Chrysler	C	1.60	4.1	4	28650	$39\frac{5}{8}$	$38\frac{1}{4}$	$38\frac{7}{8}$	$+\frac{1}{4}$
$82\frac{5}{8}$	$68\frac{5}{8}$	Chubb	CB	1.96	2.5	13	1268	$79\frac{7}{8}$	$79\frac{1}{4}$	$79\frac{3}{4}$	$-\frac{1}{8}$
$36\frac{1}{8}$	$28\frac{3}{4}$	Citicorp Inc.	CER	2.46	6.9	14	38	$36\frac{1}{8}$	$35\frac{7}{8}$	$35\frac{7}{8}$	$+\frac{1}{8}$

1. Which stock is the most expensive? _____
2. Which stock has the highest dividend? _____
3. Which stock has the highest yield? _____
4. Which stock has the lowest P/E ratio? _____
5. Which stock was traded the most? _____

Chart 7 gives you some experience in looking up actual stocks. Here are definitions of some of the terms you'll see.

- **52-Week High/Low (52 wks Hi/Lo):** The first figure in the column is the highest price the stock traded for in the previous 52 weeks. The second figure is the lowest. All prices are listed in dol-

| | 52 WKS | | STOCK | SYM | DIV | YLD | PE | VOL 100S | HI | LO | CLOSE | NET CHG |
	HI	LO										
Chemical Bank												
Colgate-Palmolive												
Disney												
Ford Motor Co.												
Reebok												

Chart 7   Reading a Stock Table. Research the Listings for These Well-Known Companies

lars and fractions of dollars. The fractions are traditionally given in eighths.

- **Stock:** The name of the company. *The Wall Street Journal* lists both the company name and its symbol. Every stock has a symbol (sym), usually consisting of from one to four letters.

- **Dividend (Div):** Corporations can pay each stockholder a dividend—a sum of money for every share each stockholder owns. A dividend is a return on investment for the stockholder. Corporations pay dividends out of the company's profits.

   A figure of 1.00 in this column means a dividend of $1 per share of stock was paid out to the company's stockholders over the course of the year. A stockholder who owned 100 shares was, therefore, paid $100 ($1 dividend × 100 shares) in dividends.

- **Yield (Yld):** The rate of return on the stock, expressed as a percentage.

Dividend/Closing Price × 100 = ROI

   The yield on a stock is low compared to the ROI on some other investments. Stocks are usually purchased with the expectation that the price will go up. Reselling the stock at a higher price is how an investor's ROI is usually made in the stock market.

- **Price/Earnings Ratio (P/E):** The P/E is the price of one share of stock divided by the earnings per share. If the price of the stock is $28, and the company earned $7 for each share of stock outstanding, the P/E ratio would be: 28 ÷ 7 = 4

   A P/E of 4 is considered low. A low P/E can indicate a stable company. A high P/E is about 20 and above. A P/E of 8 is more or less average. A zero P/E means that a company has no earnings.

   In general, the higher a P/E, the greater the risk investors are willing to take. A new company in a new field like genetic engineering will often have a high P/E because the future earnings are as yet unknown. If the company makes a scientific breakthrough, investors could earn lots of money.

- **Volume of Shares Traded (Vol 100s):** The number of shares traded (bought and sold) during the previous day's trading period. (The New York Stock Exchange trades Monday through Friday from 9:30 A.M. to 4 P.M.)

   Volume is given in hundreds of shares. Add two zeros to a number in the Vol 100s column to get the correct figure. When a very high volume of stock is being traded, it means investors are taking an interest in that stock. Volume does not indicate whether the price will go up or down.

- **Hi Lo Close:** The highest, lowest, and last prices the stock was traded for during the previous day's trading period. Again, the figures are given in fractions of dollars.

- **Net Change (Net Chg.):** The change in price from the close of the previous day's trading period.[*]

How Would You Invest in the Stock Market?[2]

Imagine you have been given $10,000 to invest in the stock market. Which of the stocks below would you choose?

Stock

American Express

American Telephone & Telegraph (AT&T)

Bethlehem Steel

Coca-Cola Company

Eastman Kodak

General Electric

IBM

McDonald's Corp.

Procter & Gamble

Sears, Roebuck

Texaco

United Technologies

Woolworth

The actual rate of return on these stocks over a ten-year period is shown on the next page.

---

[*]Additional special symbols are explained at the bottom of the published stock tables. (Answers to questions on page 132: 1. Chubb 2. Citicorp 3. Citicorp 4. Chrysler 5. Chrysler)

HOW DID YOUR INVESTMENT PERFORM?

If you had invested $10,000 in any of these stocks on January 1, 1980, the value of your investment ten years later would have been:

$10,000 Stock Investment on Jan. 1, 1980	Value of Stock on Dec. 31, 1989	Percentage ROI
American Express	$46,693	+366.9%
American Telephone & Telegraph (AT&T)	36,010	+260.1
Bethlehem Steel	8,757	−12.4
Coca-Cola Company	67,174	+571.7
Eastman Kodak	19,226	+92.3
General Electric	50,964	+409.6
IBM	14,621	+46.2
McDonald's Corp.	80,532	+705.3
Procter & Gamble	37,580	+278.5
Sears, Roebuck	21,181	+111.8
Texaco	66,625	+84.4
United Technologies	25,233	+152.3
Woolworth	50,856	+408.6

CASE STUDY: CONSIGNMENT SHOP

Do you ever throw out clothes because you're tired of them? Maybe someone else would buy clothes you don't want anymore. Maybe you would like to buy clothes one of your friends doesn't want anymore.

Business for the Young Entrepreneur

    This is the idea behind the clothing resale or "consignment" shop. A consignment shop sells used clothing. People bring in clothes they don't want anymore, and the shop sells the clothes for them. In return, the clothing donor receives a percentage of the sale, usually 30 to 50 percent. Consignment shops are becoming more popular as people search for ways to stretch their clothing dollars. You could run a consignment shop from your house (in your garage or basement) after school or work, or on weekends. Before starting any business in your home, however, you must check on local zoning and licensing laws. Call your local city hall or Chamber of Commerce.

Janet McKinstry Cort, a close friend of mine who helped me get NFTE started, runs a very popular consignment shop selling vintage and antique clothing called Cinderella's Closet, near Boston College. Her customers receive store credit for every item they bring in. This ensures a constant flow of items. Janet is a fashion designer who can repair clothes, thereby increasing their resale value. She also makes and sells her own designs in the store.

Janet says she knew the minute she saw her storefront that her business would be successful because it's located within walking distance of a college campus. She maxed out her credit cards fixing up the store, but is currently pulling in substantial sales. Her success has enabled her to replicate Cinderella's Closet on Brown University's campus in Providence, Rhode Island.

How to Buy and Sell Clothes on Consignment

- Decide how much commission you will pay on each sale.

- Have each person who brings you clothing fill out a tag with his or her name, address, and phone number. Tell every customer how much commission you are paying.

- When you sell a piece of clothing, take off the tag and write on it the amount for which you sold the garment.

- At the end of the day, make a list of whose clothes you sold and for how much.

- Call the sellers and tell them how much money you owe them. Let's say Daphne brought you a dress that you sold for $15.00. If you have agreed to pay a commission of 30 percent, you owe Daphne $4.50 ($15.00 × .30). You make $10.50 ($15.00 − $4.50).

Tips

- Only take on consignment articles of clothing that you really think you can sell. Don't take clothes that aren't in good condition or in fashion.

- Wash, or have drycleaned, all clothing before selling it, or make a rule that you'll only take cleaned clothing.

- Create a fun atmosphere when your shop is open. Play your friends' favorite music. You can even sell refreshments.

RESOURCES

Books

Jeffrey Little explores the heart of American investment in *Understanding Wall Street* (Philadelphia: Liberty Hall Press, 1991).

One of the most up-to-date books available on the stock market is *The Stock Market* by Nancy Dunnan (Morristown, NJ: Silver Burdett Press, 1990).

In *Common Sense: A Simple Plan for Financial Independence* (10th Revision) by Art Williams, the author explains the basics of investment, including compound interest and return on investment, with lively examples (Minneapolis: Park Lane Publishers, Inc., 1991).

A very helpful book on decision making for entrepreneurs is *How to Make 1000 Mistakes in Business and Still Succeed: The Small Business Owner's Guide to Crucial Decisions* by Harold L. Wright (Oak Park, IL: The Wright Track, 1990).

Another resource that should be on every entrepreneur's desk is *Mancuso's Small Business Resource Guide* by Joseph Mancuso (New York: Prentice Hall Press, 1988). It's packed with valuable contacts.

10 HOW TO READ AND USE
THE WALL STREET JOURNAL

Always do business with a man who reads.
—Andrew Carnegie (1835–1918)
American industrialist and philanthropist

The Wall Street Journal is the daily bible of American business; it's read by over two million people a day! But even *The Wall Street Journal* began as a tiny entrepreneurial venture.

In 1882, Charles Dow and Edward Jones started a service for people working in New York City's financial district. Their service provided handwritten, up-to-the-minute financial news to subscribers. Dow and Jones's first office was in a room behind a soda fountain, in a building next to the New York Stock Exchange on Wall Street. By 1889, *The Wall Street Journal* was being sold as a newspaper for two cents.

Since then, the *Journal* has developed its worldwide circulation of over two million readers. It has become the largest daily newspaper in the United States.

Anyone interested in business should read the *Journal*. It will help you think in business terms and use business vocabulary.

JOHN H. JOHNSON:
DEVELOPING BLACK JOURNALISM

Many entrepreneurs have succeeded like Dow and Jones did, by tailoring a publication to the market they know best. John H. Johnson, the son of a mill worker, became one of the richest men in the United States by starting the first magazine written by African Americans for African Americans.

In 1918, when Johnson was born in Arkansas City, Arkansas, the local high school was open to "whites only." His mother believed strongly in the value of education, however. She moved north to Chicago so her son could attend high school there. Johnson edited the high school newspaper and yearbook and was an honor student.

As Johnson became more and more interested in journalism, he saw that very few publications reported stories that were of particular interest to the black community. Many newspapers and magazines, in fact, ignored it. Johnson decided to start a publication by African American journalists for African American readers. He approached friends and businesspeople for loans to start a magazine, but got nowhere. Finally, his mother pawned her household furniture to raise $500.00 for him. In 1942, he and his mother began publishing *Negro Digest*. After just one year, the magazine was selling 50,000 copies a month.

In 1945, Johnson started *Ebony* magazine. Most of the advertisers in *Ebony* were selling hair and skin-conditioning products to African American consumers. They were eager to advertise in a magazine that targeted their market. Today, *Ebony*'s circulation exceeds 1.5 million readers.

Johnson turned his early love of books and journalism into a multimillion-dollar empire that includes *Jet* and *Ebony* magazines, a book publishing company, a nationally syndicated TV program, real estate, and a line of cosmetics. He also owns two radio stations, one of which was Chicago's first and only black-owned station.

How to Read *The Wall Street Journal*[1]

In Johnson's day, it would have been hard to find a story about an African American in *The Wall Street Journal*. Today, however, the *Journal* is much bigger and more diverse. Reading the *Journal* may seem challenging at first, because each issue contains so much. Breaking it down into its three main sections, Front Page, The Marketplace, and Money & Investing will make the paper much easier to handle.

Front Page

The front page of the *Journal* that is reproduced on page 141 has been keyed to the list below so that you can easily find the important features the *Journal* offers as openers.

1. Look first at **What's News** to get brief descriptions of the major stories of the day. Each description lists the page where the story can be found.

2. At the bottom of the front page is **Today's Contents.** This will help you find the page numbers of other features and departments.

3. Columns 1 (far left) and 6 (far right) are the spots for in-depth articles on a wide range of business topics and for profiles of business and political leaders.

4. At the top of column 4, there is usually a **performance graph** of a single aspect of the nation's economy.

5. Below the performance graph is a story about business, approached from an unusual or entertaining perspective.

6. Column 5 is reserved for what the *Journal* calls its **"Newsletter."** On Monday it deals with the economic climate in general; on Tuesday, with issues concerning labor; on Wednesday, with taxes; on Thursday, with business developments; and on Friday, with government matters affecting business, in a feature called "Washington Wire." (The *Journal* is not published on weekends.)

The front page is the first page of Section A. Here is what you'll find in the rest of Section A.

1. On page A2 is the latest economic news.

2. The middle part of Section A is generally composed of the stories listed in **What's News.**

3. The daily **Industry Focus** spotlights one company or one industry.

4. Near the back of Section A are two pages devoted to **International Reports**—business and political news from overseas.

5. In its **Leisure & Arts** section, the *Journal* reviews books and music, and covers sports news.

6. The two facing pages at the end of Section A are the **editorial pages,** where the *Journal*'s editors and publisher, as well as guest columnists, present their opinions.

7. On the back page of Section A, you'll find **Politics & Policy**—news from Washington and how it affects not only business but the country as a whole.

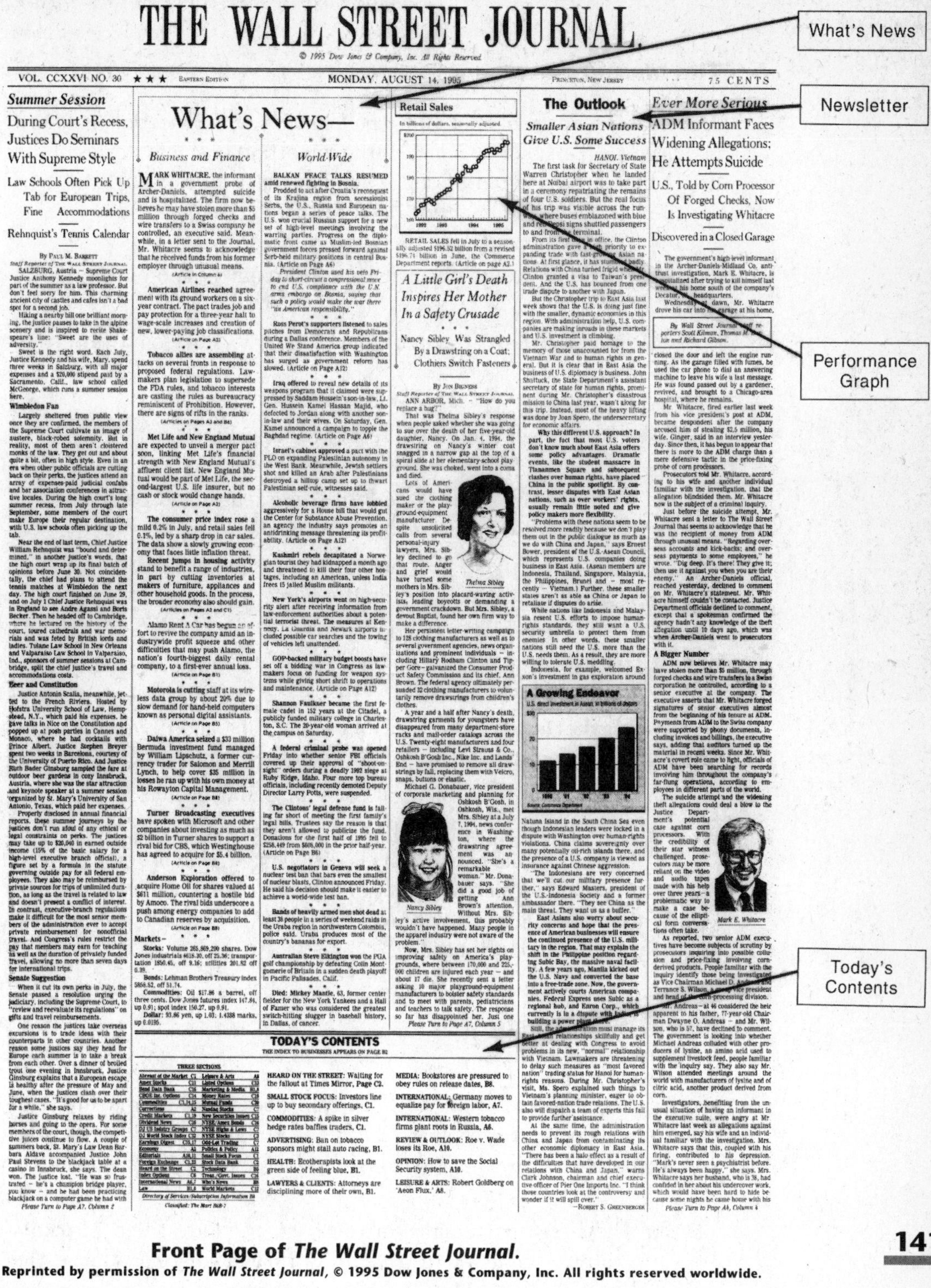

THE WALL STREET JOURNAL.

© 1995 Dow Jones & Company, Inc. All Rights Reserved.

VOL. CCXXVI NO. 30 ★ ★ ★ EASTERN EDITION   MONDAY, AUGUST 14, 1995   PRINCETON, NEW JERSEY   75 CENTS

What's News   Newsletter   Performance Graph   Today's Contents

Summer Session

During Court's Recess, Justices Do Seminars With Supreme Style

Law Schools Often Pick Up Tab for European Trips, Fine Accommodations

Rehnquist's Tennis Calendar

By PAUL M. BARRETT
Staff Reporter of THE WALL STREET JOURNAL

SALZBURG, Austria — Supreme Court Justice Anthony Kennedy moonlights for part of the summer as a law professor. But don't feel sorry for him. This charming ancient city of castles and cafes isn't a bad spot for a second job.

Hiking a nearby hill one brilliant morning, the justice pauses to take in the alpine scenery and is inspired to revive Shakespeare's line: "Sweet are the uses of adversity."

Sweet is the right word. Each July, Justice Kennedy and his wife, Mary, spend three weeks in Salzburg, with all major expenses and a $28,000 stipend paid by a Sacramento, Calif., law school called McGeorge, which runs a summer session here.

Wimbledon Fan

Largely sheltered from public view once they are confirmed, the members of the Supreme Court cultivate an image of austere, black-robed solemnity. But in reality, most of them aren't cloistered monks of the law. They get out and about quite a bit, often in high style. Even in an era when older public officials are cutting back on their perks, the justices attend an array of expenses-paid judicial confabs and bar association conferences in attractive locales. During the high court's long summer recess, from July through late September, some members of the court make Europe their regular destination.

Near the end of last term, Chief Justice William Rehnquist was "bound and determined," in another justice's words, that the high court wrap up its final table of opinions before June 30. Not coincidentally, the chief had plans to attend the tennis matches at Wimbledon the next day. The high court finished on June 29, and on July 1 Chief Justice Rehnquist was in England to see Andre Agassi and Boris Becker. Then he headed off to Cambridge, where he lectured on the history of the court, toured cathedrals and war memorials and was feted by British lords and ladies. Tulane Law School in New Orleans and Valparaiso Law School in Valparaiso, Ind., sponsors of summer sessions at Cambridge, split the chief justice's travel and accommodations costs.

Beer and Constitution

Justice Antonin Scalia, meanwhile, jetted to the French Riviera. Hosted by Hofstra University School of Law, Hempstead, N.Y., which paid his expenses, he gave talks in Nice on the Constitution and popped up at posh parties in Cannes and Monaco, where he had cocktails with Prince Albert. Justice Stephen Breyer spent two weeks in Barcelona, courtesy of the University of Puerto Rico. And Justice Ruth Bader Ginsburg sampled the fare at outdoor beer gardens in cozy Innsbruck, Austria, where she was the star attraction and keynote speaker at a summer session organized by St. Mary's University of San Antonio, Texas, which paid her expenses.

Properly disclosed in annual financial reports, these summer journeys by the justices don't run afoul of any ethical or legal constraints on perks. The justices may take up to $20,040 in earned outside income (15% of the basic salary for a high-level executive branch official), a figure set by a formula in the statute governing outside pay for all federal employees. They also may be reimbursed by private sources for trips of incidental expense, as long as the travel is related to law and doesn't present a conflict of interest. In contrast, executive-branch regulations make it difficult for the most senior members of the administration ever to accept private reimbursement for noncofficial travel. And Congress's rules restrict the pay that members may earn for teaching as well as the duration of privately funded travel, allowing no more than seven days for international trips.

Senate Suggestion

When it cut its own perks in July, the Senate passed a resolution urging the judiciary, including the Supreme Court, to "review and reevaluate its regulations" on gifts and travel reimbursements.

One reason the justices take overseas excursions is to trade ideas with their counterparts in other countries. Another reason some justices say they head for Europe each summer is to take a break from each other. Over a dinner of broiled trout one evening in Innsbruck, Justice Ginsburg explains that a European escape is healthy after the pressure of May and June, when the justices clash over their toughest cases. "It's good for us to be apart for a while," she says.

Justice Ginsburg relaxes by riding horses and going to the opera. For some members of the court, though, the competitive juices continue to flow. A couple of summers back, St. Mary's Law Dean Barbara Aldave sponsored Justice John Paul Stevens to the blackjack table at a casino in Innsbruck, she says. The dean loaned him money on a computer game he had created. The justice lost. "He was so frustrated — he's a champion bridge player, you know — and he had been practicing blackjack on a computer game that he
Please Turn to Page A7, Column 2

What's News—
* * *

Business and Finance

MARK WHITACRE, the informant in a government probe of Archer-Daniels, attempted suicide and is hospitalized. The firm now believes he may have stolen more than $5 million through forged checks and wire transfers to a Swiss company he controlled, an executive said. Meanwhile, in a letter sent to The Journal, Mr. Whitacre seems to acknowledge that he received funds from his former employer through unusual means.
(Article on Page A1)

American Airlines reached agreement with its ground workers on a six-year contract. The pact trades job and pay protection for a three-year halt to wage-scale increases and creation of new, lower-paying job classifications.
(Article on Page A2)

Tobacco allies are assembling attacks on several fronts in response to proposed federal regulations. Law-makers plan legislation to supersede the FDA rules, and tobacco interests are casting the rules as bureaucracy reminiscent of Prohibition. However, there are signs of rifts in the ranks.
(Article on Page A4)

Met Life and New England Mutual are expected to unveil a merger pact soon, linking Met Life's financial strength with New England Mutual's affluent client list. New England Mutual would be part of Met Life, the second-largest U.S. life insurer, but no cash or stock would change hands.
(Article on Pages A3 and C1)

Alamo Rent A Car has begun an effort to revive the company amid an industrywide profit squeeze and other difficulties that may push Alamo, the nation's fourth-biggest daily rental company, to a first-ever annual loss.
(Article on Page A2)

Motorola is cutting staff at its wireless data group by about 20% due to slow demand for hand-held computers known as personal digital assistants.
(Article on Page B1)

Daiwa America seized a $33 million Bermuda investment fund managed by William Lipschutz, a former currency trader for Salomon and Merrill Lynch, to help cover $35 million in losses he ran up with his own money at his Rowayton Capital Management.
(Article on Page B6)

Turner Broadcasting executives have spoken with Microsoft and other companies about investing as much as $2 billion in Turner shares to support a rival bid for CBS, which Westinghouse has agreed to acquire for $5.4 billion.
(Article on Page B1)

Anderson Exploration offered to acquire Home Oil for shares valued at $611 million, countering a bid by Amoco. The rival bids underscore a push among energy companies to add to Canadian reserves by acquisition.
(Article on Page B5)

Markets—
    Stocks: Volume 285,869,200 shares. Dow Jones industrials 4610.30, off 25.36; transportation 1850.45, off 9.16; utilities 201.92 off 0.39.
    Bonds: Lehman Brothers Treasury index 5864.82, off 11.74.
    Commodities: Oil $17.36 a barrel, off three cents. Dow Jones futures index 147.84, up 0.91; spot index 150.27, up 0.61.
    Dollar: 93.66 yen, up 1.63; 1.4388 marks, up 0.0136.

World-Wide

BALKAN PEACE TALKS RESUMED amid renewed fighting in Bosnia.

Prodded to act after Croatia's reconquest of its Krajina region from secessionist Serbs, the U.S., Russia and European nations began a series of peace talks. The U.S. won crucial Russian support for a new set of high-level meetings involving the warring parties. Progress on the diplomatic front came as Muslim-led Bosnian government forces pressed forward against Serb-held military positions in central Bosnia. *(Article on Page A8)*
    President Clinton and his veto Friday to short-circuit a congressional move to end U.S. compliance with the U.N. arms embargo on Bosnia, saying that such a policy would make the war there "an American responsibility."

Ross Perot's supporters listened to sales pitches from Democrats and Republicans during a Dallas conference. Members of the United We Stand America group indicated that their dissatisfaction with Washington has surged as government reform has slowed. *(Article on Page A12)*

Iraq offered to reveal new details of its weapons program that it claimed were suppressed by Saddam Hussein's son-in-law, Lt. Gen. Hussein Kamel Hassan Majid, who defected to Jordan along with another son-in-law and their wives. On Saturday, Gen. Kamel announced a campaign to topple the Baghdad regime. *(Article on Page A6)*

Israel's cabinet approved a pact with the PLO on expanding Palestinian autonomy in the West Bank. Meanwhile, Jewish settlers shot and killed an Arab after Palestinians destroyed a hilltop camp set up to thwart Palestinian self-rule, witnesses said.

Alcoholic beverage firms have lobbied aggressively for a House bill that would gut the Center for Substance Abuse Prevention. An agency the industry says promotes anti-drinking message threatening its profitability. *(Article on Page A12)*

Kashmiri rebels decapitated a Norwegian tourist they had kidnapped a month ago and threatened to kill their four other hostages, including an American, unless India frees 15 jailed Muslim militants.

New York's airports went on high-security alert after receiving information from law-enforcement authorities about a potential terrorist threat. The measures at Kennedy, La Guardia and Newark airports included possible car searches and the towing of vehicles left unattended.

GOP-backed military budget boosts have set off a bidding war in Congress as lawmakers focus on funding for weapon systems while giving short shrift to operations and maintenance. *(Article on Page A12)*

Shannon Faulkner became the first female cadet in 152 years at the Citadel, a publicly funded military college in Charleston, S.C. The 20-year-old woman arrived at the campus on Saturday.

A federal criminal probe was opened Friday into whether senior FBI officials covered up their approval of "shoot-on-sight" orders during a deadly 1992 siege at Ruby Ridge, Idaho. Four more top bureau officials, including recently demoted Deputy Director Larry Potts, were suspended.

The Clintons' legal defense fund is falling far short of meeting the first family's legal bills. Trustees say the reason is that they aren't allowed to publicize the fund. Donations for the first half of 1995 fell to $258,449 from $609,500 in the prior half-year. *(Article on Page B6)*

U.S. negotiators in Geneva will seek a nuclear test ban that bars even the smallest of nuclear blasts, Clinton announced Friday. He said his decision should make it easier to achieve a world-wide test ban.

Bands of heavily armed men shot dead at least 25 people in a series of weekend raids in the Uraba region in northwestern Colombia, police said. Uraba produces most of the country's bananas for export.

Australian Steve Elkington won the PGA golf championship by defeating Colin Montgomerie of Britain in a sudden-death playoff in Pacific Palisades, Calif.

Died: Mickey Mantle, 63, former center fielder for the New York Yankees and a Hall of Famer who was considered the greatest switch-hitting slugger in baseball history, in Dallas, of cancer.

Retail Sales
In billions of dollars, seasonally adjusted

RETAIL SALES fell in July in a seasonally-adjusted $196.52 billion from a record $196.71 billion in June, the Commerce Department reported. *(Article on page A2)*

A Little Girl's Death Inspires Her Mother In a Safety Crusade

Nancy Sibley Was Strangled By a Drawstring on a Coat; Clothiers Switch Fasteners

By JON BIGNESS
Staff Reporter of THE WALL STREET JOURNAL

ANN ARBOR, Mich. — "How do you replace a bag?"

That was Thelma Sibley's response when people asked whether she was going to sue over the death of her five-year-old daughter, Nancy. On Jan. 4, 1994, the drawstring on Nancy's winter coat snagged in a narrow gap at the top of a spiral slide at her elementary school playground. She was choked, went into a coma and died.

Thelma Sibley

Lots of Americans would have sued the clothing manufacturer. Despite unsolicited calls from several personal-injury lawyers, Mrs. Sibley declined to go that route. Anger and grief would have turned some mothers in Mrs. Sibley's position into placard-waving activists leading boycotts or demanding a government crackdown. But Mrs. Sibley, a devout Baptist, found her own firm way to make a difference.

Her persistent letter-writing campaign to 128 clothing manufacturers as well as to several government agencies, news organizations and prominent individuals — including Hillary Rodham Clinton and Tipper Gore — galvanized the Consumer Product Safety Commission and its chief, Ann Brown. The federal agency ultimately persuaded 30 clothing manufacturers to voluntarily remove drawstrings from children's clothes.

A year and a half after Nancy's death, drawstring garments for youngsters have disappeared from many department-store racks and mail-order catalogs across the U.S. Twenty-eight manufacturers and four retailers — including Levi Strauss & Co., Oshkosh B'Gosh Inc., Nike Inc. and Lands' End — have promised to remove all drawstrings by fall, replacing them with Velcro, snaps, buttons or elastic.

Michael G. Donabauer, vice president of corporate marketing and planning for Oshkosh B'Gosh, in Oshkosh, Wis., says Mrs. Sibley is a July 7, 1994, news conference in Washington, where the drawstring agreement was announced. "She's a remarkable woman," Mr. Donabauer says. "She got rid of getting Ann Brown's attention. Without Mrs. Sibley's active involvement, this probably wouldn't have happened. Many people in the apparel industry were not aware of the problem.

Now, Mrs. Sibley has set her sights on improving safety on America's playgrounds, where between 170,000 and 225,000 children are injured each year — and about 17 die. She recently sent a letter asking 10 major playground manufacturers to bolster safety standards and to meet with parents, pediatricians and teachers to talk safety. The response so far has disappointed her. Just one
Please Turn to Page A7, Column 5

The Outlook

Smaller Asian Nations Give U.S. Some Success

HANOI, Vietnam

The first task for Secretary of State Warren Christopher when he landed here at Noibai airport was to take part in a ceremony repatriating the remains of four U.S. soldiers. But the roar of his trip was visible across the runway, where buses emblazoned with blue and red logos shuttled passengers to and from a terminal.

From its first task in office, the Clinton administration gave a high priority to expanding trade with fast-growing Asian nations. At first glance, it has stumbled badly. Relations with China turned frigid when Mr. Clinton granted a visa to Taiwan's president. And the U.S. has bounced from one trade dispute to another with Japan.

But the Christopher trip to East Asia last week shows that the U.S. is doing just fine with the smaller, dynamic economies in this region. With administration help, U.S. companies are making inroads in these markets and U.S. investment is climbing.

Why this different U.S. approach? In part, the fact that most U.S. voters don't know much about East Asia offers some policy advantages. Dramatic events, like the student massacre in Tiananmen Square and subsequent clashes over human rights, have placed China in the public spotlight. By contrast, lesser disputes with East Asian nations, such as over workers' rights, usually remain little noted and give policy makers more flexibility.

"Problems with these nations seem to be resolved more readily because we don't play them out in the public dialogue as much as we do with China and Japan," says Ernest Bower, president of the U.S.-Asean Council, which represents U.S. companies doing business in East Asia. (Asean members are Indonesia, Thailand, Singapore, Malaysia, the Philippines, Brunei and — most recently — Vietnam.) Further, these smaller states aren't as slick as China or Japan to retaliate if disputes do arise.

While nations like Indonesia and Malaysia resent U.S. efforts to impose human-rights standards, they will want a U.S. security umbrella to protect them from enemies. In other words, these smaller nations still need the U.S. more than the U.S. needs them. As a result, they are more willing to tolerate U.S. meddling.

Indonesia, for example, welcomed Brown's investment in an exploration around

Natuna Island in the South China Sea even though Indonesian leaders were locked in a dispute with Washington over human-rights violations. China claims sovereignty over many potentially oil-rich islands there, and the presence of a U.S. company is viewed as insurance against Chinese aggression.

"The Indonesians are very concerned that we'll cut our military presence further," says Edward Masters, president of the U.S.-Indonesia Society and a former ambassador there. "They see China as the main threat. They want us as a buffer."

East Asian also worry about security concerns and hope that the presence of American businesses will ensure the continued presence of the U.S. military in the region. That may explain the shift in the Philippine position regarding Subic Bay, the massive naval facility. A few years ago, Manila kicked out the U.S. Navy and converted the base into a free-trade zone. Now, the government actively courts American companies. Federal Express uses Subic as a regional hub, and Karos Corp., which currently is in a dispute with China over building a power plant with
Please Turn to Page A6, Column 4
— ROBERT S. GREENBERGER

Ever More Serious

ADM Informant Faces Widening Allegations; He Attempts Suicide

U.S., Told by Corn Processor Of Forged Checks, Now Is Investigating Whitacre

Discovered in a Closed Garage

The government's high-level informant in the Archer-Daniels-Midland Co. antitrust investigation, Mark E. Whitacre, is hospitalized after trying to kill himself last week as his home south of the company's Decatur, Ill., headquarters.

Wednesday at dawn, Mr. Whitacre drove his car into his garage at his home,

closed the door and left the engine running. As the garage filled with fumes, he used the car phone to dial an answering machine to leave his wife a last message. He was found passed out by a gardener, revived, and brought to a Chicago-area hospital, where he remains.

The Wall Street Journal staff reporters Scott Kilman, Thomas M. Burton and Richard Gibson

These learned earlier last week from his vice president's post at ADM became despondent after the company accused him of stealing $2.5 million, his wife, Ginger, said in an interview yesterday. Since then, it has begun to appear that there is more to the ADM charge than a mere defensive tactic in the price-fixing probe of corn processors.

Prosecutors told Mr. Whitacre, according to his wife and another individual familiar with the investigation, that the allegation blindsided them. Mr. Whitacre now is the subject of a criminal inquiry.

Just before the suicide attempt, Mr. Whitacre sent a letter to The Wall Street Journal that seems to acknowledge that he was the recipient of money from ADM through unusual means. "Regarding overseas accounts and kick-backs; and overseas payments to some employees," he wrote. "Dig deep. It's there! They give it; then use it against you when you are there enemy." An Archer-Daniels official, reached yesterday, declined to comment on Mr. Whitacre's statement. Mr. Whitacre himself couldn't be contacted. Justice Department officials declined to comment, except that a spokesman confirmed the agency hadn't any knowledge of the theft allegation until 10 days ago, which was when Archer-Daniels went to prosecutors with it.

A Bigger Number

ADM now believes Mr. Whitacre may have stolen more than $5 million, through forged checks and wire transfers to a Swiss corporation he controlled, according to a senior executive at the company. The executive asserts that Mr. Whitacre forged signatures of senior executives aboard from the beginning of his tenure at ADM. Payments from ADM to the Swiss company were supported by phony documents, including invoices and billings, the executive says, adding that outfitters turned up the material in recent weeks. Since Mr. Whitacre's covert role came to light, officials of ADM have been scrutinizing the records involving him throughout the company's far-flung operations, according to employees in different parts of the world.

The suicide attempt and the widening theft allegations could deal a blow to the Justice Department's potential case against corn processors. With the credibility of their star witness challenged, prosecutors may be more reliant on the video and audio tapes made with his help over three years — a problematic way to make a case because of the elliptical conversations often taken.

As reported, two senior ADM executives have become subjects of scrutiny by prosecutors inquiring into possible collusion and price-fixing involving corn-derived products. People familiar with the inquiry identify those being investigated as Vice Chairman Michael D. Andreas — son of ADM Chairman Dwayne O. Andreas — and Terrance S. Wilson, a group vice president of the corn-processing division.

Mr. Andreas—if confirmed the heir apparent to his father, 77-year-old Chairman Dwayne O. Andreas — Mr. Whitacre, 38, is 37, have declined to comment. The government is looking into whether Michael Andreas colluded with other producers of lysine, an amino acid used to supplement livestock feed, people familiar with the inquiry say. They also say Mr. Wilson attended meetings around the world with manufacturers of lysine and of citric acid, another product derived from corn.

Investigators, benefiting from the unusual situation of having an informant in the executive suite, were angry at Mr Whitacre last week as allegations against him emerged, say his wife and an individual familiar with the investigation. Mrs. Whitacre says that this, coupled with his firing, contributed to his depression. "Mark's never seen a psychiatrist before. He's always been happy," she says. Mrs. Whitacre says her husband, who is 38, had confided in her about his undercover work, which would have been hard to hide because some nights he came home with his
Please Turn to Page A6, Column 4

Mark E. Whitacre

Nancy Sibley

A Growing Endeavor
U.S. direct investment in Asean, in billions of dollars

The Marketplace

A typical front page of Section B, the *Journal*'s second section, is shown on page 143. This section contains the important business stories of the day, which are reported in depth "with a focus on the marketplace." On the first page of the section, look for:

1. The **lead story,** given the most prominent spot at the top of the page.
2. **"The orphan"**—a short, amusing, true story on a variety of topics.

Here is what you will find in the rest of Section B:

1. **Index to Business** (page B2). This is a list, by page number, of the businesses written about in that day's issue.
2. The **Enterprise** feature is about smaller, entrepreneurial companies. (This is required reading for anyone interested in small business!)
3. **Technology** reports on "high-tech" businesses, such as computers or lasers.
4. **Marketing & Media** covers advertising and the media (television and radio, newspapers and other publications).
5. **The Law** reports on legal issues affecting business.
6. **The Mart** appears in Business Opportunities, at the end of Section B, and consists of classified pages that list employment opportunities and businesses for sale. (At the end of this chapter, you'll learn how to use The Mart to check out interesting business opportunities.)

Money & Investing

The coverage of the financial markets—in Section C, the paper's third section—is what *The Wall Street Journal* does more thoroughly than other newspapers. A typical front page of Section C is shown on page 144. It shows you why the *Journal* is so valuable to businesspeople.

1. The first two columns of the front page are titled **Markets Diary.** Activity on the five major financial markets during the

Technology: *Motorola to cut staff of wireless data group by about 20%* **Page B5.**

Law: *FDA's proposed rules for tobacco advertising prompt suits* **Page B6.**

MARKETPLACE

Who's News: *Daiwa seizes assets of fund managed by trader Lipschutz* **Page B8.**

Media: *Bantam takes a hard line on prerelease sales of books* **Page B8.**

Lead Story

HEALTH JOURNAL
By Marilyn Chase

Peanut Allergies Have Put Sufferers On Constant Alert

L IFE IS GETTING more difficult for people with a serious peanut allergy. It's a particularly vexing problem because of the ubiquity of peanuts and the severity of the allergic reaction they cause. The popularity of peanut butter and the use of nuts in creative cookery and food manufacture make peanuts difficult to avoid.

People who wouldn't go near a peanut-butter sandwich have gotten ill from egg rolls, graham-cracker pie crust or rib sauce. A lawsuit was filed last month against Bertucci's Inc. by the family of a New Hampshire woman who died in 1994 after eating a pesto sauce containing walnuts at one of the chain's restaurants. A Wesley Barks of University of Arkansas in Little Rock.

Peanuts are unique, he says, because they typically trigger potentially deadly and life-long reaction. The word for that violent reaction is "anaphylaxis" (Greek for "backward protection"). It's an overreaction by an immune system primed to recognize certain foods, drugs or insect stings as an enemy intruder. It is the body's version of friendly fire. The first known casualty, inscribed in hieroglyphics in 2640 BC, was an Egyptian pharaoh who died after a wasp sting.

Peanuts, an inexpensive and tasty protein source, are a fairly common culprit.

"What happens during a peanut-allergy reaction," says Dr. Barks, "is that the peanut allergen (protein) is absorbed into the blood stream, and goes to mouth, skin, respiratory tract and heart." Antibodies programmed to react to peanuts unleash a cascade of immune substances including histamines, which inflame tissues causing itching, swelling and obstruction.

W ITHIN SECONDS, patients experience a tingling mouth, constricting throat, stomach cramps and pooling of blood in a biochemically induced surge of anxiety. Minutes to hours later, wheezing and labored breathing may set in, with the worst cases ending in shock, cardiac arrest and death.

How to treat an accidental exposure? As with any life-threatening allergic reaction, a self-injection kit containing epinephrine (adrenalin) can be used to prevent shock. These are sold by prescription under different names, such as EpiPen and Ana Kit. Doctors advise keeping these at home or school, in a briefcase or backpack.

"Use the injections in every case — no exceptions," says John Yunginger of the Mayo Clinic. "Then go to the emergency room," and sit

out the danger period of one to several hours, because some patients seem to recover but collapse later.

Future therapy for peanut allergy may involve purified peanut proteins used for desensitization shots, but such treatments are years away, says S. Allan Bock of National Jewish Center for Immunology and Respiratory Medicine in Denver. Until then, the best strategy is to avoid peanuts and have an emergency plan.

But avoidance is tough. Many cuisines, including Chinese and

That, use peanuts. Some uses aren't obvious. In egg rolls, peanut butter is sometimes used to seal the wrapper. Re-used wok oils may transfer peanuts between dishes.

Ginger snaps and potato chips can also trigger peanut allergies. While distilled peanut oil is generally thought safe, cold-pressed oils may contain nut meat—so many allergists rule out peanut oils altogether.

"We've found peanuts in brown gravy and hot chocolate," says Anne Munoz-Furlong, founder of the Food Allergy Network. Her organization helps scan the fine print of the ingredient lists and traces product alerts.

M ANY CANDIES may contain nuts due to mingling of batches on the production line. Plain M&M's, for example, list peanuts on the label. Formerly, "reworked" chocolate from Peanut M&M's was mixed into the plain variety.

Recently, M&M's maker Mars Inc. separated its manufacturing lines to limit risk. But because all M&M's still share packaging equipment, the label warning remains—in larger, more readable type. "Our product is supposed to be fun," a spokeswoman explains. Allergic reaction "isn't part of the deal."

It takes only a milligram to provoke illness.

"I didn't realize how little it could take to set off somebody," says allergy expert Hugh Sampson of Johns Hopkins University. "We've had several cases of fatal anaphylaxis from using a jelly jar that had a knife in it previously used on peanut butter."

Even a particle of a peanut can cause havoc. David Tomich, 9, of Lynnfield, Mass., got sick from touching a peanut-bird feeder at camp and later wiping his eye. The Tomich family now funds Dr. Sampson's allergy research.

Dr. Sampson says peanut allergies may be rising because feeding peanut butter to babies sensitizes susceptible youngsters. He suggests nursing mothers in allergic families avoid eating peanuts, and not give peanut butter to kids under age three.

Howard Schwartz of Case Western Reserve University says the uninformed may dismiss this allergy with devastating results. Those seeking help can contact the Food Allergy Network of Fairfax, Va.

Ban on Tobacco Ads Might Stall Auto Racing

Jimmy Spencer, the driver of the Smokin' Joe's Racing Team, leans confidently on his yellow and blue car. "The Camel-powered car," as the announcers at the Watkins Glen, N.Y., international race

By Wall Street Journal reporters Roger Thurow, Richard Thompson and Kevin Goldman.

way say. The logo "Smokin' Joe's" jumps out in neon green; the blue hood sports an image of a large yellow camel wearing a black-and-white checkered racing scarf. Both driver and camel are here for the latest stop on the Nascar Winston Cup Series.

But despite appearances, Mr. Spencer, who has made close to $2 million racing on the Winston circuit, insists he is no cigarette pitchman for R.J. Reynolds, maker of Camels and Winstons. "R.J. Reynolds has never come to Jimmy Spencer and said 'We need to try and sell cigarettes,'" says Mr. Spencer, who himself doesn't smoke.

President Clinton sees it differently. He sees the logos and names at sporting events as contributing to the increase in smoking by children and adolescents. So last week he proposed, among other measures, prohibiting brand-name sponsorship of sporting or entertainment events by tobacco companies. As one might expect, that move is considered the pits here in the pits.

In America, sports and tobacco have been rolled together for decades. In the gilded days of baseball, back in the '30s and '40s, some big stars hawked cigarette brands. Virginia Slims, made by Philip Morris, was the main sponsor contributing to the boom in women's tennis. Today, tobacco brand names sponsor sporting events ranging from bowling to hydroplan-

ADVERTISING

ing from the Vantage golf tournament to Copenhagen Skoal Pro Rodeo. Although professional baseball, basketball and football leagues are not sponsored by tobacco companies, some of the stadiums and arenas that host games earn revenue from tobacco billboards, though they must now be out of camera view.

Nowhere, though, is the relationship as close as in auto racing, where tobacco companies began sinking money after they stopped advertising on television, and where they are the largest single advertiser. According to marketing industry figures, R.J. Reynolds, a unit of RJR Nabisco Holdings, has spent some $200 million on the National Association for Stock Car Auto Racing, or Nascar, since 1971, with much of it coming in the past decade. And Philip Morris, it is estimated, has spent at least that much on Nascar and the Indy car circuit. Both companies sponsor teams and certain races, as well as prize-money awards.

"The visibility the sponsors receive at the racing event is enormous," says Alan Friedman, editor of Team Marketing Report, a monthly newsletter in Chicago. If tobacco brands are banned from sponsorship, he says, it "will be a very serious setback for the auto-racing industry."

While motor racing has become a hot ticket for advertising dollars, Mr. Friedman says it's "doubtful" that the various racing associations would be able to find other industries capable of making up the difference if tobacco revenue is lost. For one, most advertisers interested in backing sports events already are doing so, so fresh funds are limited. Also, auto

Tobacco and Sports

Sporting events sponsored by some tobacco companies:

R.J. REYNOLDS
- Winston Cup (Nascar)
- Winston Racing (Nascar)
- Winston West (Nascar)
- Winston Select 10 Bonus Fund (Nascar)
- Winston Drag (NHRA)
- Vantage Championship (PGA)
- Smokin' Joe's Racing Team (Camel)

PHILIP MORRIS
- Marlboro auto racing
- Marlboro Grand Prix
- Virginia Slims Legends Tour (tennis, stars and musical artists, such as Gladys Knight)

U.S. TOBACCO
- Professional Rodeo Cowboys events
- Copenhagen Skoal Pro Rodeo

Includes Nascar, NHRA, Motorcycle racing and Hydroplanes

Note: Nascar=National Association for Stock Car Auto Racing; NHRA=National Hot Rod Association; PGA=Professional Golfers' Association

Source: companies

racing draws fans from particularly desirable demographics for tobacco advertisers. R.J. Reynolds, for instance, now pumps about $15 million annually into the sport, not including promotional items like hats and apparel.

"There is an old motorsport saying:

Your best sponsor is the one you already have," says Adam Saal, a spokesman for the Indy Car circuit. "Getting or losing a sponsor can be the difference between racing on Sunday or sitting on the sidelines."

Although tobacco brand names would, under the proposed regulations, have to be removed, the parent company could place its name on the event. So, gone would be the Winston Drag or the Marlboro 500 and in their places would be the R.J. Reynolds Drag and Philip Morris 500. "We would have to look very hard at whether it makes any sense for us to mount such a sponsorship," says a spokesman for R.J. Reynolds. "After all, how many people know that we make Winston?" But we haven't come to any conclusions yet."

What, say, would become of the Marlboro 500 without Marlboro?

"That's a good question," says Walt Czarnecki, executive vice president of Penske Corp., which owns several raceways, including the Michigan International Speedway that stages the Marlboro 500. "The event may still go on, but the costs of putting it on don't go down. Ticket prices would go up. That's the first thing that comes to mind."

Another thing coming to the minds of racing fans this past weekend is the specter of government interference.

At Watkins Glen, where Sunday's win also Cup race was sponsored by Budweiser, Thomas Bagatio, a 25-year-old fan from Allentown, Pa., asks, "What's going to be next? Beer advertising? Coffee?"

He has just traded a pack of Marlboros for two packs of Camels at one of the "package exchange posts" (you get two R.J. Reynolds brand packs for one competi-

Please Turn to Page B8, Column 4

HEALTH

Ecotherapists Explore the Green Side of Feeling Blue

By Timothy Aeppel
Staff Reporter of The Wall Street Journal

Having bounced in and out of therapy since college, Lisa Wessan is used to talking about her problems.

But when the 37-year-old New Yorker tried telling her therapist about the depression that hit her whenever she thought about polluted drinking water or saw pictures of birds mired in oil, the therapist cut her off. "This is was using the eco stuff to skirt the real issues—like why I didn't have a boyfriend," says Ms. Wessan, a freelance writer and radio producer.

So she switched to a therapist who melds green concerns into the treatment. Her regime now includes walking five miles a day in Central Park. "I feel better than I have in years," she says.

Everyone knows a stroll in the woods can be good for the soul. But now a handful of therapists see it as a key to mental health. The new field even has a trendy name: ecopsychology. Rather than focusing strictly on how a person feels about work, love life or family, these therapists consider their clients' relationship with the natural world in their efforts to pinpoint sources of problems. Is that lingering depression raised by a bad marriage, or is it really a subconscious mourning for lost species?

"It may be that a large amount of what's showing up in therapy—dreams, fears and environmental origins," says Theodore Roszak, a history professor at the University of California, Hayward, and one of the gurus of the movement. Mr. Roszak has published several books and puts out a newsletter on ecopsychology. He says that in addition to therapists, many environmentalists also are embracing ecopsychology as a way to better

understand how people think about green issues.

Still, ecopsychology remains on the fringe. "I'm not aware of any case where somebody's problem came directly from the environment—unless [it came] from a poison or a toxin," says Dr. Norman Clemens, a Cleveland psychoanalyst. He adds that he would let a patient talk about green issues, but he would still expect to find that the deeper problem had something to do with the patient's human relationships or experiences.

Allen Kanner, an ecopsychologist in Berkeley, Calif., takes a different approach. When one of Dr. Kanner's clients complained of dreams in which trees were screaming out in pain, he didn't "immediately reduce it to a symbolic dream about a human relationship," he says. "I didn't say, 'The trees are your mother.'"

Instead, Dr. Kanner probed the issue and discovered what he believed were the patient's deep anxieties about the destruction of the natural world. She eventually changed her lifestyle—buying less, dumping excess clothes and recycling more. "She hasn't had the dreams in a while," Dr. Kanner says, "but she's still very concerned about the environment."

While some of this sounds like common sense, a few of the techniques raise eyebrows. Dr. Kanner sometimes urges patients to use aspects of shamanism, a religion based on a belief in good and evil spirits infusing the natural world. Patients learn, for example, to consult with "animal ancestors" for advice on vexing problems.

Some psychiatrists worry ecopsychology may be used to push an environmental agenda on patients. Randall White, a psychiatrist in Atlanta, says the techniques seem to help some people but remain "very untested." For example, some ecopsychologists view overconsumption as a form of addiction, like alcoholism. "It's a very seductive notion, but there's no scientific knowledge to back it up," Dr. White says.

For their part, ecopsychologists see themselves in the same spot family therapists were in during the 1960s. Then, it was revolutionary to bring family members into therapy; now, it's routine. "Many of my patients probably don't even know that I refer to myself as an ecopsychologist," says

Please Turn to Page B5, Column 1

LAWYERS & CLIENTS

Attorneys Discipline More of Their Own

By Constance Johnson
Staff Reporter of The Wall Street Journal

Joseph A. Costino is one of a growing number of lawyers across the country who are being sanctioned for misconduct by the profession's own disciplinary authorities.

After more than four decades as a lawyer, the Buffalo, N.Y., solo practitioner was disbarred last year for transferring the stocks, bonds and home of two elderly clients into his name without advising them of the consequences of that action. (Mr. Costino declined through his son to comment.)

Disciplinary authorities are the sharp rise in attorney sanctions reflects their efforts to get tougher and respond more swiftly to complaints from clients, judges and others. [In the case of Mr. Costino, the complaint came from a social worker who was concerned about the two sisters.] "It's a reflection of an overall consumerist bent," says Frank Ricky, chairman of the New York State Bar Association's Committee on Professional Discipline.

The number of complaints filed against attorneys has risen steadily over the past decade, cresting big backlogs in some states. The complaints reflect both the booming population of lawyers—and clients' rising expectations, says Ray Trombadoro, who chairs the American Bar Association's Commission on Evaluation of Disciplinary Enforcement. Growing economic pressures have also led some lawyers to take on more cases than they can keep track of and cases they aren't qualified to handle, he says.

Until recently, though, complaints tended to languish. And most were essentially dismissed for lack of proof. Now, the lawyers are being sanctioned more sharply in many states. The number of lawyers disciplined in Texas in the year ended April 30, for example, rose 90% from two years earlier. Last year's numbers were up 54% in Ohio, 21% in New

York, 16% in Pennsylvania and 15% in California. Client neglect is the most common offense leading to sanctions. Misuse of clients' funds is a distant second.

Critics, though, still aren't convinced that disciplinary authorities are doing enough to punish errant attorneys. "It's good it's happening, but I wouldn't break open the champagne just yet," says Robert Fellmeth, who was in charge of revamping California's disciplinary system a few years ago.

Adds Bill Pry, the executive director of HALT, a Washington-based group advocating changes in the legal profession: "The basic problem is that it is still in the hands of lawyers. The system is still dominated by lawyers, and they are inclined to punish their own."

Lawyers and disciplinary authorities are required to make sure that only honest and competent people are licensed to practice law. In some cases, the disciplinary agency operates under the auspices of the state court system. In others, the bar conducts the inquiries. Whatever the system, most complaints against attorneys are dismissed for failing to disclose enough evidence to be collected to let a law breaking their course of conduct.

Please Turn to Page B5, Column 2

Though the procedures vary from state to state, the groups typically investigate complaints about alleged violations of professional rules of conduct. Lawyers found to have violated the profession's rules can be reprimanded, suspended or disbarred. (Any criminal proceedings are handled separately by law-enforcement authorities. Unhappy clients can also sue their lawyers.)

New Jersey is the only state that doesn't allow disbarred attorneys to reapply after several years, but reinstatements are rare; legal experts say. And the California State Bar is considering making disbarments permanent.

Disciplinary authorities cite several recent improvements in their procedures. Several states have added nonlawyers to their disciplinary boards to help offset concerns of a pro-attorney bias. In addition, many state disciplinary boards have beefed up their staffs, cutting down on the time it takes to resolve complaints. The state Supreme Court in New Jersey now requires the Office of Attorney Ethics to complete investigations of standard misconduct complaints within six months and more complex complaints within nine months.

In Illinois, disciplinary authorities say that 10% to 20% of the lawyers sanctioned last year were attorneys or partners at large law firms, while the rest were solo practitioners. One of them was Richard Salomon, who was a partner at Chicago's Mayer, Brown & Platt. Last year, he requested disbarment in the face of impending disciplinary charges. He would have been charged with inflating billing for clients that included Chrysler Corp., according to Illinois disciplinary authorities. He also would have been charged with dishonesty and fraudulent conduct for failing to disclose

Please Turn to Page B5, Column 3

CORPORATE FOCUS:

Rocky Road: Alamo Maps A Turnaround

By Martha Brannigan
Staff Reporter of The Wall Street Journal

For more than a decade, Alamo Rent A Car Inc. was on a roll.

By introducing such concepts as unlimited mileage, Alamo grew from a tiny regional company in the early 1980s to the nation's fourth-largest daily car-rental company in 1994—just behind Hertz Corp., Avis Inc. and Budget Rent A Car Corp. Its management used low prices and strong ties to travel agents and tour operators to dominate the rental market for leisure travelers.

But three years of turmoil have turned the car-rental industry—compounded by its own serious missteps—have hit

D. Keith Cobb

Alamo in need of a comeback. Alamo ranked fifth in first-ever rush in 1995, after recording its first-ever loss, of an estimated $18 million, at more than 170 company-owned offices, or about 25% of its Fort Lauderdale, Fla., headquarters staff. Executives concede the company may report its first annual loss in 1995.

"For Alamo, this is uncharted territory," says Anthony D'Allo, a vice president at Value Rent A Car of Boca Raton, Fla. "They've only been in sunny weather."

Michael S. Egan, the chairman and controlling shareholder of the closely held concern, has brought a fresh concern. In recent months, he has shuffled management ranks

Please Turn to Page B4, Column 1

Orphan

Theater Manager Hopes Cool Deal Can Deliver Healthy Ticket Sales

By Patricia Davis
Staff Reporter of The Wall Street Journal

Mark Cohen thinks he knows what makes a pregnant woman happy — a good film and air conditioning.

This week, Mr. Cohen, manager of the Rex Theatre in Pittsburgh's South Side, will usher in any "visibly pregnant" woman for free, as long as she's accompanied by a ticket buyer.

He got the idea for what he calls Pregnant Women Week a month or so ago, inspired by his wife, Beth, then eight months pregnant with their first child. With temperatures reaching record highs, the summer was quite uncomfortable for Mrs. Cohen. So she went to a lot of movies, as much for the air conditioning as for the entertainment. "It's one way to get out, relax and be cool," she says, "And it's cheap."

Pregnant Women Week is a way "to honor women who have carried babies through the hot summer," Mr. Cohen says.

No doctor's notes or lab tests will be required for free entry. The deal only has one limitation: "If we can't see, it's not free." Lifting of shirts to show swollen bellies isn't necessary. In fact, it's discouraged. Just a glance should do it.

Mr. and Mrs. Cohen have posted fliers in Ms. Cohen's obstetrician's office and at their Lamaze and parenting classes.

While Mr. Cohen hopes to promote the theater and celebrate his new child, he's not sure how the deal will affect attendance. "We're not expecting a whole throng of pregnant women," he says, "I don't know what to expect."

Carla Cerrito, a financial consultant who is due to deliver her first child in two weeks, says that she will go to the theater to see how many other pregnant women show up. She says she's worried some theaters over the past few months because she thought she'd be uncomfortable.

"We'll see how it is sitting in those seats," she says. "It's not often something like this is dedicated to pregnant ladies. We can commiserate."

Beth Cohen, the inspiration for Pregnant Women Week, is no longer eligible for the two-for-one deal. She had been expected to deliver the week of the promotion but she gave birth to Stephen a week and a half early, on Aug. 4.

Beth's frequent trips to the movies won't be curtailed by the baby, however. Pittsburgh's Rex Theatre has drive-ins in the family car.

Markets Diary

Abreast of the Market

Credit Markets

Small Stock Focus

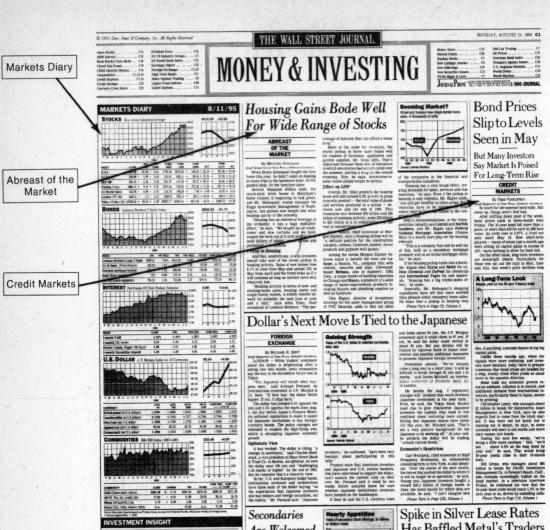

previous eighteen months and the previous week is represented in **graphs.** The markets are:

- Stocks

- Bonds

- Interest (rates)

- U.S. Dollar (compared to five foreign currencies)

- Commodities

2. Below the graphs is a **tabular summary** of the previous day's activity on the **financial markets.**

3. **Abreast of the Market, Credit Markets,** and **a focus on some aspect of the financial markets** are usually found on the first page. These features offer long-term information, analyses, and tips on how to invest and manage money.

4. An index to the contents of the rest of Section C is given at the top of the front page. The remainder of the front page is devoted to expert opinions on the previous day's financial developments and the financial world in general.

In the rest of Section C, you will find:

1. On page C2, an important financial market column, **Heard on the Street.**

2. Reports on how various financial markets, including the stock market, are performing.

You will learn about stock and corporations in Chapter 15. Corporations sell stock (shares of ownership in a company) to investors. Investors buy and sell stocks on the stock market. A single piece of stock is called a share. Back in 1889, *The Wall Street Journal* started reporting the Dow Jones Industrial Average (DJIA), an average of the prices of eleven major stocks.

Today, Dow Jones reports price averages for three types of stock and includes many more companies:

- 30 **Industrial** stocks (such as General Motors, Exxon, and IBM).

- 20 **Transportation** stocks (such as USAir and the Union Pacific Railroad).

- 15 **Utilities** stocks (such as Consolidated Edison [New York] and Detroit Edison).

The price movements of these stocks are averaged at the end of each day. These averages are called the "Dow Jones Averages." You've probably heard them announced during the business news on television or on the radio. The DJIA is watched by casual investors. Changes in the leading industrial stocks are an important indication of how the entire stock market is performing.

Chart 8 compares the DJIA in 1896 (twelve companies were listed then) with the thirty companies that now yield the industrial average.

Other financial markets covered in Section C of the *Journal* are:

- Mutual Funds.
- International Stocks.
- Foreign Currencies.
- Credit Markets.
- Futures & Options.

THE MART

Look in The Mart section of *The Wall Street Journal* for a business for sale that interests you. Call the person selling the business and ask

The 1896 DJIA	The Current DJIA		
American Cotton Oil	Allied-Signal	General Electric	Texaco
American Sugar	Alcoa	General Motors	Union Carbide
American Tobacco	American Express	Goodyear Tire	United Technologies
Chicago Gas	AT&T	IBM	Walt Disney
Distilling & Cattle Feeding	Bethlehem Steel	International Paper	Westinghouse Electric
General Electric	Boeing	McDonald's	Woolworth
Laclede Gas	Caterpillar	Merck & Company	
National Lead	Chevron	3M	
North American Co.	Coca-Cola	J.P. Morgan	
Tennessee Coal & Iron	Du Pont	Philip Morris	
U.S. Leather Preferred	Eastman Kodak	Procter & Gamble	
U.S. Rubber	Exxon	Sears Roebuck	

Chart 8   The Dow Jones Industrials in 1896 and in 1995

some questions that would help you decide whether the business is worth buying. Some good questions to ask are:

- What is the product (or service) that you sell?
- How do you define one unit of your product or service?
- Do you have audited financial statements (statements that have been reviewed by an independent accountant)?
- What is your revenue? Your gross profit? Your profit before tax? Your net profit?
- How have your sales been over the past five years?
- What are your sales and profit forecasts?
- Do you have a business plan that you can send me?

SAMPLE AD

Look at this Mart advertisement from the *Journal,* March 23, 1995. The wording is simple and direct:

THE MART

INTERNATIONAL/NATIONAL/REGIONAL

Small Family Business

in Central Virginia with annual sales of $200,000. Owner interested in selling or in finding someone interested in investing in the business as a partner.
Call Frank V. at (804) 352-7191

If you were to call the owner/seller, your dialogue might go like this:

YOU: What is the product (or service) that you sell?

SELLER: This is a commercial printing company. We make printed stationery, envelopes, and other items. We define one unit of printing service as one hour. Our price per job is based on how long we think it will take, plus the cost of the paper and ink we will need.

YOU:　　Do you have audited financial statements?

SELLER:　　Yes, we do.

YOU:　　What is your revenue?

SELLER:　　Our revenue is approximately $200,000 per year.

YOU:　　Your gross profit?

SELLER:　　It's approximately $95,000 per year.

YOU:　　Your net profit?

SELLER:　　Our net profit was $72,000 this year.

YOU:　　How have your sales been over the past five years? What are your sales and profit forecasts?

SELLER:　　Our sales have been steadily increasing over the past five years. We expect our sales and profits to increase by about 10 percent per year over the next five years.

YOU:　　Are these numbers audited? Who's your accountant?

SELLER:　　Yes, our financials were prepared by Ernst & Young.

YOU:　　Do you have a business plan that you can send me?

SELLER:　　Yes, I do.

**Business
for the Young
Entrepreneur**

CASE STUDY: YARD WORK

John has about thirty-five customers who depend on him to keep their yards clean. He gets out of bed before dawn to mow lawns in the summer, rake leaves and resoil in the fall, and shovel snow in the winter.

John started his company, John's Four Season Care, at age fourteen, while participating in the Young Entrepreneurs of Minnesota program. "People give me business because they really like to see kids working hard—not just hanging out doing drugs, ripping off," John says. "Too many kids want to make money illegally," he adds. "This way you can do it legally and be proud."

John says the most important thing a young entrepreneur can be is reliable. "People won't ask you back if you show up late or don't do a good job," John says. "They won't recommend you to their neighbors, either," he adds. Much of John's business comes from repeat customers and referrals.

Yard work is available year-round. If, like John, you live in a four-season region, each season offers different business opportunities:

Summer	Fall	Winter	Spring
Cut grass	Rake leaves	Shovel snow	Clean up winter debris
Weed flower beds	Mulch	Salt sidewalks	Plant flowers

How many more yard work chores can you imagine?

Each season, John makes flyers announcing his services. He puts one flyer in each mailbox in his neighborhood. A week later, he visits each home that received a flyer and tries to sign up customers.

Tips

- Work quickly, but be thorough. Never leave a job until you've completely finished what the customer asked you to do.
- Always clean up after yourself. Don't leave mud or plant clippings on the sidewalk, for example!
- Don't forget to put away tools. Younger children can hurt themselves if shovels, rakes, or hedge clippers are left lying around. If it rains when they're left outdoors, they'll rust and have to be replaced.

RESOURCES

The Wall Street Journal is available on newsstands and by subscription. To have it mailed or delivered to you, call: (800) 628-9320.

For a more detailed look at *The Wall Street Journal*, see *The Dow Jones-Irwin Guide to Using the Wall Street Journal* by Michael B. Lehmann (Homewood, IL: Dow Jones-Irwin, 1987).

11

THE ESSENCE OF
SELLING IS TEACHING

HOW TO MAKE A GREAT SALES CALL

When there's nothing to lose and much to gain by trying, try.
—W. Clement Stone (b. 1902)
American sales expert and author

BUSINESS IS BASED ON SELLING

All business is based on selling products or services for money. Direct selling is when you are face-to-face with a potential buyer, trying to convince him or her to make a purchase.

Salespeople often become successful entrepreneurs because they hear what the consumer needs and wants on a daily basis. If the customer is dissatisfied, it is the salesperson who hears the complaint.

FROM SALESPERSON TO ENTREPRENEUR

Many of America's great entrepreneurs started out in sales:

- Ray Kroc, founder of McDonald's, was selling milkshake machines when he was inspired to turn the McDonald brothers' hamburger restaurant into a national operation.
- King C. Gillette was a traveling salesman when he invented the safety razor that millions of people use.
- William C. Durant, the founder of General Motors, began his career as a buggy salesman. He said, "The secret of success is to

have a self-seller, and if you don't have one, get one." Durant was from my hometown, Flint, Michigan; I should have remembered his advice when I started selling.

One of the first products I tried to sell was a bicycle lock from Taiwan. I was representing the lock exporter. After many phone calls, I finally secured a meeting with an importer who might order thousands of the locks. My commission on the sale would have been $5,000 a month. The importer picked up one of the locks and yanked it as hard as he could. It broke. I learned the importance of finding a self-seller— a product in which I really believed.

DURANT FINDS HIS "SELF-SELLER"

From 1878 to 1886, Durant started a variety of entrepreneurial ventures, primarily in the fields of insurance, real estate, and construction. None of them really took off. He had yet to find his "self-seller." When he was twenty-five, however, Durant hitched a ride to work with a friend. He noticed that his friend's new buggy rode smoother than any he had been in. His friend explained that the smooth ride was due to a new design in the buggy's springs. Durant was so impressed that he decided he wanted to own the company that made this new kind of carriage.

Durant learned that the Coldwater Road Cart Company made the buggies with the improved springs. The very next day, Durant went to Coldwater, Michigan. The owner of the cart company was willing to sell it for $1,500. Durant insisted that the deal include the patent for the springs. In two days, the deal was closed. This transaction demonstrated Durant's business philosophy: "Decide quickly, make your pitch, nail down the details, and don't worry about the money."

MAKING BUGGIES

When Durant made the deal, he didn't even have $1,500, but he didn't let that deter him from his vision. Durant borrowed $2,000 from the Citizens National Bank of Flint and made two sample buggy carts. He transported one of them to a county fair in Madison, Wisconsin. His entrepreneurial hunch was correct. The cart sold itself; within a week he had orders for 600 buggy carts.

The business was a great success. By 1893, the original $2,000 had grown to $150,000. By 1901, his company was the biggest buggy manufacturer in the country.

FEATURES BECOME BENEFITS

The essence of selling is teaching *how* and *why* the outstanding features of your product or service will benefit your customers. When Durant took his buggy cart to the county fair, he was able to teach potential customers how the cart's unique feature—it's extra-springy seat—could benefit them by making them more comfortable during a buggy ride.

Let's say you sell hats that last long, are washable, fold without wrinkling, and come in many great colors. These features create the product's benefits: a durable hat will not have to be replaced soon; an easy-to-clean hat will save money; a hat that fits into a pocket or bag will be used often. The benefits sell the hat, not the features.

The features of a product are facts about the product. The creative art of selling is teaching customers how the features will benefit them.

THE BUICK PARTNERSHIP: DURANT FINDS HIS SECOND "SELF-SELLER"

David Dunbar Buick, a Scottish immigrant who ran a plumbing supply business in Detroit, formed the Buick Manufacturing Company in 1902. He was not having much success, however, and constantly needed capital. In 1904, the Buick Company turned to Durant, both as a fresh source of capital and for his famed selling abilities.

Durant took a ride in the still experimental "Buick." He became immediately enthusiastic about the car, which he believed was one of those natural "self-sellers" he was always on the lookout for. He agreed to come in only if he could have absolute managerial control. Durant took over the Buick Company on November 1, 1904.

Once in, Durant infused the operation with his own energy. At the 1905 auto show in New York, he "sold" 1,108 cars when the company had actually manufactured only 37. By 1906, the Buick Company was worth $3 million.

PRINCIPLES OF SELLING

Like Durant, every entrepreneur has to be able to sell his or her product or service and make an effective sales call. The following principles of selling were used by Durant throughout his life. Durant was one of the great direct salespeople of this century. These principles apply to any product or service:

1. *Make a good personal impression* when selling your product or service. Prepare yourself physically. Be neat and clean.

2. *View selling as teaching*—it's your chance to teach the customer about the product or service. Explain the benefits of your product or service to your customer.

3. *Believe in your product or service.* Good salespeople believe in what they are selling.

4. *Know your product or service.* Understand how its features can benefit the consumer.

5. *Know your field.* Read the trade literature. Learn about your competitors.

6. *Know your customers.* What are their needs? How does your product or service address these needs?

7. *Prepare your sales presentation.* Know ahead of time how you want to present your product or service.

8. *Think positively.* This frame of mind will help you deal with the rejections you may experience before you sell your product or service.

9. *Keep good records.* Have your record-keeping system, including invoices and receipts, set up before you go on your first sales call.

10. *Make an appointment.* People are more likely to listen when they have set aside time to hear your sales pitch. They will be less patient if you interrupt their day unannounced.

11. *Stay in touch with your customers and potential customers.* Cultivate your customers for repeat sales. Build relationships.

The essence of selling is teaching.

Rule of Thumb

THE SALES CALL

A sales call is an appointment with a potential customer to explain or demonstrate your product or service. During the sales call, you will want to:

- Make the customer aware of your product or service.
- Make the customer *want* to buy that product or service.
- Make the customer want to buy it from *you*.

PREQUALIFY YOUR SALES CALL

Before calling to make an appointment for any sales call, ask yourself these questions:

- Is this person in my market?
- Does this person need my product?
- Can this person afford it?

If the answer to any of these questions is No, making a sales call on that person may be a waste of time. Asking yourself these questions is called "prequalifying" a sales call.

THE SEVEN-STEP SALES CALL

Many people don't realize how strong you have to be mentally to conduct sales calls. I went on over 1,100 sales calls while running my import–export business. I went on 400 calls before I closed my first sale of more than $1,000. This experience allowed me to hone my ability to make a sales call. I still make frequent sales calls today, only now I'm selling the NFTE mission to potential donors. I use the same seven steps when talking to billionaire donors that I used when I was trying to sell wooden carvings.

1. *Preparation.* Prepare yourself mentally. Think about how your product or service will benefit this customer. Have the price, discounts, all technical information, and any other details "on the tip of your tongue." Be willing to obtain further information should your customer request it.

2. *Greeting.* Greet the customer graciously. Do not plunge immediately into business talk. The first few words you say can be the most important. Keep a two-way conversation going. Maintain eye contact and keep the customer's attention.

3. *Showing the product or service.* Try to "personalize" it. Point out the benefits for this particular customer. Use props and models (or the real thing) where appropriate.

4. *Dealing with objections.* Always acknowledge objections and deal with them. Don't pretend you didn't hear. Don't overreact to objections and don't be afraid to listen. A famous real-estate entrepreneur, William Zeckendorf, said, "I never lost money on a sales pitch when I listened to the customer."

5. *Closing the sale.* Review the benefits of your product or service. Narrow the choices the customer has to make. Close the sale. Don't overstay your welcome. There is a rule of thumb that if a customer says No three times, you still have a chance. If he or she says it the fourth time, it's really No. If the answer is No, take it gracefully. You may make a sale to this customer in the future.

6. *Follow-up.* Make regular follow-up calls to find out how your customer likes the product or service. Ask if you can be of any further help. If the customer has a complaint, don't ignore it. Remember, *the most successful business is built on repeat customers.*

7. *Ask for references.* If you did a good job for customers who needed your product or service, ask them to refer you to other potential customers.

THE ONE-MINUTE SALES CALL

Another good suggestion is to keep your sales calls under one minute. Believe it or not, it's a challenge for most people to pay attention to someone for more than a minute. Write down your sales pitch and practice delivering it to a friend or relative. Have your listener time you. You'll be shocked at how fast a minute can go by!

Here's an example to get you started. Let's say you make baby food from organic fruits and vegetables. You are trying to convince the owner of Johnson's General Store to buy some of your baby food to sell in his store.

YOU: Hello, Mr. Johnson. Thank you for agreeing to see me today. I'm excited about this product and think you and your customers will be, too.

I brought you a jar of our baby applesauce. It's nicely packaged, don't you think? You hand-decorate each jar. They make nice gifts for new or expecting parents. The eye-catching ribbons will be sure to attract your customers.

We use only organic fruits and vegetables, no sugar, and very little salt. Our label explains that some babies are sensitive to the additives and dyes found in some commercial baby foods. These may give sensitive babies headaches or upset stomachs. Our food is very gentle on the baby—and that makes the parents' life much easier!

I understand your concern that our baby food costs twenty-five cents per jar more than the brand you presently stock. I think your customers will pay more for our high quality and for knowing that their babies are protected from harmful additives or high levels of sugar and salt. Because we add very little water to our product, we actually offer more food for the money than some cheaper brands.

I really think you could start a trend by stocking our baby food here, Mr. Johnson. There's been a shift in the food market toward healthy food for adults—and those adults are looking for healthy baby food. Our products combine an eye-catching look with healthy ingredients that new parents and their friends and relatives won't be able to resist. How many jars would you like to order?

SANDRA KURTZIG:
LISTENING TO THE CUSTOMER

In the late 1960s, Sandra Kurtzig made hundreds of sales calls. She was selling computer time for General Electric. In those days, there were no personal computers. Computers were enormous machines called mainframes that many people shared by buying computer time. As a result, using a computer was a complicated and time-consuming process. If you wanted to solve a problem using a computer, you had to hire a computer programmer to write a program that would solve your problem.

Kurtzig's customers complained frequently that they wanted a more efficient way to use computers. She realized that what her customers wanted was programs that were already written to meet their needs. In 1971, Kurtzig started her own company, ASK Computer Systems, Inc., to develop software programs that would meet this consumer need.

Kurtzig started ASK in a spare bedroom in her house with $2,000.00 when she was twenty-four. By 1973, ASK had developed a simple, universal program that could be used by thousands of manufacturers to keep track of their inventory. No one had done this before. Business software that people everywhere use today had not yet been invented.

By the end of the decade, ASK was worth $400 million. ASK became the first high-tech company owned by a woman to sell stock and the largest company founded and run by a woman.

Kurtzig has said that almost every ASK product evolved from customer requests or suggestions. One important ASK invention was financial software (developed when a customer asked for help managing his financial accounts). You can never go wrong by listening to the customer, Kurtzig recommends.

Turning Objections into Advantages

Initially, Kurtzig's customers were worried that paying ASK to design software for them would be too expensive. Kurtzig did not respond by arguing with the customer's perception of the software as expensive. Rather, she explained that the expense reflected the product's high quality and ASK's commitment to making sure that it worked when installed and that it would satisfy the customer's needs.

The key to selling is to show the customer that his or her objection to buying a product is really an advantage. Remember this acronym[1] during your sales call:

Smile, Agree, Deflect Objection, Next Offer
"SAD - O - NO"

Sales Commission

Many salespeople are paid sales commissions—percentages of each sale made. A car salesperson who makes a 10 percent sales commission, for example, would earn $1,000 after selling a car for $10,000.

$$.10 \times \$10{,}000 = \$1{,}000$$

I earned a 5 percent sales commission on any products I sold for my friends from Africa and Bangladesh.

DIRECT SALES

The Direct Selling Association (DSA) is the national trade association of companies that manufacture and distribute products and services sold directly to consumers. Its membership includes Avon Products, Mary Kay Cosmetics, Artistic Impressions, Amway, Tupperware Worldwide, and many other popular direct sellers.

Direct selling companies tap into the entrepreneurial dream by training people who want to build their own businesses. A Mary Kay salesperson, for example, purchases skin-care products and makeup from Mary Kay Cosmetics at a 40 to 50 percent discount. The salesperson gives facials and skin-care classes in her home or at a customer's home to attract customers, and sells the products directly to them.

A Mary Kay salesperson can also recruit people to sell Mary Kay products. The recruiter receives a percentage of the sales of her recruits. In this way, direct selling has enabled thousands of people to build very profitable businesses with very little capital investment.

Some disreputable companies focus almost exclusively on the recruiting aspect of direct sales, luring salespeople with promises of instant riches. The DSA has been instrumental in educating the public about the dangers of these so-called pyramid schemes. The primary purpose of a direct selling company should be to sell products that meet consumer needs. Before getting involved with any direct sales company, call or write the Direct Selling Association.

THE SALES RECEIPT

When you make a sale, don't forget to fill out a receipt for the customer. A sample receipt is shown in Chart 9.

The receipt must include the date of the sale, the amount of the sale, and the item. The receipt is the customer's proof that the item or service was purchased. The carbon copy is a record of income for you.

GINA'S T-SHIRT CO.

Date _June 13_   19_95_

Sold to: _George Braxton_

Address: _123 E. Orange St._

Reg. No.	Clerk		
1	_1 red T-shirt (#28)_	_$10.99_	_$10.99_
2			
3		_Tax_	_.61_
4			
5		_Total_	_$11.60_
6			
7			
8			
9			
10			

Style 1200   **495-1**

Chart 9   A Typical Sales Receipt

CASE STUDY: TURNING YOUR SPECIAL RECIPES INTO CASH

Business for the Young Entrepreneur

What do Paul Newman, Debbi Fields, and a group of high school students from Los Angeles have in common? They've all turned their favorite recipes into profitable businesses. Newman's Own popcorn, pasta sauces, and salad dressings raise funds for his favorite charities. Debbi Fields has turned her teenage chocolate-chip cookie recipe into Mrs. Fields Cookies, a multimillion-dollar international enterprise. And thirty students from Crenshaw High School have formed a company called Food From The 'Hood that markets one of the hottest selling items in southern California—Straight Out The Garden salad dressing. They were mentored by their teacher, Tammy Bird, who was recently trained as a NFTE teacher, and a publicist named Melinda McMullen, who actually took a leave of absence from her job to help get Food From the 'Hood off the ground.

The students had already been selling produce from their school garden when they decided to concoct a dressing. They wanted the dressing to be low in fat and salt because diseases linked to high sodium diets, such as high-blood pressure, are prevalent in their urban community.

Next, the students met with Rebuild L.A., a nonprofit organization formed to help L.A. businesses recover from the 1994 riots. Rebuild L.A. introduced them to the owners of a minority investment firm, who helped the students write a business plan. The plan landed the budding entrepreneurs a partnership with Sweet Adelaide Enterprises, a large salad dressing packer.

In 1994, the students were awarded a grant from Rebuild L.A. to help them to get their product into local grocery stores. Today, Straight Out The Garden is sold by over 2,000 grocery stores in southern California. All profits go toward college scholarships for the student owners. The college fund expects to award over $200,000 in scholarships in 1995.

Tips

- To place your product in grocery chain stores requires some clout. Crenshaw students consulted Bromar, a professional food broker, for advice on how to get their product accepted by grocery chains.
- Believe in your product. The other thing Newman, Fields, and the Crenshaw students have in common is a tremendous belief in the quality of their products.

RESOURCES

Books

Some of the best books published about selling are:

The Joy Of Selling by J. T. Auer (Holbrook, MA: Adams, Inc., 1991).

Swim with the Sharks Without Being Eaten Alive by Harvey Mackay (New York: William Morrow & Co., 1988).

How To Sell Yourself by Joe Girard (New York: Warner Books, 1988).

Face-to-Face Selling by Bart Breighner (Indianapolis, IN: Jist Works, Inc., 1995).

If you think a career in sales might interest you, or just want to read the latest theories on selling, check out *Sales and Marketing Magazine* at your library or call (800) 253-6708 to subscribe.

Associations

The Direct Selling Association has a wealth of information on the craft of direct selling and on how to contact direct sales firms.

Direct Selling Association
1666 K Street, NW, Suite 1010
Washington, DC 20006-2808
(202) 293-5760
Fax (202) 463-4569

12 MARKETING INSIGHTS AND EFFECTIVE ADVERTISING

In my factory we make cosmetics, but in my stores we sell hope.
—Charles Revson (1906–1975)
American founder of Revlon Cosmetics, Inc.

When you go on a sales call, you are bringing the product to the customer. **Marketing** is the art of getting the customer to come to the product. It is the plan an entrepreneur develops for introducing a product or service to the market. Revlon Cosmetics, Inc. sells cosmetics. It distributes cosmetics to stores where customers can buy them. But Revlon also markets cosmetics. It convinces customers that cosmetics offer a benefit—that the customers will look more beautiful after using them. Customers, therefore, seek out Revlon cosmetics.

To market a product successfully, ask yourself: What does the customer need this product to do? The answer to that question identifies a benefit. Show your customer that your product produces that benefit.

Why does a customer go to a hardware store to buy a drill? Because he or she needs to make a hole. The *hole* is what the customer needs, not the drill. If the hole could be bought at the hardware store, the customer wouldn't bother to buy the drill. If you are marketing a drill, therefore, you should explain to the customer what good holes your drills make![1]

TURNING A MARKETING INSIGHT
INTO A FORTUNE: MCDONALD'S

Many great fortunes have been based on a single marketing insight. Ray Kroc, the president of McDonald's, did not invent or even improve the hamburger. He invented a new way of *marketing* hamburgers. He realized that customers cared more about fast service, consistent product, and a low price than they did about the ultimate hamburger. These were the benefits that brought them to the product. By marketing those benefits, Kroc made McDonald's the huge success it is today.

The original McDonald's restaurant was a small hamburger stand in San Bernardino, California. Two brothers, Maurice and Richard McDonald, run the stand. Kroc was a fifty-two-year-old salesman of Multimixers, the mixers the McDonald brothers used to make their shakes. When Kroc received an order for eight Multimixers—enough to make forty milkshakes at once—from this hamburger stand on the edge of the desert, he flew out to see the business for himself.

With sales of over $350,000 a year, McDonald's was one of the most successful little restaurants in America. Customers loved the simple, cheap food and the fast service. The McDonald brothers knew they had a hot business that they could expand around the country, but there was just one problem—both brothers hated to fly. When Kroc flew in and offered to form a partnership with them and take care of franchising their business, they signed on the dotted line.

In 1961, Kroc bought out the brothers for $2.7 million, but he followed rigidly their original recipes for their hamburgers, fries, and shakes. Kroc wanted every McDonald's customer, from Anchorage to Miami, to get an identical product. According to Bill Bryson's fascinating book *Made in America,* Kroc "dictated that McDonald's burgers must be exactly 3.875 inches across, weigh 1.6 ounces, and contain precisely 19 percent fat. Big Mac buns should have an average of 178 sesame seeds."

RUSSELL SIMMONS: MARKETING
AFRICAN AMERICAN CULTURE TO EVERYONE

The goal of marketing is to successfully introduce a product or service to a new market or to enlarge the original market. Kroc introduced fast-food restaurants to consumers around the globe. Russell Simmons turned them on to rap. Simmons was one of the first rap promoters to realize rap culture could be marketed to white consumers, not just to black audiences. From this marketing insight, Simmons has built his $50 million entertainment empire, Rush Communications.

Simmons began his career promoting rap concerts at the City University of New York. At the time, rap was considered a passing fad, but Simmons believed rap could become extremely popular. In 1983, he befriended Rick Rubin, another rap-obsessed student promoter—who was white. Simmons and Rubin formed Def Jam Records with $5,000. They produced hits with Run DMC and LL Cool J.

In a 1992 interview in *Worth* magazine, Simmons said that he's never made "records, music, or television for black people, but for people who consume black culture." Simmons used this marketing concept to push hip-hop culture so far into the mainstream that his artists sold millions of records.

DEF COMEDY JAM

In 1990, Simmons turned his attention to television. On his nightly trips out to see new musical talent, he had noticed that many discos and rap clubs had comedy nights that were always sold out. He wanted to put those comedians on television.

Simmons produced *Russell Simmons' Def Comedy Jam,* a series of eight half-hour comedy specials, for HBO. The show was HBO's most popular late-night comedy show ever, attracting 1.7 million viewers.

Simmons continues to find new talent and think up new ways to promote urban culture. He has started a management company to secure endorsements for professional athletes, as well as a modeling agency and a line of clothing called Phat Fashion.

MARKETING GIVES YOUR BUSINESS DIRECTION

Both Kroc and Simmons have built their entire careers on marketing. Kroc decided that consumers cared more about fast service and a low price than the ultimate hamburger. Every decision he made about McDonald's was a direct result of that marketing direction. McDonald's will never branch into gourmet food, for example.

Simmons's marketing decision was to sell black urban culture to the entire world. Every decision he has made about Rush Communications has stemmed from that vision.

All your decisions about your business should reinforce your marketing decision, too. To reach your marketing decision, decide what is the most important benefit the customers in your market will receive from your product or service. All your advertisements and other promotions should tell your customers about this benefit. Next, choose the four essential elements of your marketing plan. These are called "The Four Ps."

THE FOUR "Ps" OF MARKETING

1. **Product**—the product (or service) should meet or create a consumer need.
2. **Price**—the product (or service) has to be priced low enough for the public to buy it and high enough for the business to make a profit.
3. **Place**—the product (or service) should be sold where there will be a demand for it and where customers can easily find it. Don't try to sell bathing suits in Alaska in February! Location is extremely important. Ideally, you'll want your store or business to be in a place where *your* market is.
4. **Promotion**—advertising and publicity.

PREPARING A MARKETING PLAN

Once you've chosen the Four Ps of your business, you will be ready to complete a marketing plan for your business. Fill out the marketing plan shown in Chart 10. Use Y for Yes and N for No.

PROMOTION = PUBLICITY + ADVERTISING

Your marketing plan indicates how you plan to promote your business. Entrepreneurs use **promotion** to attract customers and increase sales. Promotion is the use of **publicity** and **advertising.** Publicity is free; advertising is purchased. If your business is providing an unusual service, for instance, you might be able to get a local newspaper to do an article on your business. That article would be publicity for your business—you didn't pay for it. If you buy an ad in that newspaper, you're

MARKETING PLAN LOCATIONS (WHERE TO SELL)

S E L L I N G M E T H O D S	Door to Door	Flea Markets	School/ Church Functions	Street (Street Vendors)	Through Local Stores	Your Own Home	Other
Business Cards							
Posters							
Flyers							
Phone							
Sales Calls							
Brochure							
Mailings							
Other							

Chart 10   Sample Marketing Plan

using advertising to promote your business. Publicity is sometimes referred to as public relations or "PR."

Valuable promotions include:

- **Business cards.** Your business card bears the name, address, and phone number of your business, as well as your name and title. Carry some cards with you wherever you go.

- **Discount coupons.** Give a discount, or price break, to first-time customers or to all customers for a limited time. This will encourage potential customers to try your product or service.

- **Flyers.** Flyers are one-page ads you can create by hand or on a typewriter or computer. Photoprint your flyer and distribute it at school, at church functions, at sporting events, or on the street. Chart 11 shows a simple but explicit flyer.

- **Promotional items.** T-shirts or caps bearing the name of your business can turn you and your friends into walking advertisements for your business. You can even put the name of your business on your shopping bags.

Chart 11   Advertising via a Flyer

VISUALIZE THE CUSTOMERS

There is one more step to take before you begin following your marketing plan: visualize your customers. How old are they? What kind of income do they earn? What benefit of your product or service would attract your ideal customer? Make that benefit the center of your promotion plans.

If you are advertising a rap concert, for example, it would be a waste of money to take out an ad in a magazine for senior citizens. By visualizing your customer, you avoid wasting money on advertising to customers who aren't interested in your product or service.

Turning a Knack for Marketing into a Successful Business

If you have a knack for marketing, that in itself can be your business. When Doug Mellinger was in college, he knew some computer programmers and engineers whose ability to sell themselves was not nearly as developed as their technical skills were. He decided to start a business that would market them to businesses that needed their services.

Doug's PRT Corp. of America acts as a go-between for corporations that need to hire people who are skilled in advanced computer technology for various projects. PRT secures the job, puts the technical team together, and makes sure everything runs smoothly between the client and the technicians.

Since its inception in 1989, PRT has successfully completed projects in artificial intelligence, data security, imaging, and other high-tech areas for over forty Fortune 200 companies in the United States, Japan, and Europe. Today Doug is widely acknowledged as one of the most successful young entrepreneurs in America.

One of the reasons Doug is so successful with PRT is that he had already run a number of small businesses while in college. He visited a NFTE class in the South Bronx and gave a very inspirational talk about how his experiences as a young entrepreneur had prepared him to handle PRT's incredible growth (the company grew from 1 to 100 employees in four years and saw revenue increases of over 100 percent during each of those years). Today, he is one of NFTE's strongest supporters. He serves on a number of advisory boards to government agencies, and public and private universities that are committed to improving educational and career opportunities for economically disadvantaged youth.

EFFECTIVE ADVERTISING

An effective ad for a small business typically concentrates on the aspect of the product or service that is most important to the customer. That aspect is usually one of these three:

1. Price.
2. Product/Service.
3. Location.

THE MEDIA

There are many places to advertise your business. These are referred to collectively as the **media.** The main types of media are print, television, and radio.

- **Print.** Newspapers, magazines, and newsletters are examples of print media. A good spot for a print ad is the Yellow Pages. Consider running a coupon in your neighborhood or school newspaper.
- **Television.** Even though commercial TV rates are very expensive, a young entrepreneur can sometimes get low rates or even a free mention (publicity) of his or her business on local cable stations.
- **Radio.** University and local stations are usually willing to mention a young person's business venture.

To generate publicity, consider mailing to the local media a **press release**—a few paragraphs that give information about your business. Chart 12 gives you a model to imitate.

A PRINT AD'S FIVE PARTS

A print ad in a newspaper or magazine has five basic parts:

1. Headline (title).
2. Deck (subhead).
3. Copy (text).
4. Graphics (photos or drawings).
5. Logo (symbol or distinctive design feature).

You can find all five parts in the ad pictured in Chart 13.

LOGOS AND TRADEMARKS

A **logo** (short for logotype) is an identifying symbol for a product or business. The logo is printed on the business's stationery, business cards, and flyers. Some logos appear on the products as well. When a

For Immediate Release   **For More Information Contact:**
May 24, 1995   **John Davies—(718) 555-7839**

SOUTH BRONX HIGH SCHOOL
STUDENT OPENS TIE-SELLING BUSINESS

Sixteen-year-old John Davies of 34 Fordham Road, in the
South Bronx, announced today the creation of "John's Tie
Service." A junior at Longfellow High School, John
purchases his ties from the wholesale market and orders
them through catalogs. He will be selling ties on weekends
at the Mott Haven Flea Market.

John is starting his own enterprise as a way to learn about
business and supplement his income. His short-term goal is
to raise enough capital to help pay for his college
education. John's long-term plan is to own a string of soul-
food restaurants in urban communities.

John believes that creating a successful business is a great
way to help not only himself but his community.

For interviews with this young entrepreneur, please call
(718) 555-7839.

Chart 12   Format for a Press Release to the Media

There Is No Substitute For Tacoma Cowboy Boots

But This Is Close.

Sierra Cowboy boots are not Tacoma Cowboy boots. But they *are* close.

They are designed by Tacoma and crafted to Tacoma's exclusive specifications. They are backed by Tacoma. Continually refined and enhanced by Tacoma's extensive research and development program.

Naturally, we believe that there is no substitute for a pair of Tacoma boots—even if it is *our* substitute.

So we designed Sierras to have their own unique look and feel. To be handcrafted to their own high standards of quality and workmanship. To share the Tacoma tradition of excellence, while being affordable to as many different budgets as possible. Including yours.

In the Tacoma tradition

Chart 13   A Classic Five-Part Print Ad

logo has been registered with the United States Patent Office to protect it from being used by others, it is called a **trademark.**

A company uses a trademark so that people will recognize its product instantly, without having to read the company name or even having to think about it. The Nutrasweet™ red swirl is an example of a trademark most people recognize. Rights to a trademark are reserved exclusively for its owner. To infringe on a trademark is illegal.

To file for a trademark, request an application from the **Patent and Trademark Office.** Call **(703) 557-4636.** After you receive the application, gather these items into one packet:

1. The completed application form.
2. A drawing of the trademark.
3. Three specimens showing the actual use of the mark on or in connection with the products or services.
4. A filing fee ($200).

Send your application packet to:

Patent & Trademark Office
U.S. Department of Commerce
Washington, DC 20231

LOGOS HELP CUSTOMERS MAKE QUICK DECISIONS

Customers don't have a lot of time to study different companies before deciding where to spend their money. If you consistently offer a quality product or service and create a logo that represents your company attractively, you are on your way to success. Over time, your logo will become associated with your product or service. It's up to you to make sure that your customers think of quality when they see your logo. This association gives you an advantage over your competition.

McDonald's golden arches are a famous trademark. When people see the golden arches, they expect fast service, inexpensive prices, and a specific type of food. The logo gives McDonald's restaurants a competitive advantage over less recognizable restaurants. Customers head for the golden arches because they know what to expect.

CASE STUDY: PUBLIC RELATIONS FIRM

Business for the Young Entrepreneur

Keeya Branson is a student of mine who started her own public relations company, Wide Awake Publicity, when she was twenty-three. She had graduated from DePaul University with a degree in philosophy and had spent a year looking for a job. Between job interviews, she served as an intern at an advertising agency. Keeya also wrote press releases for the Young Entrepreneurs Program (YEP) run by the University Community Outreach Program (UCOP) at the University of Pennsylvania's Wharton School of Business, and she helped some other community organizations with their publicity. Keeya had gone through YEP's program herself as a senior in high school.

Suddenly, Keeya says, "It clicked." She realized, "Why am I spending this energy looking for a job? I have a job." YEP became Wide Awake Publicity's first client. Today, Keeya is generating publicity for several other nonprofit groups and various individuals.

Wide Awake Publicity's most important tool is the media kit, Keeya says. The media kit is a folder that holds a black-and-white photograph that represents the client, a press release, a biography of the business or individual, and copies of any press coverage the client has already received. Keeya sends the media kit to newspapers and to radio and television stations she thinks might be interested in spotlighting the client's business. She always follows up with several phone calls. The most important aspect of her business, in fact, is her relationship with "the press."

Keeya says entrepreneurship is a viable alternative to the unemployment so many recent college grads face. "You can't always live and die in a company anymore. The only person you can count on is yourself," Keeya says. She adds, "Entrepreneurship is not an impossibility; in fact, it's a definite possibility."

Tips

- Consider serving an internship in the field of your choice. Although interns are not usually paid (some receive stipends), the experience and networking opportunities are invaluable. Many companies hire from their pool of interns before looking to outside applicants to fill a position.

- Most small publicity firms specialize in certain types of clients. Some may represent only rock bands, for example. Others, like

Wide Awake, focus on meeting the needs of nonprofit organizations. Specialization will make it easier for your firm to build strong media ties.

RESOURCES

Books

Since a small business is by definition a "do-it-yourself" project, learn how from *Do-It-Yourself Advertising: How To Produce Great Ads, Brochures, Catalogs, Direct Mail, and Much More* by Fred Hahn (John Wiley & Sons, Inc., 1993).

Bill Bryson's often hilarious book, *Made in America: An Informal History of the English Language in the United States* (New York: William Morrow, and Co., 1995) tells the stories of many American entrepreneurs as it explores American linguistics.

Another valuable source is *The Handbook of Small Business Advertising* by Michael Anthony (Addison-Wesley Publishing Co., 1981).

Other Resources

The bible of Madison Avenue is *Advertising Age* magazine. It's available on newsstands and in libraries. For a subscription, contact:

> *Advertising Age*
> Crain Communications
> 740 N. Rush Street
> Chicago, IL 60611
> (800) 678-9595

MARKET RESEARCH

13

GETTING TO KNOW YOUR CUSTOMERS

If you give the consumer a snapshot where he could see himself as he really is and the way he wants to be portrayed, people really respond to it. That emotionalism translates into behavior in the marketplace.

—Thomas Burrell (b. 1939)
Founder of the largest African American-owned advertising agency, Burrell Communications Group

MARKET RESEARCH HELPS YOU GET TO KNOW YOUR CUSTOMERS

We've talked about the importance of knowing your customers and marketing your product or service to them. But we haven't talked about *how* to get to know your customers.

Market research is the process and technique of finding out *who* your potential customers are and what they want.

Through market research, business owners ask consumers questions and listen to their answers.

TYPES OF MARKET RESEARCH

A large corporation might hire an advertising agency to conduct market research for it, or the corporation may have its own marketing division.

You can—and should—conduct some market research for your business. Market research can vary from a simple survey of friends and neighbors, which can be completed in one day, to detailed statistical studies of a large population over a long period of time.

The three main types of market research are:

1. **Surveys.** People are asked directly, in interviews or through questionnaires, what they would think about a product or service if it were available. At NFTE, for example, we often form focus groups with young people or with teachers. A focus group is comprised of people who do use or might use a product. The focus group is typically led by a facilitator trained in market research, who questions the group about a product or service. We've used feedback from our focus groups to help us make many decisions—from what color the BizBag™ should be to how to improve our textbooks.

2. **General research.** Businesspeople check libraries, city agencies, or other resources for information. If you want to start a sporting goods shop in a neighborhood, for instance, you will need to know how many sporting goods shops are already in that area.

3. **Statistical research. Statistics** are facts collected and presented in a numerical fashion—in percentages, for instance. Market research companies keep records of the typical consumers in a given area. They can then provide statistics based on age, occupation, geographic location, income, and ethnic or religious background. Market researchers also delve into consumers' hobbies and interests and find out whether they own or rent their homes. Consumer statistics that deal with the behavior of groups of people are called **demographics.**

Large corporations with nationally distributed products will spend a great deal of time and money on market research in order to get a product "just right."

Ford and Chrysler each spent millions on market research *before* producing, respectively, the Mustang and the minivan. It was worth millions of dollars to these companies to determine whether the public wanted these vehicles, because producing them was going to cost *tens* of millions.

Both the Mustang and the minivan were successful. One of the best-known examples of market research failure, however, was Ford's 1956 Edsel. The car was introduced with great fanfare, but was so poorly made and clumsily designed that very few were purchased. When the Edsel made its national debut on a live television special, in fact, it wouldn't start. Two years and $450 million later, Ford pulled the plug on the Edsel assembly line.

MARKETING TO AFRICAN AMERICANS

To market a product or service to a particular group of people, you have to know exactly what those people want. In the late 1960s, major corporations became more conscious of the potential clout of black consumers but were unsure how to reach them.

In 1971, Thomas Burrell opened one of the first black-owned advertising agencies in the United States. By 1972, Burrell had convinced McDonald's that Burrell Advertising Inc. could help the huge company expand its inroads into the African American market. Today, Burrell Advertising is the fastest growing and largest black-owned advertising agency in the United States, with annual billings over $60 million.

Burrell Advertising has created over one hundred commercials for McDonald's. The list of Burrell's corporate clients includes Coca-Cola, Ford Motor Company, Johnson Products, Joseph Schlitz Brewing, Blockbuster Entertainment, Procter & Gamble, Jack Daniel Distillery, Polaroid, Stroh Brewing, and First National Bank of Chicago.

Burrell Advertising specializes in advertising for special market segments, such as African American consumers. The company is always first or second on the short list of companies seeking to target the African American market. Burrell himself could probably quote the demographics of the African American market off the top of his head. By combining his company's detailed market research with his own experiences as a black man, he has created powerful appeals to that market.

Burrell describes his marketing philosophy as "positive realism." He adds, "We wanted to make sure the consumer understood the advertiser was inviting that consumer—that black consumer—to participate as a consumer of their product. Black consumers have not felt they were being extended an invitation."

RESEARCHING MARKET SEGMENTS

Burrell also caters to nonminority consumers. Within this large category are groups that require "target advertising"—that is, advertising tailor-made to their particular needs, values, and lifestyles. Among these groups are the youth market, the "mature" (or older) market, and the urban market.

In 1988, Burrell founded two related companies: Burrell Public Relations Inc. and Burrell Consumer Promotions Inc. Together with Burrell Advertising, the three companies provide clients with a total marketing package. The three companies' revenues total over $70 million annually, ensuring Burrell's reputation as a world-class player in the field of marketing communications.

The public relations company helps clients communicate more effectively with their target markets. In 1989, for example, Burrell Public Relations created a Hispanic Marketing Division in order to respond more effectively to the needs of Hispanic consumers.

Burrell's second entrepreneurial extension was Burrell Consumer Promotions Inc. This arm designs promotional packs, in-store sampling, direct mail, sweepstakes and contests, and other promotions for clients.

BURRELL THE ENTREPRENEUR: BREAKING THROUGH THE RACE BARRIER

Burrell still considers himself, first and foremost, an entrepreneur. A fit and imposing man at 6′4″, Burrell speaks candidly of the two influences that originally triggered his entrepreneurial energy. One was his mother, who, from the time he was a child, encouraged him to be self-reliant. The other was the fact that he is African American. It is not surprising that a powerful five-foot-tall statue of Martin Luther King, Jr. stands in the waiting room of his office.

Burrell himself best describes why being African American encouraged him to try entrepreneurship: "I felt that no matter how successful I might have been at that time [the late 1960s], there was a ceiling that would certainly prevent me from going all the way in someone else's company. And even if I could go all the way it would still not be my company. I felt I had something special to say. I had a special approach to running an advertising business that I could do best in my own establishment. And, I figured I had nothing to lose."

Despite the original orientation of his firm toward the African American market, Burrell feels his agency has proven by now that it can handle advertising to any market. "It's an unfortunate thing," he says, "that being a black-owned company means, for some people, that you should be limited to addressing blacks only. I've got to believe that who owns an ad agency will at some point become irrelevant. What will matter will be the kind of advertising the agency does, how capable the agency is."

Smiling, he adds, "I've been a black person all my life and I will be for the rest of my life. The only thing I know how to do is stay positive. You stay positive and something good will happen."

COLLECTING DATA

No matter what market a Burrell Advertising campaign is targeting, market research is the first step. Market research identifies the Four Ps discussed in the previous chapter: (1) Product, (2) Price, (3) Place, and (4) Promotion.

You can collect market research data by interviewing your friends, neighbors, and relatives. Here are a few questions you can adapt to your own product or service:

1. Would you buy this product/service?
2. How much would you be willing to pay for it?
3. Where would you buy it?
4. How would you improve on it?

Say you created a design and silkscreened it on five dozen plain white T-shirts. After six weeks, you have only sold six. Friends tell you they would have bought your product if:

- The shirt came in red or blue.
- The shirt was available in a different size.
- The shirt came in a different style.
- The shirt was silkscreened with a different design.

With a little market research, you could have determined your customers' needs and wishes *before* you made the shirts. You would have sold many more.

COMPETITION

Your market research should include collecting data about your competition. Have you found out who else offers your product/service in your area? List the names of these competitors and the prices they charge. Compare your quality to theirs.

Name of Competitor	Product/Service	Price	Quality
1. _____	_____	_____	_____
2. _____	_____	_____	_____
3. _____	_____	_____	_____
4. _____	_____	_____	_____

Why is your product/service going to beat the competition?

STUDIO TWIST: MARKETING TO THE MIDDLE

When Dan Hoyt decided to renovate the recording studio he had built from scratch in the basement of his Manhattan storefront, he knew he wanted to turn it to a world-class facility. His original Studio Twist had catered to the hundreds of unsigned bands on the Lower East Side. Although the studio was adequate for recording demo tapes for these bands, Hoyt knew that in order to have the record-producing career he wanted, he needed a high-quality studio.

Hoyt and his partners (Richard Mishell, who was financing the renovation, and Mark Humphrey, who handled promotion for the studio) were worried, however. If they built a studio that was less than perfect, signed recording artists would bypass it for the slick multi-million-dollar studios uptown. If it was too expensive, however, Studio Twist would lose its base of up-and-coming bands. The partners' solution was to conduct lots of market research.

"For about four months, we asked every client we had ever recorded to come in and tell us what they would like to see in the new studio," Hoyt explains. "Then we called every engineer and producer we knew and asked them to come tell us what kind of facility and what kind of equipment would attract them," he continues. "Eventually," Hoyt says, "we uncovered our market niche. We realized that there were many recording artists whose labels were not giving them big enough budgets to afford the uptown studios, but who still needed to sound great. That was our market—the artists in the middle."

A WIN–WIN AGREEMENT PROVIDES HIGH-TECH RESULTS

To make sure he could deliver the desired level of quality, Hoyt made an agreement with Robert Van Der Hilst, a studio designer who had designed some of the best studios in the world. Normally, Van Der Hilst would have been far too expensive for Studio Twist, but Hoyt knew Van Der Hilst was looking for a facility to test new mixing speakers he had co-invented. Van Der Hilst also wanted to test his acoustical design ideas. Hoyt offered Van Der Hilst free rein to design Studio Twist to his specifications. In return, Van Der Hilst would be building his own acoustical lab. Van Der Hilst agreed to lower his fee.

THE PRICING DECISION

When the studio was almost finished, the partners repeated the market research process. This time, though, they showed the studio to potential clients, engineers, and producers, and asked them what they would pay to work there. "Pricing was very important," Hoyt says. "We needed to be expensive enough to cover our overhead, but cheap enough to avoid losing clients to the high-end studios."

The owners finally settled on an hourly rate of $50. To avoid alienating demo-tape clients accustomed to the previous $35-an-hour rate, Studio Twist offered a three-song special that included recording tape; ten cassettes, complete with color covers and labels; and twelve hours of recording time—all for $600.

PROMOTION

To promote the new studio, Humphrey designed a brochure illustrated with photos, including a detailed equipment and rate list, and a coupon for the three-song special. He mailed it to every client, engineer, producer, and record label in Studio Twist's rolodex. The slogan on the front of the brochure perfectly captured the essence of Studio Twist's marketing plan: "The Only High-End Studio In The East Village *And* The Best Rates In New York."

Conducting market research as Studio Twist was being constructed helped the owners make intelligent decisions every step of the way. Whenever you are unsure how to handle the next step in the growth of your business, market research will tell you what to do.

CASE STUDY: SELLING COMPUTERS FROM HOME

Business for the Young Entrepreneur

One advantage many young entrepreneurs have is low overhead. Rob, for example, started his business, RFS Computer, in a room in his parents' Long Island home when he was only fourteen. Rob does pay his parents some rent, but overall his operating costs are much lower than they would be if he were renting an office.

At eighteen, Rob combines his low overhead with his four years of experience buying and selling computer software and hardware, and secures great deals for his customers.

"I sell almost anything people want," Rob says, "Go get a price somewhere else; I can beat that price 80 percent of the time. The only places I can't beat are the huge mail-order firms."

Rob advertises his company online via computer bulletin boards. He also runs print ads in church circulars and local newsletters. Some ads include discount coupons. Rob also keeps track of accounts receivable for his dad's floor-covering company.

Tips

- Consider starting a business in your home or a relative's home. If the business takes off, you can always move to an office. Starting a business with very low overhead is a good way to protect it from insolvency during the lean times any new business will face.

- Like Rob, don't limit yourself to one service if your equipment can handle more than one. If you silkscreen T-shirts, for example, you have the equipment to silkscreen posters, invitations, shorts, and so on. Concentrate on your main business, but don't overlook other money-making opportunities.

RESOURCES

Book

For the full story of Ford's Edsel fiasco, see *Made in America: An Informed History of the English Language in the United States* by Bill Bryson (New York: William Morrow and Co., 1995). This book offers a wealth of fascinating anecdotes about American businesses.

Other Resources

If you need help analyzing your market, or want to expand your business into a market with which you are not familiar, a demographic consultant can be useful. Demographic information is usually not cheap, so check prices carefully before you order any. American Demographics, Inc. is one of several market research organizations that sells demographic information. Contact:

American Demographics, Inc.
P.O. Box 68
Ithaca, NY 14851
(800) 828-1133

Another resource is Business Demographics, an on-line service that offers market reports tailored to geographical regions.
Business Demographics can be contacted at *CompuServe::go BUSDEM*.

If you're thinking about a career in marketing and would like some brochures or other instructive materials, contact:

The American Marketing Association
25 S. Wacker Drive, Suite 200
Chicago, IL 60606
(312) 648-0536

14 PRACTICAL GENIUS

DEVELOPING AND PROTECTING INVENTIONS

Don't ask whether something can be done; find a way to do it.
—An Wang (b. 1920)
Chinese-American inventor
and founder of Wang Laboratories

AN WANG: PRACTICAL DAYDREAMING

Conducting market research might inspire you to try to imagine new products or services for your market. Everyone daydreams, but entrepreneurs daydream with a market in mind. Some entrepreneurial daydreams have become inventions that have changed the world.

Computer scientist and entrepreneur An Wang, who founded Wang Laboratories, has patented forty inventions in his lifetime. He described his best ideas as "presented to me by my subconscious almost as a gift."

Wang came to the United States from China in 1945, when he was twenty-five. While working at the Harvard Computation Laboratory, An Wang invented the magnetic memory core. This invention, which Wang patented, made computer memory possible. At twenty-eight, Wang gave up his job and started Wang Laboratories with a few hundred dollars, in a small loft above a garage.

Sometimes, Wang and his wife encountered discrimination because he was Chinese. Wang said this made him more determined to succeed: "A small part of the reason I founded Wang Laboratories," he said, "was to show that Chinese could excel at things other than running laundries and restaurants."

Eventually, IBM purchased the rights to the magnetic memory core Wang had invented. Wang used the money from the sale to start marketing some of the new devices he had invented, including desk-top calculators. The calculators led to Wang Laboratories' growth in sales to $39 million by 1972. By 1984, Wang was the fifth richest American, with a net worth of $1.6 billion.

DEVELOP YOUR OWN PRACTICAL DAYDREAMING

Many successful small businesses have started with practical daydreams that an entrepreneur carefully protected and developed. My friend Sylvia Stein has invented several products, including The Nose™, an eyeglass holder. When I asked her how she jump-starts her imagination, she said she tries to complete this sentence:[1]

I wish someone would make a _____ that _____.

Another way to start thinking like an inventor is to imagine solutions to problems in your neighborhood or community or in the world. Write or sketch your solutions, pretending that anything is possible.

TURNING AN IDEA INTO A REAL PRODUCT

Once you've come up with an idea for a product, make a model of it. This model can be rough. Use cheap materials such as paper, wood, paint, cloth, or plaster of Paris. You may go through many models.

Conduct some market research by showing the model to friends, acquaintances, and storekeepers. Collect ideas and suggestions, and use any suggestions that will improve your design. Don't be afraid to experiment.

Once you've perfected your model, the next step is to have a **prototype** made. A prototype is an exact model of the product, made by the manufacturing process that would be used in actual production of your invention. This can be an expensive step: prototypes cost many times the final production cost per item. If you are serious about turning your invention into a business, however, you will need a prototype to show investors or buyers.

To find a manufacturer for your prototype, check your library for the *Thomas Register of American Manufacturers*. This reference lists all U.S. manufacturers.

USING THE *THOMAS REGISTER OF AMERICAN MANUFACTURERS*

The *Thomas Register* is published every year and contains twenty-six volumes. It is an excellent source for names of manufacturers you can contact about having a prototype of your invention made. You should be able to find the *Thomas Register* in the reference room at a public library. If you can't find it, don't hesitate to ask the reference librarian. It's a good idea, in fact, for budding entrepreneurs to be nice to their local reference librarians! I've relied on them greatly for help on many occasions.

The twenty-six volumes are divided into three groups:

- Group One—Volumes 1–16 are a list of categories of products and services arranged alphabetically. Within each product or service category, you can look up companies alphabetically by state and city. Use Group One to locate manufacturers in your area that make products similar to your invention.

- Group Two—Volumes 17 and 18 give profiles of different companies, listed alphabetically by company name. After you find a manufacturer (in Group One) that looks interesting, look up its profile in Group Two. The profile will include the manufacturer's address, telephone numbers, and office locations, and the names of company officials.

- Group Three—Volumes 19–26 offer catalogs arranged alphabetically by company name. These catalogs include product information such as drawings, photos, and statistics.

REALITY CHECK

- Does your invention solve a big enough problem—that is, a problem faced by many people?
- Can you locate these people easily?

- Is the manufacturing cost too high?
- Is there competition? Is someone else selling a similar product? How is yours better? Different?
- Try **test marketing.** Put a display, along with the product, in a store and see how it sells.

PATENTS

Once you have developed a good invention, you can either go into business for yourself or sell the idea to a manufacturer. Before taking either step, however, you must protect your rights as inventor by patenting the invention.

A **patent** grants to the inventor the exclusive privilege of making, using, selling, and authorizing others to make, use, and sell his or her invention. A patent can be obtained for any original and useful device or process and is valid for seventeen years. After that time, anyone may sell the invention, without paying the inventor.

Thomas Jefferson wrote: "The issue of patents for new discoveries has given a spring to invention beyond my conception." Later, Abraham Lincoln said, "The Patent System added the fuel of interest to the fire of genius." The first patent and copyright law was passed in 1790. The United States Patent Office was established in 1836.

WHEN FILING A PATENT IS NECESSARY

A patent cannot be obtained on a mere idea or suggestion. Your invention must be fully developed and working consistently before you can seek patent protection. You will have to prepare detailed drawings showing exactly how it works.

You don't need to obtain a patent unless you:

- Invent a product that you intend to market yourself or sell to a manufacturer *and*
- Believe that someone else could successfully sell the product by copying your invention.

On average, a patent takes about two years to obtain. A patent search has to be undertaken to make certain that the idea is not **infringing** on, or violating, someone else's patent. Obtaining a patent is a complex legal process. Before starting it, see a registered patent attorney.

A patent application must include the following:

1. An in-depth description of the invention.
2. A drawing of the invention.
3. A completed "Declaration for Patent Application."
4. A notarized statement from the inventor to the effect that he or she is the original inventor of the subject of the application.
5. The filing fee ($370).

The completed packet of the above five items should be sent to:

Patent & Trademark Office
U.S. Department of Commerce
Washington, DC 20231
(703) 557-4636

A PATENT CAN BUILD A FORTUNE: FRED C. KOCH

When Fred C. Koch patented a process in the 1920s for making gasoline out of heavy crude oil, it transformed the oil industry and made Koch a very wealthy man—but not without a fight.

The major oil companies, which used competing technologies, immediately sued Koch for patent infringement. Some 40 suits were filed and Koch eventually won them all.

During his legal battle, though, Koch took his process to the Soviet Union, where he helped upgrade 15 oil refineries. This provided him with the capital he used in 1940 to build his first refinery, once he could finally use his technology, in the United States. Under the leadership of Fred's son, Charles Koch who has pioneered many management techniques, Koch Industries has grown from a company with annual revenues of $177 million in 1966 to almost $24 billion in 1994.

PUBLIC DOMAIN

Failure to obtain a patent can prevent an inventor from profiting from his or her invention. If an invention is put into use by the inventor for more than one year without obtaining a patent, the invention is considered **public domain** and a patent will no longer be granted.

An unfortunate example of public domain is the case of Louis Temple, an African American of New Bedford, Massachusetts, who invented the toggle harpoon in the early 1800s. This invention greatly increased the efficiency of whaling at a time when whale oil was extremely valuable for lighting lamps and making candles.

To test the harpoon, Temple gave prototypes to several New Bedford ship captains. In those days, whaling voyages took about two years. By the time the ships returned and reported the harpoon's great success, Temple's invention had become public domain. Temple was never able to profit from his invention and died in poverty.

> **Don't go to the trouble and expense of applying for a patent unless your invention is unique and you intend to sell it.**

Rule of Thumb

COPYRIGHTS

Literary, artistic, and musical works also need protection from copycats, but they cannot be patented. A **copyright** is the form of legal protection offered to literary, musical, and artistic works. The owner of a copyright has the sole right to print, reprint, sell and distribute, revise, record, and perform the work under copyright. The copyright protects a work for the life of the author/artist plus fifty years thereafter.

To file for a copyright, request forms from the Copyright Office. The forms are easy to fill out. To secure a copyright, send a completed form and two examples of the work, with a registration fee of $20, to:

Copyright Office
Information and Publications Section, LM-455
Library of Congress
Washington, DC 20231

These are the phone numbers you'll need:

Public information: (202) 707-3000
To order forms: (202) 707-9100

AFRICAN AMERICANS BEGIN PATENTING THEIR INVENTIONS

Like Temple, many African American inventors made important contributions to American business, yet failed to profit from them. Nobody knows how many inventions were thought up by slaves before the Civil War, for example, because credit for them was taken by their masters. There were probably quite a few, because ideas for making a job easier or faster often come to those who have to do the actual work.

In 1895, an African American Congressman, George Washington Murray, read into the Congressional Record a list of ninety-two patents that had been issued to Americans of color. Murray wanted the general public to know that African Americans had made important contributions to the industrial revolution. Murray himself received eight patents for farm machinery improvements.

EARLY AFRICAN AMERICAN INVENTORS

After the Civil War, many African Americans went to work for the railroads. Some received patents for inventions to make the trains run more smoothly. In 1872, for example, Elijah McCoy invented a device for the self-oiling of railroad locomotives. This invention saved a great deal of time and money. Before it was available, the train's foreman had to get out of the cab and oil the parts by hand so they would not wear out prematurely.

McCoy was inspired to invent this device because he had often been assigned to do this tiresome job. The railroad was the only reliable form of long-distance transportation at the time, so McCoy's invention was very important. When Elijah McCoy died in 1929, he was both financially secure and respected by the engineering community.

Another African American's invention revolutionized the shoe industry. Jan E. Matzeliger invented an automatic shoe-stitching machine, called a "lasting" machine, in 1883. In could stitch 700 pairs of shoes a day, instead of the few pairs a day that could be sewn by hand. This invention greatly reduced the price of the average pair of shoes.

INVENTOR OF THE LIGHT BULB

Few people know that an African American named Lewis H. Latimer invented the light bulb that made the practical application of Edison's electric light system possible. Latimer worked closely with Edison and installed the first city electric light systems in New York, Philadelphia, London, and Montreal.

Dr. George Washington Carver is one black inventor who was internationally known during his lifetime. Born at the end of the Civil War, Carver completely transformed farming in the South by developing ways to use the peanut (peanut butter being only the most famous), the sweet potato, and the soybean. Because of his efforts, the South's dependency on cotton as the only exportable cash crop ended. Although Dr. Carter did not become rich from his work, he did receive honor and fame.

MORE RECENT SUCCESS STORIES

In this century, African American inventors have been better positioned to profit directly from their inventions. When Garret A. Morgan invented a gas mask in 1914, he already had a very profitable business based on a hair-straightening cream he had accidentally discovered and successfully marketed. Although his gas mask was originally meant for use in mines and tunnels, the U.S. Army used it extensively in World War I. In 1923, Morgan invented the first three-way traffic signal, the forerunner of today's traffic light. General Electric paid him $40,000 for the rights to his signal, a considerable sum at the time.

In the 1960s, Dr. Meredith Gourdine developed a million-dollar company based on inventions in the field of "electrogas dynamics"—converting gas into electricity. Even though Dr. Gourdine became blind in 1973, he is still very active in the company he founded.

WOMEN INVENTORS

Like the stories of early African American inventors, the stories of women inventors are finally coming to light as interest in women's history has increased. Nuclear fission, solar heating, bras, drip coffee, the ice cream cone, the Barbie doll, dishwashers, rolling pins, windshield wipers, medical syringes—these are just some products invented by women.

Many early women inventors created new products to help them where they spent most of their time—in the home—cooking, cleaning, and sewing. Mary Kies became the first woman patentee in 1809. She invented a process for weaving straw with silk or cotton thread. Her idea was instrumental in boosting New England's hat-making industry. When the War of 1812 cut off supplies of hats from Europe, New England hat makers used the Kies process to take over the hat market.

As women began to work outside the home as secretaries, they invented helpful office products. Bette Graham invented "Liquid Paper," or whiteout, which saves secretaries the trouble of typing over an entire page when they make a typing error.

WOMEN INVENTORS TODAY

As women move into traditionally male fields, such as medicine and science, their inventions in these areas are increasing. In 1988, for example, Gertrude Elion became the first woman inducted into the Inventors' Hall of Fame. During the thirty-nine years she worked for Burroughs-Wellcome, a drug company, Elion patented forty-five medical compounds. She shares the 1988 Nobel Prize for medicine with George H. Hitchings. They invented a compound that prevents transplant patients' immune systems from rejecting transplanted organs.

Ann Moore's invention of the child-carrying Snugli™ is more like the stereotypical "women's invention," yet it led to a valuable medical application. The Snugli can be seen on almost every American street, but Moore got the idea for it during her service with the Peace Corps in Africa in the 1960s. In Togo, West Africa, mothers carry their babies around with them all day in a fabric harness. Moore developed this concept into a pouchlike child carrier that is comfortable and washable. Moore began selling the Snugli in 1979. By 1984, annual sales were $6 million—and rising. Moore has used her Snugli technology to develop the Airlift™—a padded, portable oxygen tank carrier for patients who need a steady supply of oxygen.

IMMIGRANT INVENTORS

As they establish themselves in this country, Asian, Hispanic, and other new Americans are inventing important new products and processes.

Dr. Eloy Rodrìguez, for example, has developed some important drugs from tropical and desert plants. His formulas are being tested against viruses and cancer. He was drawn to these discoveries by noting that monkeys and other primates eat certain plants when they are sick. Dr. Rodrìguez has established a new biology field called "Zoopharmacognosy"—the study of self-medication by primates.

Another recent medical breakthrough by a Hispanic American is the invention, by Dr. Lydia Villa-Komaroff and her team of researchers, of the process of harvesting insulin from bacterial cells.

SOME POPULAR INVENTIONS

Listed below are some popular products and their inventors. The interesting stories behind many of these inventions can be found in the NFTE book *Inventions In Profile*.

Product	Inventors
Post-It notes	Silver/Fry/Nichols
Frisbee	Walter Morrison
Silly Putty	James Wright
Slinky	Richard James
Band-Aids	Earle Dickson
Vaseline	Robert Chesebrough
The Nose	Sylvia Stein
Yo-Yo	Donald Duncan
Toothpick	Charles Forster
Safety razor	King Gillette
Motorcycle	Sylvester Roper
Safety pin	Walter Hunt
Drive-in theater	Richard Hollingshead
Bathtub	Michael Kohler
Levi jeans	Levi Strauss
Shopping cart	Sylvan Goldman

CASE STUDY: HEALTHY SNACKS

Although many great businesses have been built on inventions, you don't need to be a brilliant inventor to be a brilliant entrepreneur. Sometimes, just repackaging an existing idea and selling it in a fresh way or in a new place can generate big bucks.

Douglas Chu, 27, and Scott Samet, 26, expect to generate over a million dollars this year from sales of health-food snacks in movie

Business for the Young Entrepreneur

theaters. Their company, Taste of Nature, sells trail mix, dried fruits, and yogurt-covered snacks in over 1,000 movie theaters in twenty-five states.

Taste of Nature revenues grew slowly but steadily after the company was founded in mid-1992 with $15,000. The snacks first appeared at Metropolitan Theaters' Santa Barbara operations and spread to snack counters at nearly two dozen other chains, including AMC, General Cinema, Edwards, Cineplex Odeon, and Sony. Sales skyrocketed, however, after news reports uncovered the high saturated-fat content of movie popcorn. Chains that were testing Taste of Nature products in a few theaters quickly added it in additional theaters.

Sales were also goosed by the new merchandising the partners had developed. At first, the owners sold prepackaged snacks. Customers were bored with the packages, Doug said. Doug and Scott conducted several market research surveys and learned that moviegoers wanted to be able to purchase healthy snacks at the movies but needed to be enticed by fun packaging.

Doug and Scott consulted with Bill Hughes, vice president of theater concessions with Metropolitan Theaters. He helped them design Plexiglass bins to display their snacks. Customers scoop up the snacks and pour them into bags. One scoop costs $2.25. Moviegoers enjoy the novel presentation, and theater owners love to have the product at their snack counters.

RESOURCES

Books

The U.S. Patent and Trademark Office offers a booklet called *General Information on Patents*. It can be ordered by calling the U.S. Government Printing Office at (202) 512-1800.

Here are three books that cover the basics of obtaining patents, copyrights, and trademarks:

The Copyright Handbook: How To Protect and Use Written Works by Stephan Fishman (Berkeley, CA: NoLo Press, 1991).

Inventing and Patenting Sourcebook by Richard Levy (Detroit, MI: Gale Research, Inc., 1992).

Trademark: How to Name Your Business & Product by Kate McGrath and Stephan Elias (Berkeley, CA: NoLo Press, 1992).

Feminine Ingenuity: How Women Inventors Changed America by Anne L. Macdonald (New York: Ballantine Books, 1992) is a very entertaining and informative look at American female inventors.

Other Resources

Many public libraries provide trademark searches for a small fee. Or, you can contact:

United States Trademark Association
6 East 45th Street
New York, NY 10017-1487
(212) 986-5880

15 WHAT TYPE OF BUSINESS YOU'RE STARTING AND HOW TO MAKE IT LEGAL

When two men in a business always agree, one of them is unnecessary.

—William Wrigley, Jr. (1861–1932)
American businessman

FOUR BASIC BUSINESS TYPES

An entrepreneur may start many different kinds of businesses during his or her lifetime, but all businesses fall into one of four basic categories:

1. **Manufacturing**—a business that makes a tangible product.
2. **Wholesale**—a business that buys products from manufacturers and sells them to retailers.
3. **Retail**—a business that sells directly to the final consumer.
4. **Service**—a business that sells intangibles such as time or expertise.

As you will see when you start working on your business plan, each type of business has different accounting, marketing, and promotional needs. That's why it's important to be able to categorize your business.

As I've mentioned previously, my first small business was an import–export business. This was a service business. I represented manufacturers from West Africa, Pakistan, and Bangladesh. I was providing a service to them by taking their products around to dealers in New York City and trying to sell them. I was selling the manufacturers my time and my familiarity with New York.

Today, I am the president of NFTE, which is also a service business. We provide expertise in the teaching of entrepreneurship.

MANUFACTURING

A **manufacturing** business is one that makes a tangible product. A manufacturer rarely sells its products directly to the consumer. It typically sells large quantities of its product to wholesalers, or it may hire a manufacturer's representative to sell its products directly to retailers. Some examples of manufacturing businesses are:

- Kohler, Inc., which manufactures plumbing fixtures. You've probably seen faucets imprinted with the Kohler name.
- Sony Corporation. Sony manufactures the Sony Walkman™, the Trinitron™ television, and other consumer electronic products.

WHOLESALE

A **wholesale** business rarely sells directly to the public, and it doesn't manufacture anything. It buys products from manufacturers in bulk and sells smaller quantities to retailers from warehouses. Some wholesalers also have store outlets, but they will not sell to consumers. If you see a store with a sign that reads "To the Trade Only," it is a wholesaler. A wholesaler is sometimes called a **middleman.** Wholesalers perform the business activity between manufacturers and retailers. Here are some examples of wholesale businesses:

- Dial-A-Floor buys carpets from manufacturers and sells them to carpet retailers.
- Hudson Wholesale buys clothing from manufacturers and sells it to boutiques.
- Butler Lumber, Inc. sells lumber to hardware stores and lumber companies.

RETAIL

Retail businesses sell directly to the consumer. Retailers buy products from a wholesaler and sell them directly to the final consumer. Retailers run stores or other selling units that are open to the public. Examples of retail businesses are:

- The Body Shop, Inc. Body Shop stores sell to consumers a variety of skin care products made from natural ingredients.
- Mrs. Fields Cookies. Although Mrs. Fields Cookies bakes its own cookies, the company sells them directly to consumers from its retail stores.
- East Side Sports. In Chapter 20, you'll read about this sporting goods store started by a NFTE graduate.

SERVICE

A **service** business provides intangibles such as time, skills, or expertise in exchange for a fee. Examples of service businesses are:

- H & R Block, Inc., the largest preparer of federal income tax returns for individuals. H & R Block prepares over 10 million returns each year.
- Charles Schwab & Company, which provides stock trading service.
- Wide Awake Publicity. Keeya Branson's firm helps clients secure publicity.

The above examples are *retail* service businesses because they sell directly to the end consumer. There are also service businesses that serve wholesale or manufacturing customers.

THE FOUR PARTS OF BUSINESS

Each business is composed basically of four parts. Large businesses (or corporations) employ many experts who oversee different aspects of these four parts. An entrepreneur, though, might have to handle all four parts alone. These parts are:

1. **Production**—making or obtaining the product.

2. **Financing**—securing and efficiently using money to develop the business.

3. **Marketing**—developing strategies for getting the consumer interested in the product or service.

4. **Customer service**—maintaining and servicing a product or service once it has been sold; the art of keeping customers happy and loyal to the business. Don't confuse customer service with a service business. Every kind of business should pay attention to customer service. If your business offers good customer service, your customers will become repeat purchasers. They will return to your business again and again. Repeat customers make a business successful.

In their book *Fast Cash for Kids* (Hawthorne, NJ: Career Press, 1995), Bonnie and Noel Drew suggest that young entrepreneurs take these three steps to excellent customer service:

1. **Get a written agreement.** Discuss the price of your product or service with the customer before agreeing to a transaction. Write down on an order form:

   - The work you are going to do or the product you are going to deliver.

   - The amount you will be paid.

   - The date the job is to be completed or the product is to be delivered.

   Have the customer sign the order form.

2. **Underpromise and overdeliver.** Always "expect the unexpected." For instance, if you think you can do a job in three days, tell the customer you'll have it done in five days. In that way, you're covered if you run into a problem. If you can finish "early," the customer will be pleasantly surprised.

3. **Make your customers your number-one priority.**

   - Do something extra without being asked.

   - Offer a money-back guarantee on your product or service.

   - Thank the customer for the business.

   - Keep appointments; if you can't keep an appointment, call and explain why.

- Follow up on every sale. Check with the customer to make sure he or she is satisfied with your product or service. A follow-up call or visit can often lead to another sale.

LEGAL BUSINESS STRUCTURE

After you pick the kind of business you want to be in, you will have to choose a legal structure. There are five basic legal business structures:

1. Sole proprietorship.
2. Partnership.
3. Corporation.
4. Subchapter S corporation.
5. Nonprofit corporation.

Sole Proprietorship

A **sole proprietorship** is owned by one person, who may also be the only employee. The owner receives all the business profits and must bear all the losses. Most student businesses are sole proprietorships.

The sole proprietor is personally **liable,** or responsible, for any lawsuits that arise from accidents, faulty merchandise, unpaid bills, or other business problems. This means the winner of a lawsuit against a sole proprietor can not only collect money from the business but also ask a court to force the owner to sell private possessions. The owner could lose his house or car, for example.

To avoid lawsuits, a young person starting a business should sell only products or services that are highly unlikely to hurt anyone. Avoid selling skateboards, for example, or offering rock-climbing lessons!

Partnership

A **partnership** consists of two or more owners who make decisions for the business together and share profits, losses, and liability. Partners can bring different strengths, skills, and resources to the business. You may need a partner to make your business idea a reality. Herbert, for example, had a business plan for a T-shirt screening business, but he had no place to set up a business. He formed a partnership with Koung because Koung had a garage.

Sometimes, partnership disagreements can destroy a business. We recommend that partners always see a lawyer and draw up a **partnership agreement** that carefully defines the responsibilities of each partner. Before Herbert and Koung went into business together, I warned them that their partnership could ruin their friendship. I counseled them to write down all their agreements. They did, and their business (and friendship) has lasted seven years so far.

Corporation

The word "corporation" is derived from *corpus,* Latin for "body." A **corporation** is a legal body composed of stockholders united under a common name. Corporations issue stock and elect a board of directors, who manage the company.

The corporate legal structure offers two key advantages:

1. A corporation may issue stock to raise money. Essentially, the company sells pieces of itself to stockholders, who then become owners of the company. This is called selling **equity** (ownership) to raise money.

2. A corporation has limited liability. Unlike sole proprietorships and partnerships, the owners of a corporation cannot have their personal assets used to pay business lawsuit settlements or debts. Only the assets of the corporation can be used to pay corporate debts.

The main disadvantage of corporations is that corporate income is taxed twice. First, the corporation must pay corporate income tax on its earnings. Later, when the corporation distributes its earnings as dividends to stockholders, the stockholders must include the dividends as personal income on their tax returns.

A business needs to incorporate when the owner wants to raise money by selling equity or when the owner needs protection from being liable for lawsuit settlements or debts that could be incurred by the business.

When Harold started his DJ business at age sixteen, he was spinning records for local parties. Today, his Nu X-Perience Sound and Lighting Company provides sound and lights for parties and parades. Now that he's dealing with sound and lighting equipment that could conceivably hurt someone in an accident, Harold has incorporated to protect his personal assets.

Subchapter S Corporation

This type of corporation limits the number of stockholders to thirty-five. It offers most of the limited liability protection of the corporation, but Subchapter S corporate income is taxed only once—as the personal income of the owners. Many small companies are Subchapter S corporations because it's a good way for a small company to avoid the double taxation of corporations.

Nonprofit Corporation

A nonprofit corporation is set up with a specific mission to improve society. Churches, museums, charitable foundations, and trade associations are examples of nonprofit corporations.

Nonprofit corporations are **tax-exempt.** They do not pay taxes on their income because the income is being used to help society. On the other hand, nonprofits may not sell stock or pay dividends. No one owns a nonprofit corporation.

WHY NFTE IS A NONPROFIT CORPORATION

NFTE is a nonprofit corporation with a mission that I believe will improve society: to teach young people to start and operate their own small businesses. Indeed, initial research conducted by Brandeis University has indicated that our programs do have a positive effect on the lives of young people by teaching them entrepreneurship. We hope to prove through our research what I, and other NFTE teachers, have observed—our students seem more likely to avoid unwanted pregnancies, graduate from high school, develop self-esteem, and go to college. Something about learning to start and operate one's own small business is very inspiring for both adults and young people.

Initially, I funded my entrepreneurship program with personal savings. When I saw how well young people were responding to learning about business through hands-on experience, I decided to build a national movement so that every child born into poverty could have the opportunity to start his or her own business.

In 1987, I registered NFTE as a nonprofit corporation. As a "nonprofit," I could ask for donations. I wrote to everyone on the list of the 400 wealthiest people in America, published by *Forbes* magazine, and told them about my mission. Raymond Chambers, a wonderful entrepreneur from Newark, New Jersey, responded to that letter. After I met with him and his adviser, Barbara Bell, he agreed to finance NFTE for its first year at the Boys and Girls Clubs of Newark.

Certain types of businesses lend themselves to the nonprofit structure; educating kids is certainly one of them. NFTE does work closely with several for-profit companies, however. We've had a long-term partnership with Koch Industries and the Koch family, and we are just beginning a partnership with Microsoft. We also work closely with Babson College and other educational institutions, including Columbia University, the Wharton School of Business, the University of California at Berkeley, the University Community Outreach Program, and Harvard Business School.

MANAGEMENT

As a small business grows, it will reach a point where the entrepreneur and a few employees cannot handle the business efficiently. At that stage, the business needs **management.** Management is the art of planning and organizing a business so it can meet its goals.

Many successful entrepreneurs are creative people who tend to get bored with the everyday details of running a large business. I'm that way, myself. Successful entrepreneurs realize this and hire managers to actually run the business. Once NFTE outgrew my home office and moved into our headquarters in downtown Manhattan, I began a search for a tough, experienced entrepreneur to become executive director for NFTE. I eventually hired Mike Caslin who was a perfect choice because he had worked in high-level management for several charities and he had *also* run his own small businesses. I also hired Mike to help me with fund-raising and strategy. Mike has been my partner since 1988 and is responsible for much of NFTE's success. So is Chris Meenan, the first, and one of the finest, teachers I ever hired. Today Chris oversees NFTE's teachers worldwide.

As a nonprofit, NFTE had to raise money from funders to hire Chris and Mike, but entrepreneurs with growing *for-profit* corporations can raise capital by selling stock. These entrepreneurs can use some of the capital they raise to hire managers who can organize their businesses. The entrepreneurs can then spend less time managing and more time thinking up new business ideas.

DEBBI FIELDS LEARNS TO DELEGATE

Some entrepreneurs will fail to hire adequate management because they don't want to give up overseeing the daily details of their businesses. Debbi Fields, the owner of Mrs. Fields Cookies, made this mistake in the late 1980s. By 1987, Fields had opened over 500 stores in six countries. The rapid growth, combined with Debbi's unwillingness to let other people take much responsibility, almost caused the business to fall apart in 1988.

Too many new stores had opened too close to existing ones, and sales were falling as a result. Fields was forced to close ninety-seven stores that year. She realized that she would have to find good managers and trust them with helping her and her husband, Randy, run the business. She hired a chief financial officer from a top accounting firm and a head of operations who had long experience in the food business. She delegated the day-to-day details of running the business to them.

This left her free to develop new ideas. The name Mrs. Fields meant top-quality baked goods to customers all over the world, so she began thinking up ways to use the name for more than just cookies and brownies. Fields made a deal with Ambrosia Chocolate to make and market Mrs. Fields semisweet chocolate chips, and she began testing recipes for muffins, bread, sandwiches, and soups for her new Mrs. Fields Bakeries. Soon, the stock price began to recover and profits improved.

Letting go of the daily details also gave Fields more time to read every comment sent to the company by customers and to travel around visiting her stores and meeting with local managers. She learned the hard way that a successful entrepreneur should not try to do everything alone.

MOTIVATIONAL MANAGEMENT: SAM WALTON AND WAL-MART

No matter what legal structure you use for your business or what managers you hire, motivating yourself and your employees is very important. One of the masters of motivation was Sam Walton, who built Wal-Mart, the largest retailer in the world, from a single five-and-dime store.

Walton grew up during the Great Depression in the small, hardscrabble town of Bentonville, Arkansas. He picked up entrepreneurship from his mother, who started a small milk business to help the family make ends meet. Walton began selling magazine subscriptions when he was only eight years old, and he had paper routes from seventh grade through college. He also raised and sold rabbits and pigeons, "nothing unusual for country boys," as he noted in his autobiography, *Sam Walton: Made in America* (with John Huey, New York: Doubleday, 1992).

Although Walton passed away in 1992, his folksy style remains the key to a business that is now worth over $50 billion. Even when *Forbes* named him America's richest man in 1985, Walton preferred pickup trucks to Rolls Royces, and hunting and fishing to attending celebrity-studded events.

Walton expected his managers and executives to share his aversion to flashy spending. This wasn't just a billionaire's quirk; it was part of his motivational strategy. In his autobiography, he said, "if American management is going to say to their workers that we're all in this together, they're going to have to stop this foolishness of paying themselves $3 million and $4 million bonuses every year and riding around everywhere in limos and corporate jets like they're so much better than everybody else."

Walton Introduces Profit Sharing

Walton wasn't just paying lip service to this idea. He put money behind it. In 1970, Walton introduced profit sharing for Wal-Mart managers. By 1971, he had extended it to every "associate" (as he called his employees) in the company. Using a formula based on profit growth, Wal-Mart contributes a percentage of each associate's wages to a profit-sharing plan, which the associate can take along—in either cash or Wal-Mart stock—when he or she leaves the company. In 1991, for example, Wal-Mart contributed $125 million to the profit-sharing plan.

The profit-sharing plan has created significant wealth for many Wal-Mart employees. More importantly, it makes each employee eager to work hard and come up with innovations to improve the profitability of the company. In *Sam Walton: Made in America,* a Wal-Mart truck driver notes that he worked for one large company for thirteen years and left with $700. After working for Wal-Mart for twenty years, he has built up over $700,000 through profit sharing. "When folks ask me how I like working for Wal-Mart," he says, "I tell them about my profit sharing and ask them, 'How do you think I feel about Wal-Mart?'"

Profit sharing was just one of Walton's motivational innovations. No matter how enormous the company became, his door was open to any employee who needed to talk to him. He constantly visited stores and made people feel that they were an important part of the Wal-Mart team. He encouraged and rewarded healthy competition among his stores.

I visited the Wal-Mart museum in Bentonville recently. People there are still sad about Walton's passing. His office has been reconstructed, and a copy of the profit-sharing plan hangs on the wall. Although he didn't have a computer in his office, Walton was a great proponent of technology. An incredible inventory control system has helped Wal-Mart keep prices low. The chain also uses video technology to train people across the country. (I'm going to be visiting one of their directors of internal training, to learn how to apply this technology to the training of NFTE teachers.)

I'm sure Walton would approve. He wrote that "our country desperately needs a revolution in education. Without a strong educational system, the very free enterprise system that allows a Wal-Mart or an IBM or a Procter & Gamble to appear on the scene and strengthen our nation's economy simply won't work."

CASE STUDY: NETWORK SERVICE

Business for the Young Entrepreneur

By the time she was twenty-one, Jennifer Kushell had already owned three small businesses. She had noticed that young entrepreneurs can feel more isolated than older entrepreneurs. Even if they've never started a business before, older entrepreneurs may already be "in the loop" because they've built up many business contacts over the years. Jennifer decided that her fourth business would help young entrepreneurs network.

In November 1993, Jennifer and her partner, Benjamin Kyan, began producing The International Directory of Young Entrepreneurs (IDYE). Today, the directory includes around 500 members from thirty countries. The entrepreneurs listed range in age from ten to early thirties. The directory also includes information on professional business resources such as venture capital groups.

Jennifer and Benjamin are currently preparing a quarterly newsletter for their members. Eventually, Jennifer says, "We want to be the number-one resource for everything a young entrepreneur would need—whether it's travel services or convention planning. We also want to do a four-color magazine and eventually start a business consulting service."

The growth of Jennifer's business is a natural result of her knowledge of her market. The directory was a great way for her to research her market while providing it with an important service. As you get to know your market better, ideas for expanding your business will multiply.

RESOURCES

Books

The Partnership Book: How to Write a Partnership Agreement by Dennis Clifford and Ralph Warner (Berkeley, CA: NoLo Press, 1991).

The Small Business Incorporation Kit by Robert L. Davidson, III (New York: John Wiley & Sons, Inc., 1992).

One of the most popular books on customer service is *Delivering Knock Your Socks Off Service* by Kristin Anderson and Ron Zemke (New York: American Management Association, 1991).

Jennifer Kushell's directory for young entrepreneurs is available from:

The International Directory of Young Entrepreneurs
100 Linden Street, Suite 9
Boston, MA 02134
(800) 455-IDYE
(617) 562-8616
Fax (617) 562-8617

Other Resources

Starting and Operating a Small Business in [name of state]. Packets under this title have been prepared for each state. Each packet includes up-to-date information regarding both federal and state laws and regulations that affect small business. Contact:

Oasis Press/PSI Research
300 North Valley Drive
Grant's Pass, OR 97526
(800) 228-2275

The National Association for the Self-Employed (NASE) keeps track of tax issues for small business owners. It also arranges bulk discounts for small businesses. More than 88 percent of its 300,000 members are business owners with five or fewer employees. The NASE offers a toll-free small business advice hotline and other helpful services. Contact:

National Association for the Self-Employed
1023 15th St., NW, Suite 1200
Washington, DC 20005-2600
(202) 466-2100
Fax (202) 466-2123
(800) 232-NASE

Women who need advice starting their own business can contact:

American Women's Economic Development Corporation (AWED)
641 Lexington Avenue, 9th Floor
New York, NY 10022
(800) 222-AWED

SELECTING YOUR BUSINESS

16

LET YOUR TALENTS LEAD YOU

> The propensity to truck, barter, and exchange one thing
> for another . . . is common to all men, and to be found in
> no other race of animals.
>
> —Adam Smith (1723–1790)
> Scottish economist

LET YOUR TALENTS LEAD YOU: HOW SPIKE LEE BUILT BUSINESSES ON THE SUCCESS OF HIS FILMS

You may think of yourself as more artistic than businesslike. You may have no idea what kind of business you could start. You may wonder whether you could ever be a successful entrepreneur.

Spike Lee's business success disproves the notion that a creative artist can't also be a shrewd businessperson. Lee began selling merchandise connected with his films through an informal mail-order operation after the success of his first feature film, *She's Gotta Have It*. By the time Lee's movie *Do the Right Thing* became a huge hit, he was selling $50,000 worth *a month* of T-shirts and baseball caps. To sell his merchandise, Lee opened a store called Spike's Joint, in Fort Greene, Brooklyn, a few blocks from where he was raised.

Lee's style-setting ability was confirmed by the incredible popularity of the "X" cap he designed to promote the film *Malcolm X* in 1991. So many imitation "X" caps flooded the market, however, that Lee was forced to become more serious about properly promoting and protecting his merchandise and fashion ideas.

In June 1992, Macy's opened a Spike's Joint in its Manhattan store. This was soon followed by Spike's Joints in sixteen other Macy's stores. Lee even opened a Spike's Joint on trendy Melrose Avenue in Los Angeles, and he began negotiating a licensing deal to open five Spike's Joint stores in Japan. Lee began developing three lines of sportswear. He also opened his own record company, 40 Acres and a Mule Musicworks.

Lee equates owning a business with freedom and power. He strongly believes that African Americans should become entrepreneurs. He has said, "For so long, we African American people have been taught to work for other people and not to build our own businesses . . . but anytime you're in business and you can unify things, it gives you that much more power."

TURNING HOBBIES, SKILLS, AND INTERESTS INTO BUSINESSES

The possibilities for young people starting businesses are almost limitless. If you still haven't settled on a business idea, list some of your hobbies and skills below. What you enjoy doing in your spare time might be turned into a profitable business. Making money through doing what you enjoy is a winning combination.

Match up business opportunities with your hobbies, interests, and skills.

Hobbies and Interests	Business Opportunities

Skills	Business Opportunities

Anita Roddick, the founder of The Body Shop, Inc., suggests that new entrepreneurs ask themselves three questions when trying to choose a business to pursue:

1. What makes me mad?
2. What am I good at?
3. What separates me from the pack?

> **When selecting your business, choose something you enjoy doing.**

Rule of Thumb

THINGS TO CONSIDER WHEN CHOOSING A BUSINESS

Imagine yourself for a moment in the business of your choice. Is it a "good fit"? Are you going to stay interested in it and enthusiastic about it for a long time?

Consider keeping your business simple. This is going to be your very first enterprise, so don't bite off more than you can chew. Many successful entrepreneurs start more than one business over the course of their lifetimes. *Start with something simple that you know you can do well.* View yourself as growing into business by starting small. Choose something you are going to enjoy selling.

For now, if you choose a simple business and follow these three rules, your business should succeed:

1. Satisfy a consumer need.
2. Buy low, sell high.
3. Keep good records.

Successful entrepreneurs listen to what people in the community are saying. What do the people you know like? What do they want? What do they need? Could you fill one of their needs? Consider what your friends, family, and schoolmates want and need. They are your market.

By now, you may have several ideas and can't decide which one would be best. Try writing down several possible businesses. Eliminate them one by one until you end up with the business you like best.

If you haven't yet come up with a business idea you like, this chapter may help. Several good books are available that are packed with money-making ideas for the young entrepreneur. Check out the resources at the end of the chapter.

Throughout this book, I have included detailed examples of businesses run by young entrepreneurs. I hope these narratives will help you select a business of your own. Below is a list of some of the most common businesses run by young people.

Baby-Sitting Service

Are you reliable and responsible? Do you like children? Provide a baby-sitting service.

Baking

Do you like to bake? You can sell freshly made bread, cookies, cakes, and pastries. This is a business where "word of mouth" is truly the best advertising!

Bicycle/Auto/Appliance Repair

Are you mechanically inclined? Fix bicycles, cars, appliances, or other machinery that you know well.

Catering

Are you into cooking in a big way? Start a catering business and supply whole meals or buffets for parties and other occasions.

Distributing Flyers

Do stores in your neighborhood need people to hand out flyers? These can be distributed on the street, put on car windshields, or given out at social functions. This service could be offered to shopkeepers on a regular basis.

Entertaining

Are you a natural ham who enjoys being in front of a audience? Do you know any magic tricks or have any acting experience? You might like being a magician or a clown and entertaining at birthday parties and other events. If you have musical talent, you could get a band together and play for weddings and parties.

Gardening/Lawn Cutting

Do you like working outdoors? From the street, you can often spot lawns and gardens that are not being kept up by their owners as well as they should be. You could also shovel snow in the winter (if you live in a four-season area).

Growing Plants

Is there a room in your house or apartment that gets a lot of sunlight? You can grow herbs, flowers, or other plants for sale. This can be a good "second" business because plants don't have to be watched every minute of the day.

Handicrafts

Do you like to make jewelry, leather goods, or other handicrafts? Do you have friends who make nice handicrafts but don't want to be involved in the selling process? Sell your own crafts and, for a commission, your friends' crafts, too.

Holiday Selling

Do you have spare time during the holidays? Try selling seasonal specialties, such as Christmas decorations or Valentine's Day candy, which have short but intense sales seasons. If you are willing to put in the time, you can make a lot of money in a relatively short period.

House/Office Cleaning

Do you like to see things clean and neat? Houses and offices need to be cleaned. Many people and businesses do not have time to clean.

Laundry Service

Do you have access to a good washer and dryer? Doing laundry (like dog walking and house cleaning) is another chore many people do not have time to do.

Messenger Service

Do you enjoy running around? Try a messenger/small-package delivery service. This business has low start-up costs. The service can expand rapidly as you build up a reputation for reliability.

Music Lessons

Do you play an instrument well enough to teach someone else? Even if you have only intermediate knowledge of an instrument, you could probably teach young beginners.

Painting/Furniture Refinishing

Do you like to paint? Paint rooms and apartments; repaint or refinish old furniture.

Pet Care

Do you like animals? Dog walking or taking care of pets are possibilities.

Photography

Do you have a good camera or a camcorder? More and more, people are having their weddings, birthdays, parties, and other events photographed or videotaped (or both). You'll need samples of your work to show to prospective clients.

Plant Care

Offices sometimes hire a service to come in once a week or so to water, clean, and fertilize plants. As more and more people work outside the home, there is more demand for household plant care, too.

Translating

Are you bilingual? Translate ads, flyers, signs, and other printed media for local shopkeepers who want to reach customers who speak different languages.

T-Shirts

Are you artistically inclined? Design and print your own customized T-shirts.

Tutoring

Do you know one of your school subjects well enough to teach other students? Do you know how to dance, act, sing, or draw well enough to teach it to young children? Giving lessons (tutoring) requires patience, but you will discover the rewards and satisfaction of teaching.

Typing Service

Are you a fast and accurate typist? If you can type well or use a word processor, there is a wide variety of services you can offer: typing up papers for other students, organizing and printing out mailing lists, or making up brochures, newsletters, or flyers.

Wake-Up Service

Are you an early riser? Start a wake-up service for your fellow students.

Naming Your Business

Once you've selected a business, the next step is to name it. The name of a business represents the character of the enterprise to customers, investors, and advisers.

It is common for entrepreneurs to name their businesses after themselves. Using your first name to identify your business—showing the pride you take in it—can be a good idea (Joe's Pizza, for example).

Attaching your last (family) name to your business is not such a good idea. If you name your business with your last name, several risks are involved:

- If the business fails, your name is now associated with a failed business. This can hurt you if you decide to start a new business and potential investors remember that your earlier business failed.
- If the business succeeds, you might decide to sell it for a tidy profit. But what if you hate what the new owner does with it? What if he or she engages in dishonest business practices? Your name is still on the door.

Business owners can get carried away when naming a business. Naming a photography studio "Timeless Expression," for example, is creative but doesn't give customers any information about the business. A more straightforward name, such as "The Portrait Place," might draw more customers.

The best name is one that tells customers what the company does, sells, or makes. As Mancuso says in his best-selling book, *Have You Got What It Takes? How To Tell If You Should Start Your Own Business* (Englewood Cliffs, NJ: Prentice-Hall, 1982). "Naming the company is the first move of many in which you should keep the customer's needs first and foremost in mind." NFTE's name—The National Foundation For Teaching Entrepreneurship, Inc.—for example, explains that we teach entrepreneurship nationally and that we are a nonprofit foundation.

REGISTERING A SOLE PROPRIETORSHIP

To sell a product or service legally, you need to register your business. In most areas, it is easy and inexpensive to register a sole proprietorship. Once you do, you will have a real business! Contact the county courthouse or local Chamber of Commerce to find out which licenses and permits are necessary in your area.

Registration usually takes the following steps:

1. Choose a name for your business.
2. Fill out a "Doing Business As" (DBA) form, indicating the name of your business and your name. The certificate in Chart 14 is an example of a standard DBA. The state will then have a record of the name of the person doing business.
3. Be prepared to have an official conduct a name search to make sure the name you've chosen isn't already being used.

BUSINESS CERTIFICATE

I HEREBY CERTIFY *that I am conducting or transacting business under the name or designation*

of

at

City or Town of   *County of*   *State of New York*

My name is*

and I reside at

I FURTHER CERTIFY *that I am the successor in interest to*

the person or persons heretofore using such name or names to carry on or conduct or transact business.

IN WITNESS HEREOF, *I have this*   *day of*   19   *, made and signed this certificate*

....

*Print or type name.
*If under 21 years of age, state "I am .... years of age."

STATE OF NEW YORK
COUNTY OF   } *ss.:*

On this   *day of*   19   *, before me personally appeared*

to me known and known to me to be the individual described in and who executed the foregoing certificate, and he (she) thereupon duly acknowledged to me that he (she) executed the same.

....

Chart 14   A Standard DBA Form

4. Fill out a registration form and pay the fee required in your area.

5. Find out whether a **notary public** must witness your signature on the DBA. A notary is a person authorized to witness the signing of documents and to certify them as valid. Most banks have a notary or can refer you to one. There may be one at the registration office. You will have to show the notary photo identification.

SALES TAX IDENTIFICATION NUMBER

In most towns, every business must obtain a sales tax identification number and collect sales tax. To find out what sales taxes are required in your area, call your state's sales tax office. The office can send you an application for a sales tax number. Chart 15 will familiarize you with the format of the application.

BUSINESS CARDS

Once you have registered your business, you should have business cards made. A business card bears your name, title, business name, and phone and fax numbers. The card should fit into the credit-card section of your wallet. Always carry business cards with you. Give them to business contacts and prospective customers.

Business for the Young Entrepreneur

CASE STUDY: ON-LINE SERVICE[1]

The most important lesson I hope you'll take from this book is that starting and operating your own small business should be fun. Pick something you love to do and let your imagination lead you.

That's exactly what Omar Wasow, 24, and Peta Hoyes, 25, did when they began New York OnLine, an on-line service all about New York City. Omar and Peta were raised in New York and love the city's ethnic diversity and cultural offerings. The pair met at Stanford University and decided to return to New York after college. New York On-Line started operating from Omar's Brooklyn brownstone apartment in April 1994.

Omar borrowed most of the $50,000 start-up capital from his parents. Today, three computer terminals and twenty-five phone lines are

AP-100-2
(Rev. 10-93/14)

TEXAS APPLICATION
• SALES TAX PERMIT   • USE TAX PERMIT
• MIXED BEVERAGE TAX ACCOUNT SET-UP

NOTE: *Where space indicators are shown, please enter only one letter or number in each space and skip one space between words.*   Page 1

If you are visually impaired, would you like special assistance from the Comptroller's Office before you are mailed notices?   ☐ Yes   ☐ No

¿ Si necesita informacion sobre impuestos prefiere usted hablar con una persona que habla español? _____   ☐ Si   ☐ No

TAXPAYER IDENTIFICATION

1. Legal name of owner *(Sole owner or partners, first name, middle initial and last name; corporation or other name)*

2. Mailing address *(Street & no., P.O. Box or rural route and box no.)*

City   State   ZIP Code

County

3. If you are a sole owner, enter your home address *(Street & number, city, state, ZIP code)* if it is different from above.

3a. Enter the daytime phone number of the person
primarily responsible for filing tax returns.   (Area code and number) ____ / ____ — ____

4. Enter your Social Security Number if you are a sole owner. ____ **2** ____ — ____ — ____

5. Enter your Federal Employer's Identification (FEI) Number, if any, **1** ____ — ____
assigned by the United States Internal Revenue Service. ____

3 ____

6. If you are incorporating an existing business,
enter the taxpayer number of the existing business. ____

7. Enter your taxpayer number for reporting any Texas tax OR your Texas Vendor
Identification Number if you now have or have ever had one. ____

OWNERSHIP

8. Indicate how your business is owned. ☐ 1 - Sole owner   ☐ 2 - Partnership   ☐ 3 - Texas corporation
☐ 7 - Limited partnership ☐ 6 - Foreign corporation ☐ 4 - Other (explain)

9. If your business is a Texas corporation,   Charter Numr   Charter date (Mo., day, year)
enter the charter number and date. ____

10. If your business is a foreign corporation, enter home state, charter number, Texas Certificate of Authority Number & date.
Home state   Charter Number   Texas Cert. of Auth. No.   Cert. of Auth. date (Mo., day, year)

11. If your business is a limited partnership,   Home state   Identification number
enter the home state and identification number. ____ — ____

PROPRIETORS

12. List all general partners or principal officers of your business. If you are a sole owner, skip Item 12. *(Attach additional sheets if necessary)*

Name *(First, middle initial, last)*

Social Security or Federal Employer's Identification (FEI) No.   Title   Phone *(Area code & no.)*   ____ / ____ — ____

Home address *(Street & no., city, state, ZIP code)*

Name *(First, middle initial, last)*

Social Security or Federal Employer's Identification (FEI) No.   Title   Phone *(Area code & no.)*   ____ / ____ — ____

Home address *(Street & no., city, state, ZIP code)*

Name *(First, middle initial, last)*

Social Security or Federal Employer's Identification (FEI) No.   Title   Phone *(Area code & no.)*   ____ / ____ — ____

Home address *(Street & no., city, state, ZIP code)*

(Continue on Page 2)

For Comptroller's Use Only

JOB NAME - SALEAPP

Spanish/Visually impaired indicator

☐   • **01150**
   ☐ 0 - None
   ☐ 1 - Spanish
   ☐ 2 - Visually impaired
   ☐ 3 - Spanish and Visually impaired Indicator

Master name change

☐   • **01170**
   ☐ 0 - Send
   ☐ 1 - Do not send

Master account set up

☐   • **01100**

Master mailing address change

☐   • **01180**

County code

Master phone number add/change

☐   • **01185**
   QF ☐   ☐ NR
   ☐ ☐
   ☐ ☐
   ☐ ☐
   ☐ ☐

State employee - A

Individual recipient -B

Ownership type

• ⌐_⌐

• ⌐0 ¦0 ¦0 ¦0⌐

Partnership set up

☐   • **01140**
   ☐ ☐
   ☐ ☐
   ☐ ☐

Chart 15   One State's Application Form for a Sales Tax Identification Number

hooked up in his living room. Omar and Peta (who has a degree in mechanical engineering) taught themselves how to wire everything.

Subscribers to New York OnLine pay a base charge of $6 a month. In return, they get access to restaurant, movie, and television reviews, and trendy magazines like *Wired* and *Vibe*. Users also participate in debates on subjects dear to New Yorkers' hearts—such as why Pat Riley *really* quit coaching the Knicks.

Peta and Omar have tried to attract a young, ethnically diverse crowd and seem to be succeeding. Although they had only around 1,200 subscribers as of July 1995, the company seems poised for a serious growth spurt because of intense advertising interest in its demographics. While most on-line services attract mostly white males, 40 percent of New York OnLine's users are female and 50 percent are people of color. Omar and Peta have been written up in local newspapers and Japanese magazines, and Omar was invited to address a Harvard conference for editors and publishers, regarding their concern about how the digital revolution will affect journalism.

The information highway offers tremendous business opportunities for young people. In an interview with *New York Newsday* (Rita Ciolli, July 6, 1995), Nicholas Negroponte, director of MIT's Media Lab, said New York OnLine is an example of a business started with little capital that can become very valuable to its community.

To contact New York OnLine, call (800) 845-1195.

RESOURCES

Books

Better Than a Lemonade Stand: Small Business Ideas for Kids by Daryl Bernstein (Hillsboro, OR: Beyond Words Publishing, Inc., 1992).

Fast Cash for Kids: 101 Money-Making Projects for Young Entrepreneurs, 2nd Edition by Bonnie and Noel Drew (Hawthorne, NJ: The Career Press, 1995).

Other Resources

Call your local Chamber of Commerce to find out whether any youth entrepreneurship clubs or programs are being run in your town. You might also check with your local Boys & Girls Club.

For a list of programs that NFTE runs nationally, contact:

The National Foundation for Teaching Entrepreneurship, Inc.
120 Wall Street, 29th Floor
New York, NY 10005
(212) 232-3333
Fax (212) 232-2244

For information on the fine entrepreneurship education programs run by the University Community Outreach Program, contact Lisa Hoffstein at:

UCOP
Milken Institute
401 City Avenue, Suite 204
Balacynwyd, PA 19004
(610) 668-5330

The Kauffman Foundation runs an entrepreneurship program, called Y.E.S. Contact:

Marilyn Kourilsky
Ewing Marion Kauffman Foundation
4900 Oak
Kansas City, MO 64112-2776
(816) 932-1000

Entrepreneurship programs are also run by EDTECH. The directors of Edtech, George Walters and Aaron Bocage, mentored me in the early 1980s when I was a teacher. Contact:

EDTECH
313 Market Street
Camden, NJ 08102
(609) 342-8277

Joline Godfrey runs business summer camps for teen women. For more information, contact:

An Income of Her Own
Joline Godfrey, Director
P.O. Box 987
Santa Barbara, CA 93102
(800) 350-2978

17 FINANCING STRATEGY

BORROW OR SELL?

**We [at Polaroid] grow and grow and grow not on the basis
of the bottom line but on the basis of the faith that if you
do your job well, the last thing you have to worry about is
money, just as if you live right, you'll be happy.**

**—Edwin Land (b. 1909)
American founder of Polaroid, Inc.**

Anita Roddick didn't expect The Body Shop, Inc. to change the cosmetics industry, be a force for social awareness, *and* make millions of dollars—but it has done all of these. The Body Shop would have never gotten that far, though, if Roddick hadn't sold half the company to her friend Ian McGlinn for his £4,000 (around $7,000) investment in her company. Local banks refused to lend Roddick money because she had been in business for only a few months. In return for his investment in Roddick's business, McGlinn received a share of The Body Shop's profits.

Today, McGlinn's investment is worth over £140 million (around $240 million). Roddick says she has no regrets. Without McGlinn's financing, she would not have been able to grow her company.

FINANCING

Financing is the use and manipulation of money. Raising money for a business is one aspect of financing.

If an entrepreneur cannot personally supply the necessary amount of money, another option is **other people's money** (OPM). There are two ways to raise OPM. Each affects a business differently.

1. **Debt.** The business borrows the money and pays it back over a set period of time at a set rate of interest. Corporations sell debt in the form of bonds. You could borrow money from family and friends to finance your business. Roddick was unable to raise any debt financing for her business so she turned to equity.

2. **Equity.** The business gives up a percentage of ownership for money. Like McGlinn, the equity investor receives a percentage of future profits from the business, based on the percentage of ownership purchased. Corporations sell equity in the form of stock. You cannot sell stock unless your business is incorporated, but you *can* sell equity. You can offer ownership and a share of your future profits in exchange for financing.

DEBT

To finance through debt, the entrepreneur borrows from a person or an institution that has money. The entrepreneur signs a promise to repay the borrowed sum with interest. That promise is called a **promissory note.**

Interest is figured by multiplying the **principal** by the interest rate. The principal is the amount of the loan, not including interest payments. If $1,200 is borrowed at 10 percent to be paid back over one year, the interest on the loan is $1,200 \times .10 = 120.

One advantage of debt is that the lender has no say in the future or direction of the business as long as the loan payments are made. Another is that the loan payments are predictable.

The disadvantage of debt is that if the loan payments are not made, the lender can force the business into bankruptcy to get the loan back, even if that loan is only a fraction of what the business is worth. The lender can even take the home and possessions of the owner of a sole proprietorship, or of a partner in a partnership, as substitutes for the money owed.

Borrowing should be carefully considered by the beginning entrepreneur. It often takes a long time for a new business to show a profit. *The risk of debt is that failure to make loan payments can destroy the business before it gets the chance to prove itself.*

Advantages of Debt Financing (Loans, Bonds)

1. The lender has no say in the future or direction of the business as long as the loan payments are made.

2. Loan payments are predictable—they do not change with the fortunes of the business.

Disadvantages of Debt Financing

1. If loan payments are not made, the lender can force the business into bankruptcy.

2. To settle a debt, the lender can take the home and possessions of the owner of a sole proprietorship or a partner in a partnership.

EQUITY

Equity means that, in return for money, the investor receives a percentage of ownership in the company. For the $1,200 investment we discussed above, an equity investor might want 10 percent ownership of the company, which would give the investor 10 percent of the business's profits. The investor is hoping that, over time, 10 percent of the profits will provide a high rate of return on the initial investment of $1,200.

The equity investor assumes greater risk than the debt lender. If the business doesn't make profits, neither does the investor. An equity investor cannot force a business into bankruptcy to get back the original investment. If a business is forced into bankruptcy by its creditors, they get paid off first from the sale of the business assets. Equity investors have a claim on whatever is left over after debt investors have been paid.

Although the equity investor's *risk* is higher than that of the debt lender, so is the potential for *return on equity.* The equity investor could make the investment back many times over if the business prospers. For that reason, he or she accepts a higher level of risk than the debt lender. The debt lender's risk of losing his or her investment is lower, but so is the debt lender's return.

With equity financing, the money doesn't have to be paid back unless the business is successful. However, through giving up ownership, the entrepreneur can lose control of the business to the equity holders.

Advantages of Equity Financing (Stock, Percentage of Company)

1. If the business doesn't make a profit, the investor does not get paid. The equity investor cannot force the business into bankruptcy in order to get paid.

2. The equity investor has an interest in seeing the business succeed and may, therefore, offer helpful advice and valuable contacts.

Disadvantages of Equity Financing

1. Through giving up ownership, the entrepreneur can lose control of the business to the equity holders.

2. Equity financing is riskier for the investor, so the investor frequently wants both a say in how the company is run and a higher rate of return than a lender.

FINANCIAL RATIOS

Large companies are usually financed by both debt and equity. The mix of debt and equity is grasped quickly by dividing equity into debt to obtain a debt-to-equity ratio.

The financial strategy of a company is expressed by its **debt-to-equity ratio.** If a company has a debt-to-equity ratio of one-to-one (expressed as 1:1), this means that for every dollar of its debt the company has one dollar of assets.

$$\frac{\text{Debt}}{\text{Equity}} = \text{Debt-to-equity ratio}$$

Another ratio that gives a picture of financial strategy is the **debt ratio**—the ratio of debt to assets. A debt ratio of .50 means that every dollar of assets is financed by 50 cents of debt and 50 cents of equity.

$$\frac{\text{Amount of debt}}{\text{Amount of assets}} = \text{Debt ratio}$$

Example:

$$\frac{0.50}{1.00} = 0.50$$

Whether a ratio is good or bad depends on the amount of debt considered acceptable in a given industry. In general, however, companies with lower debt ratios are considered more solvent because they have fewer creditors if they go bankrupt.

DONALD TRUMP: THE DANGERS OF HEAVY DEBT FINANCING

Companies that rely heavily on debt financing are described as "highly **leveraged.**" Leveraged means financed with debt. This financial strategy works well only when business is very good. When business is slow, debt payments are more difficult to meet.

Reliance solely on debt is very dangerous for a company. Creditors can force the company into bankruptcy or take over company property.

Businesses sometimes are in this position because the business owner has been unwilling to give up any control of the company by issuing equity and has relied too heavily on debt financing.

Real estate tycoon Donald Trump made exactly this mistake in the 1980s. Trump invested millions of dollars in revitalization of Atlantic City's gambling strip. He also bought New York's landmark Plaza Hotel and built Trump Tower, a skyscraper of ultraluxurious apartments purchased by oil sheiks and movie stars. As you'll see when we take a closer look at Trump's financing strategy on page 227, by 1988 Trump owned some very valuable properties. He was also deeply in debt, however.

Trump did not want to give up managerial control by selling stock when he needed to raise money to build a new casino or buy a hotel. Because of his reputation, banks were willing to lend him a great deal of money. The lender banks took several of Trump's important assets and properties when the economy took a downturn in the late 1980s and he couldn't make his loan payments. Trump was forced by the banks to sell off his airline, Trump Shuttle, and some of his casinos. By pruning his real estate holdings and paying off some of his debt, Trump has been able to make a comeback in the 1990s.

STEVEN JOBS: LOSING CONTROL OF APPLE

Relying too heavily on equity can also be the downfall of a business owner. Steve Jobs, co-founder of Apple Computer, made that mistake. Because Jobs and his partner, Stephen Wozniak, were young men with very little money, debt financing was out of their reach. To raise money, they sold off chunks of the company.

By the late 1980s, Apple was very successful—so successful that Jobs was able to hire a prominent Pepsico executive, John Sculley, to take over as Apple's chief executive. Unfortunately for Jobs, Sculley set out to convince Apple's board of directors that Jobs was a disruptive influence on the company. Eventually, a vote was taken. The number of votes each shareholder had was related to the number of shares he or she owned. Jobs didn't own enough of Apple's equity to fight off Sculley's effort to fire him. He was outvoted and thrown out of the company he had started.

EVALUATING DONALD TRUMP'S FINANCING STRATEGY

Below is Donald Trump's balance sheet (in millions) as of December 31, 1988.[1] Calculate the debt ratios for each of his properties, then answer questions 1 through 7.

| Assets | Millions of Dollars | | | |
	Estimated Worth of Assets	Debt	Net Worth	Debt Ratio*
Taj Mahal	$834	$834	$ 0	1
West Side Yards	480	172	308	_____
Trump Plaza Casino	637	273	364	_____
Trump Casino	606	410	196	_____
Trump Shuttle	400	400	0	_____
Trump Tower	200	100	100	_____
Cash	130	157	−27	_____
Trump Condos	111	6	105	_____
Marketable securities	88	75	13	_____
Trump Palace	77	77	0	_____
Trump Plaza	70	48	22	_____
Grand Hyatt (50%)	70	30	40	_____
Trump Regency	63	85	−22	_____
Trump Plaza Co-ops	46	0	46	_____
Trump Air	41	0	41	_____
Personal transportation	37	0	37	_____
Personal housing	30	39	−9	_____
Total	$____	$____	$____	_____

*Debt ratio $= \dfrac{\text{Debt}}{\text{Estimated worth of assets}}$

1. What was Trump's highest-priced asset?

2. What was Trump's net worth for the Trump Shuttle? Why?

3. On which asset was Trump's net worth the greatest?

4. Which asset carried the most debt?

5. Which properties did Trump own free of debt?

6. On which properties did Trump owe one dollar of debt for each dollar of the asset?

7. Why do you think Trump separately incorporated each of his properties?

ANSWERS: EVALUATING DONALD TRUMP'S FINANCING STRATEGY

The debt ratios for each of Donald Trump's properties as of December 31, 1988, were:

| Assets | Millions of Dollars | | | |
	Estimated Worth of Assets	Debt	Net Worth	Debt Ratio*
Taj Mahal	$ 834	$ 834	$ 0	1.00
West Side Yards	480	172	308	.42
Trump Plaza Casino	637	273	364	.44
Trump Casino	606	410	196	.68
Trump Shuttle	400	400	0	1.00
Trump Tower	200	100	100	.50
Cash	130	157	−27	1.20
Trump Condos	111	6	105	.05
Marketable securities	88	75	13	.85
Trump Palace	77	77	0	1.00
Trump Plaza	70	48	22	.66
Grand Hyatt (50%)	70	30	40	.43
Trump Regency	63	85	−22	1.35
Trump Plaza Co-ops	46	0	46	0
Trump Air	41	0	41	0
Personal transportation	37	0	37	0
Personal housing	30	39	−9	1.30
Total	**$3,920**	**$2,706**	**$508**	**.69**

*Debt ratio = $\dfrac{\text{Debt}}{\text{Estimated worth of assets}}$

1. Highest-priced asset: The Taj Mahal.

2. The net worth for the Trump Shuttle was zero because it was financed completely with debt.

3. Asset with greatest net worth: Trump Plaza Casino.

4. Asset with most debt: The Taj Mahal.

5. Properties owned free of debt: Trump Plaza Co-ops, Trump Air, personal transportation.

6. Properties with dollar-for-dollar debt: The Taj Mahal, Trump Shuttle, Trump Palace.

7. Trump separately incorporated each of his properties in order to protect them from creditors. His creditors on The Taj Mahal, for example, could not force him to sell Trump Air to pay them. They could only force him to sell The Taj Mahal.

CASE STUDY: HOME-BAKED GOODS

Business for the Young Entrepreneur

Debbi Fields, of Mrs. Fields Cookies, Inc., built a multimillion-dollar business from cookies. Do you bake anything really well? Cookies? Banana bread? You can sell your home-baked goods at flea markets, garage sales, or school events.

When Fields was nineteen, she married an older man who was a brilliant economist. Being the wife of an older man who was getting a lot of attention for his career made Fields want to accomplish something, too. Fields had baked her popular chocolate chip cookies for friends and families since she was thirteen, so she decided to start a business selling her cookies to the public.

No one—not her family, not her friends, not even her husband—thought this was a good idea. Her cookies were soft and chewy, not crisp like store brands. They needed to be eaten fresh to taste their best.

Fields refused to abandon her idea, so her husband decided to give her his full support, even though he thought it would never work. The banker who had given her and her husband the mortgage on their house arranged a loan. He, too, told her that her business would never work, but he trusted the Fields to pay back the loan.

Fields opened a small store in Palo Alto, California, in August 1977. On her first day of business she hadn't sold a single cookie by noon. Trying not to panic, Fields loaded up a tray with cookies and walked around the shopping arcade offering them to shoppers for free.

Her strategy worked: within an hour, customers were at her store buying cookies. She sold $50.00 worth that day and $75.00 worth the next. She was in business and she had discovered a strategy. To this day, Mrs. Fields stores give customers free samples to encourage them to buy cookies.

The business grew rapidly, but most of the profits were earmarked to pay off bank loans used to open new stores. Despite her success, Fields constantly had to fight for financing from the banks. Again and again she was told that selling cookies was not a "real" business like selling steel or cars.

In 1986, her husband quit doing economic consulting and joined her business. Although the company was now profitable, bank loans were still needed to open new stores. The Fieldses were very tired of dealing with bankers so they set out to try to replace their debt financing with equity financing. They decided to sell shares in the company to the public and use the cash to pay off the banks and finance further expansion.

The Fieldses sold stock on the London Stock Exchange's unlisted securities market first, because this approach was easier and cheaper than selling stock on the American market. The stock was offered in London in the spring of 1986. It did not do well at first because the company was not that well known in Britain, but eventually the stock price did improve.

When the stock was offered in the United States the following year, it did very well. Today, Mrs. Fields Cookies is financed with a blend of debt and equity. The Fieldses have more flexibility than when they relied exclusively on debt financing.

Tips for Starting a Business with Home-Baked Goods

- Don't get too elaborate. Stick to one or two products that you can consistently make really well.

- Figure out your cost of goods sold—the cost of making one additional unit (your unit might be one cookie or one cake, for example). Set your price high enough to cover your cost of goods sold and your labor.

- Offer a baking service to busy families. Make up a flyer that advertises your service. You could offer to supply fifty cookies a week, for example.

- Buy ingredients in bulk at warehouse or grocery club stores. Bulk purchases are cheaper.

- Make your baked goods extra-irresistible by packaging them attractively. Tie a yellow ribbon around banana bread, or sell cookies in colorful boxes. Make up batches of special items around holidays—green cookies for St. Patrick's Day, or heart-shaped cakes for St. Valentine's Day.

- Give away samples to attract customers.

These tips also apply to businesses selling homemade soups, jams, and jellies, or any other food item you might make that people really like.

RESOURCES

Books

A particularly good book on creative entrepreneurship financing is *Guerrilla Financing: Alternative Techniques to Finance Any Small Business* by Bruce Brechman and Jay Conrad-Levinson (Boston: Houghton Mifflin, 1991).

Another excellent resource is *Money Sources for Small Business: How You Can Find Private, State, Federal, and Corporate Financing* by William Alarid (Santa Maria, CA: Puma Press, 1991).

If you'd like to learn more about Donald Trump's flamboyant career, look for *The Art of the Deal* (New York: Random House, 1988), and *Surviving at the Top* (New York: Random House, 1990).

Debbi Fields tells her story in *One Smart Cookie* (New York: Simon & Schuster, 1987).

Other Resources

The National Association of Small Business Investment Companies is an association of companies that give financial assistance to small businesses. A membership directory is available for $1.00.

National Association of Small Business Investment Companies
1156 15th Street, N.W., Suite 1101
Washington, DC 20005
(202) 833-8230

18 FROM THE WHOLESALER TO THE FLEA MARKET

Commerce is the great civilizer. We exchange ideas when we exchange goods.

—R. G. Ingersoll (1833–1899)
American lawyer

Chrissie had no room for a dog or cat in the basement apartment she lived in with her little girl, so she bought a fish. This gave the NFTE student the idea for a business she calls "The Best Pet." Chrissie brought home some brandy snifters from the distribution house for which she worked. She filled each snifter with colored sand and added a fish that matched the color of the sand.

Chrissie took ten of her "Best Pets" to the flea market that her class was participating in at the Mall of America, in Minnesota. To her surprise, she sold all ten and received orders for four more. Today, Chrissie sells ten to twenty Best Pets a week while she attends technical college. Between attending college and taking care of her child, Chrissie can devote only a few hours a week to her business, but she estimates that those few hours bring her about four times more income than she would earn from a part-time job. Best of all, Chrissie can make her Best Pets while she's home with her daughter.

A flea market is a great place for a budding entrepreneur to test-market a product and launch a business. This chapter outlines how to buy goods from a wholesaler and resell them for a profit at a flea market. This experience will allow you to practice many concepts you have studied so far, including salesmanship, negotiation, and the preparation of an income statement.

FINDING A WHOLESALER

Wholesalers buy goods in large quantities from manufacturers and sell those goods in smaller quantities to retailers. If you live in a city, there will be wholesale stores close enough for you to visit in person. Find them by looking through your local *Business-to-Business Directory*. This is a Yellow Pages publication in which businesses advertise the products and services they offer to other businesses.

If you live in a small town or rural area that has no wholesale suppliers nearby, pick the major city nearest you and look in its *Business-to-Business Directory*. You can call wholesalers whose products interest you and order goods from them through the mail.

In addition, NFTE is launching a wholesale catalog and mail-order business called NFTE On Broadway. Entrepreneurs who don't live near a wholesale district can use the catalog to order products for resale. The business is run by NFTE students, overseen by Janet McKinstry Cort and Lou Sussan of NFTE. The catalog includes a variety of products from New York City's wholesale district. All products are marked up only slightly from the original wholesale price. Young entrepreneurs will also be able to advertise their products in the catalog.

Another way to locate wholesalers is to contact manufacturers' representatives. To do so, write to or call the Manufacturers' Agents National Association. It can direct you to wholesalers in your area that carry the products you are seeking.

Manufacturers' Agents National Association
23016 Millcreek Road
Laguna Hills, CA 92653
(714) 859-4040

Most major product lines (lingerie, candy, and so on) have trade associations located in Washington, DC. These associations are listed in the Washington phone book and will be happy to tell you about wholesalers in your area. Most public libraries have phone books from around the country in their reference sections.

SELLING AT THE FLEA MARKET

A flea market is an open-air market made up of entrepreneurs who rent space by the day or by the season. The space may be free, on a first-come, first-served basis. More often, there is a fee for renting a space.

Traditionally, prices at flea markets are low. Consumers shopping at flea markets are looking for bargains.

You can get a list of flea markets in any community by calling the local Chamber of Commerce.

Rule of Thumb

> ## FLEA MARKET SALES RULES
>
> 1. **Arrive early to get a spot where as many people as possible will see your merchandise.**
>
> 2. **Have plenty of business cards and flyers to give away, even to people who don't buy anything.**
>
> 3. **Display posters or other eye-catching advertisements.**
>
> 4. **Bring plenty of change.**
>
> 5. **Keep track of your merchandise on inventory/record sheets.**
>
> 6. **Write a sales receipt for every sale.**
>
> 7. **Put on your "sales personality"—be outgoing and friendly.**

INVENTORY SHEETS

Use an inventory sheet to keep track of the sales you make at the flea market. An inventory sheet also shows at a glance how much profit you made on each sale. This record will make it easy to prepare an income statement for your flea market day.

Inventory sheets also keep track of the markup—the difference between what you paid for an item and the amount you get when you sell it—on each unit you sell. Markup is expressed as a percentage. To calculate markup, divide the wholesale cost per unit into the gross profit per unit and multiply by 100:

$$\text{Markup} = \frac{\text{Gross profit per unit}}{\text{Wholesale cost per unit}} \times 100$$

Chart 16 shows a sample inventory sheet. Notice how easily the income statement falls out of the information on the inventory sheet.

FLEA MARKET INVENTORY SHEET (SAMPLE)

Product	A $\times$ Units Sold (make mark for each sale)	B Wholesale Cost Per Unit	C = Total Cost of Goods Sold	D Selling Price Per Unit	E (A $\times$ D) Total Sales
Hat	IIII	$9.00	$45.00	$15.00	$75.00
Lipstick	IIII I	.50	3.00	2.00	12.00

MY INCOME STATEMENT

My total sales are:	$87.00	($75.00 + $12.00)
My total cost of goods sold is:	48.00	($45.00 + $ 3.00)
My gross profit is:	$39.00	($87.00 − $48.00)
My operating costs are:		
My fixed costs are:	$4.00	
My variable costs are:	0	$ 4.00
My net profit/(loss) is:	$35.00	($39.00 − $4.00)

Chart 16   Flea Market Inventory Sheet and Income Statement

Remember: This information is for your eyes alone. Never place your records where your customers can see them.

TRADE SHOWS

Another great opportunity to sell is the trade show. A trade show is, in essence, an industry-specific flea market. Trade shows are usually run by industry or artist associations. For entrepreneurs who can't afford to—or don't want to—open their own stores, a trade show is an excellent way to show products off to store buyers.

Sue Scott[1] is a sculptor who made her living working in galleries, but really wanted to support herself with her art. She never thought of herself as the entrepreneurial type, but knew she was unhappy with her life. One day she experimented with putting a light in one of her sculptures. She was so taken with the result that she decided to go into business designing lights. Scott used her credit cards for capital to make samples of her novelty lights.

Scott named her company Primal Lite and went to trade shows to display her samples. Ninety-five sales representatives across the country snapped up her line of dinosaur, fried egg, lizard, and other lights. Today, Primal Lite's annual sales are almost $10 million.

To find out about trade shows in your area, call your local civic center. A schedule of upcoming trade shows should be available there. To learn about important trade shows in major cities, check out trade publications. Your public library should have a list of trade publications that you can contact. Local wholesalers and trade associations may also be able to direct you to information about trade shows nationwide.

CASE STUDY: PET CARE

Business for the Young Entrepreneur

Believe it or not, some very profitable businesses have been built around animal waste. In *Fast Cash for Kids,* Bonnie and Noel Drew report that Richard Scott started a "pooper scooper" business in Seattle. Richard launched Dog Butler when he was twenty-four. Four of his employees pick up waste from 500 dogs at 160 homes and kennels. He charges each client $22 per month. That adds up to revenues of $11,000 per month!

If you love animals, there are lots of money-making services you can offer. Here are some ideas:

- **Dog walker.** Many people are too busy to walk their dogs every day. But you could walk several dogs at one time! Is there a dog run in your neighborhood park? Arrange to take several neighborhood dogs to the dog run each afternoon. This is a good way to meet more busy dog owners who might need your service!

- **Cleaning aquariums.** Fish tanks are beautiful but require regular cleaning and care. This service requires some knowledge about caring for fish. A fish tank is a delicate environment. If disturbed by the wrong chemicals, fish can die. This is a good business idea, therefore, only if you already love fish and are willing to learn to take care of tanks. You will need to know how to clean both freshwater and saltwater tanks. You will also need cleaning supplies and fish food.

- **Pet sitter.** You can take care of pets for people who are on vacation. Before accepting a job, though, go to the home and meet the pet. Make sure it's an animal you feel comfortable handling by yourself. Before the owners leave, ask how to contact them in an emergency. You should also get the phone number and address of the animal's veterinarian.

- **Pet grooming.** If you love to play with animals, pet grooming can be fun and profitable. Cats and dogs need regular baths and flea treatments. If you have a good pair of clippers and have learned to use them correctly, you can also offer haircuts for dogs. Veterinarians usually offer free booklets on care and grooming of pets. A veterinarian or pet store can direct you to the safest bath and flea products to use.

RESOURCES

Book

A great primer on how to enjoy selling (and buying) at flea markets is *The Flea Market Handbook* by Robert G. Miner (Rudner, PA: Chilton Book Company, 1990).

Other Resources

To familiarize yourself with the trade show universe, check out *Trade Show Week Magazine.* Contact:

Trade Show Week Magazine
249 West 17th Street
New York, NY 10011
(800) 826-7887

19

KEEPING YOUR MONEY SAFE

YOUR BANK ACCOUNT AND YOUR RELATIONSHIP WITH YOUR BANKER

Put not your trust in money, but put your money in trust.
—Dr. Oliver Wendell Holmes (1809–1894)
American writer and physician

PUT YOUR MONEY IN A SAFE PLACE

Every evening, after he finished his shift at a neighborhood supermarket, Damon would tend to his remote control car repair business. The small, brightly colored cars were extremely popular with children in Damon's neighborhood on Manhattan's Lower East Side. He repaired about twenty cars a week and charged $6 per repair. Damon didn't have a bank account because he didn't think he needed one. He cashed his supermarket check at a local check cashing office and conducted his car repair business entirely in cash. It wasn't until he was mugged and lost an entire week's earnings from his business that Damon decided to get a bank account.

Once you start making money with your own small business, you will need a safe place to put your earnings. When you have a bank account, you have a safe place to store your money. People who do not have bank accounts have to carry all their money around at all times or hide it where they live. Both solutions are risky and dangerous. Your money is safer in a bank.

Bank deposits are protected by the Federal Deposit Insurance Corporation. Individual accounts are protected up to $100,000—even if the bank fails.

Banks offer two basic kinds of accounts: (1) savings accounts and (2) checking accounts.

DEVELOP A GOOD RELATIONSHIP WITH A BANKER

Banks are a major source of business financing. You should begin a relationship with a banker early in your business career. One of my students opened a bank account when she started her lingerie business during her senior year in high school. Tanya bought lingerie from wholesalers and sold it at parties she threw for friends.

Tanya introduced herself to the manager of her bank and kept him up to date on her business as it developed. As a result, the manager recommended that she apply for a $4,000 college scholarship the bank planned to award to a local high school senior. Tanya won the scholarship, largely because she had such positive recommendations from the bank manager and other adults she had met while conducting her business. If she ever needs a loan to expand her business, she probably won't have too much trouble getting approval from her bank.

In *How to Get a Business Loan Without Signing Your Life Away* (Englewood Cliffs: Prentice-Hall, 1990), best-selling entrepreneurship author Joe Mancuso says: "I recommend that you make your banker your best friend; in fact, start to think of him as the key person in your company. When you think about it, you will realize that your banker is really the key to building a good company, but too many of us do a poor job of cultivating this crucial relationship."[1]

SELLING ART LIKE TUPPERWARE: ARTISTIC IMPRESSIONS

Some people don't start their first business until they've tired of their career—but when they do, they find out how important their banker can be. Bart Breighner had spent twenty years with World Book, where he set many sales records and became executive vice president.

Breighner's hobby was collecting art, so he heard about companies that were selling original oil paintings and prints to customers through home parties. He became intrigued with the idea of entering this business but doing it on a much broader scale. He wanted to make a wider variety of art available and become the dominant company in the industry.

To finance his dream, Breighner went to his banker, who helped Breighner mortgage his house and raise over a million dollars in debt. Breighner signed personally for the debt. He also cashed in his children's college funds. In other words, he was taking a big risk because he hoped to reap a big reward.

Breighner started Artistic Impressions, Inc. in 1985. Today, the company's annual sales are roughly $20 million. Instead of just hiring salespeople, Breighner taps into the entrepreneurial dream by hiring people who want to own and build their own businesses. He understands that people are motivated by ownership. Over 1,350 art consultants in 42 states sell art for Artistic Impressions. Breighner, who serves on NFTE's board of directors, has received national recognition from the Direct Selling Association for his efforts to encourage women and minorities to join his company. A big believer in entrepreneurship, Breighner and his consultants hold benefit art auctions for NFTE, donate a portion of their sales to us, hold a NFTE "Walk-A-Thon" and co-sponsor our Chicago program.

SAVINGS ACCOUNTS

The very first bank account you will need is a **savings account.** When you deposit money in a savings account, not only is the money safe, but the bank pays you interest. The rate of return is low compared to some other investments, but there is virtually no risk that you will lose your money. A savings account is a low-risk, low-yield investment.

Banks make their profits by taking the money of their depositors and lending it. Compared to the amount they pay on the deposits, the banks receive a higher interest rate on the money they lend out.

A savings account also provides you with **liquidity.** Liquidity is the ease with which you can retrieve your savings as cash. You can withdraw your money anytime from a savings account without having to pay the bank anything. Many savings banks offer 24-hour cash machines.

To open your savings account, visit your local bank and bring along the money you wish to deposit. Bring your Social Security card. You will also need identification with your photo on it, such as a driver's license, state ID, or passport.

Rule of Thumb

Develop the good habit of always depositing 10 percent of your income in a savings account.

CHECKING ACCOUNTS

Paying by check, not cash, is the professional way to do business. It is safer to carry checks instead of cash. When you write a check, you are authorizing the bank to pay someone from your account.

Each month, the bank sends you a statement, along with the checks the bank has paid. These canceled checks provide you with proof that you have paid your bills. Don't discard them for at least seven years.

Shop around carefully before you decide where to keep your **checking account.** Different banks have different costs and requirements. Some demand that you keep a large minimum balance in your account. Others require a minimum balance for you to write checks for free. If your balance is lower, the bank charges you a fee for each check. Look into what different banks offer. Choose the checking account that best suits your needs or you could wind up paying expensive bank charges.

THE CHECK

Chart 17 shows a typical check. The circled numbers correspond to these explanations:

1. Your name and address. These lines will be preprinted on your blank checks by the bank.

2. Bank number and branch number.

3. Check number—also preprinted on the checks. Always use your checks in numerical order.

4. Date you made the check out to someone.

5. Payee—the person or business to whom the check was written.

6. The amount of the check in numbers. Be sure to start the amount right next to the dollar sign so no one can sneak in another number.

7. The amount of dollars in words and the amount of cents as a fraction of 100. Fifty cents would be written as 50/100. Start writing at the beginning of the line. Draw a line to fill any space left after you have written the amount. These steps will prevent another person from altering the check. If the amount

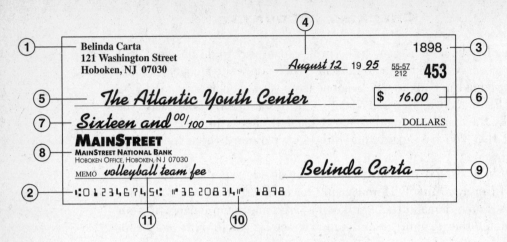

Chart 17   The Key Parts of a Check

written in numbers differs from the amount written in words, the bank will pay the amount written in words.

8. Drawee—your bank branch.

9. Drawer—you. The check is no good unless you sign here.

10. Electronic scanning number used by the bank to process your check.

11. Memo—you don't have to fill this in for the check to be valid, but it's a good place to write a note to yourself as a reminder of the purpose of the check.

DEPOSITING YOUR MONEY

To deposit money—cash or checks—in your checking account, fill out a deposit slip like the one in Chart 18. Simply write in the amounts of each item and the date. You don't need to sign it.

You do, however, need to sign the back of any checks you wish to deposit and write your account number on them. Your signature on the back of the check is called an endorsement. Underneath your endorsement and the account number, write "for deposit only," so no one can try to cash the check. Chart 19 shows a completed endorsement.

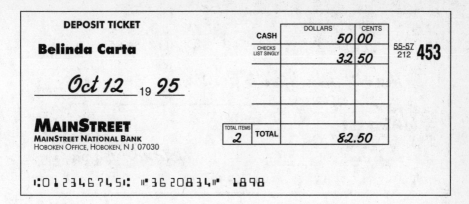

Chart 18   A Deposit Slip for Placing Cash and Checks into Your Checking Account

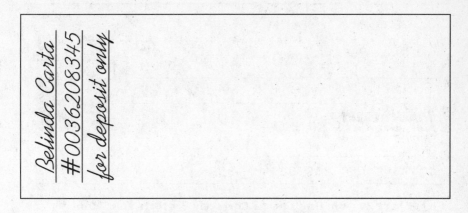

Chart 19   An Endorsed Check

WRITING A CHECK

Study the sample in the top portion of Chart 20. Then fill out the bottom check. Pretend you are paying a $37.50 phone bill to New Jersey Bell.

Before you write any checks, be sure you have enough money in your account to pay out the amount of the check. If any of your checks are rejected by your bank for having "not sufficient funds" (NSF), you will be charged a fee. If you are frequently listed as having NSF, it could negatively affect your chances to get a bank loan from your bank or any other.

1898

August 12 19 95 $\frac{55\text{-}57}{212}$ **453**

The Atlantic Youth Center $ 16.00

Sixteen and 00/100 —————————————— DOLLARS

MainStreet
MainStreet National Bank
Hoboken Office, Hoboken, N J 07030
MEMO *choir dues*   *Yolanda Baxter*

⑈012346745⑈ ⑈3620834⑈ 1898

1899

_____ 19___ $\frac{55\text{-}57}{212}$ **453**

$

—————————————————— DOLLARS

MainStreet
MainStreet National Bank
Hoboken Office, Hoboken, N J 07030
MEMO _____

⑈012346745⑈ ⑈3620834⑈ 1899

Chart 20   Writing Checks Correctly Protects Your Money

**Business
for the Young
Entrepreneur**

CASE STUDY: MESSENGER SERVICE

NFTE Solutions, Inc. is a nonprofit organization established by Maximo Blake-DeCastro in the South Bronx, in January 1993, with support from NFTE and seed funding from the J. M. Foundation. Blake-DeCastro is well known for successfully putting high-risk youth to work and teaching them valuable job skills. Before founding his company, he trained New York State prison system convicts in building renovation and contracting.

When Max and I met, we realized there was a lot we could accomplish together. We started by providing his workers with an entrepreneurship education. Some of our students, in turn, are learning renovation and contracting from Max. In addition, NFTE Solutions is building storefronts equipped with office furniture and equipment that it has salvaged. Our goal is for NFTE students to be able to move their new businesses into these "business incubators."

NFTE Solutions, Inc. runs three businesses with six young people aged 18 to 23:

1. Renovation/Contracting—low-cost housing and office alterations for nonprofits, government agencies, and commercial properties.
2. Recycling—used office furniture, computers, books, and surplus construction materials are repaired and used on NFTE Solutions renovations.
3. Messenger service—packages are delivered on foot and by bicycle transport throughout upper Manhattan.

The messenger service was started because so many recycling and renovation customers in Harlem and the South Bronx complained that there was inadequate messenger service to upper Manhattan. Most messenger services concentrate on the downtown Wall Street area or on midtown Manhattan.

Is there a part of your community that could use a messenger service but is not being served by existing companies? If you're fast on your feet or your bicycle and know your way around town, you could start a messenger service, too. Offer your service to local businesses and offices. Let them know what hours you can be available—from 3:30 P.M. to 6 P.M. on weekdays, for example. NFTE Solutions charges a flat fee for a delivery anywhere in Manhattan. Set your fee to reflect what you think your market is willing to pay.

What You'll Need to Get Started

- Waterproof knapsack for carrying items to be delivered.
- Receipt book. When you deliver an item, always have the person who takes it sign for it. Bring the receipt back to the person who ordered the delivery. It is proof that you brought the package to the correct person or company.
- Maps. Carry street maps, subway maps, bus maps, and so on in your knapsack.

- A reliable watch.
- If you're using a bicycle, a current license.

Tips

- Make flyers advertising your service. Put them up in office buildings, gyms, or stores. Leave one with each person who accepts a delivery.
- Start looking for customers by asking your parents or your parents' friends if they work in a company or a part of town that might need your messenger service.

RESOURCES

Books

These books explain how banks borrow and lend money and how compound interest works:

Capitalism for Kids by Karl Hess (Chicago: Dearborn Financial Publishing, 1992).

Making Cents: Every Kid's Guide to Money by Elizabeth Wilkinson (Boston: Little, Brown & Co., 1989).

What You Need to Know About Taxes

20

To tax and to please, no more than to love and to be wise,
is not given to men.

—Edmund Burke (1729–1797)
Irish philosopher and statesman

Your Legal Obligation as a Successful Business Owner

Paying taxes is the last thing a struggling new business owner may want to think about. Neglecting your taxes, however, may cost you not only your business, but your business career.

David opened a small café near a college when he was twenty-two. He didn't set up his accounting system or apply for a tax ID number right away. He figured he'd have more time to do it once he got the business off the ground. Unfortunately, after his business had been open a few months, the Internal Revenue Service (IRS) did a spot check and found that he was not collecting sales tax. The IRS closed his business and put liens on his personal assets. This meant the IRS could seize his personal belongings and sell them if David did not pay his tax bill. This derailed David's business career before he had gotten a firm start.

A **tax** is the percentage of your gross profit or income that you are required by law to pay to the government. The government uses taxes to support schools, the military, police and fire departments, and many other public services.

Most states impose an income tax. City and other local governments are supported primarily by taxes on property. The federal government is financed by personal and corporate income taxes.

SALES TAX

States usually raise money from a **sales tax** on the sale of goods (but not services). The sales tax is a percentage of the cost of the item sold and is included in the amount paid. In New York State, the sales tax is 8.25 percent. Tax on a $10.00 item is $0.83, so the total paid by the consumer is $10.83.

A SOLE PROPRIETOR PAYS INCOME TAX AND SELF-EMPLOYMENT TAX

You may already be paying income tax if you have a job. If your small business earns more than $400 a year, you will have to pay self-employment tax on your business income.

Income Tax

Tax forms are available at your local post office or bank. Forms can also be ordered from the Internal Revenue Service (IRS), which is the federal government agency responsible for collecting federal taxes. The IRS can charge you penalties and even put you in jail for **tax evasion,** if you fail to file tax returns.

    You can call the IRS at 1-800-829-3676 to order forms. Your forms must be filed—sent to the IRS with your payment—by April 15th each year.

Form 1040EZ

You will probably want to use Form 1040EZ for filing your income tax return. It is the simplest tax form to complete (see Chart 21). To qualify for Form 1040EZ, you must:

- Be single and younger than 65.
- Have only one dependent (yourself) or be claimed as a dependent by your parents.
- Earn less than $50,000 gross income.
- Earn less than $400 in interest income.

Department of the Treasury - Internal Revenue Service

Form 1040EZ

Income Tax Return for Single and Joint Filers With No Dependents 1995

OMB No. 1545-0675

Use the IRS label
(See page 11.)
Otherwise, please print.

L A B E L   H E R E

Print your name (first, initial, last)

If a joint return, print spouse's name (first, initial, last)

Home address (number and street). If you have a P.O. box, see page 12.   Apt. no.

City, town or post office, state and ZIP code. If you have a foreign address, see page 12.

Your social security number

Spouse's social security number

See instructions on page 2 and in Form 1040EZ booklet.

Presidential Election Campaign
(See page 12.)

Note: Checking "Yes" will not change your tax or reduce your refund.

Do you want $3 to go to this fund? ▶

If a joint return, does your spouse want $3 to go to this fund? ▶

Yes No

Income

Attach Copy B of Form(s) W-2 here. Enclose, but do not attach, any payment with your return.

Note: You **must** check Yes or No.

1 Total wages, salaries, and tips. This should be shown in box 1 of your W-2 form(s). Attach your W-2 form(s).   1

2 Taxable interest income of $400 or less. If the total is over $400, you cannot use Form 1040EZ.   2

3 Add lines 1 and 2. This is your **adjusted gross income.** If less than $9,000, see page 15 to find out if you can claim the earned income credit on line 7.   3

4 Can your parents (or someone else) claim you on their return?
☐ **Yes.** Do worksheet on page 2; enter amount from line G here.
☐ **No.** If **single,** enter 6,250.00. If **married,** enter 11,250.00. For an explanation of these amounts, see page 2 of form.   4

5 Subtract line 4 from line 3. If line 4 is larger than line 3, enter 0. This is your **taxable income.** ▶   5

Dollars Cents

Payments and tax

6 Enter your Federal income tax withheld from box 2 of your W-2 form(s).   6

7 **Earned income credit** (see page 15). Enter type and amount of nontaxable earned income below.
Type $ 7

8 Add lines 6 and 7 (don't include nontaxable earned income). These are your **total payments.**   8

9 **Tax.** Use the amount on **line 5** to find your tax in the tax table on pages 28-32 of the booklet. Then, enter the tax from the table on this line.   9

Refund or amount you owe

10 If line 8 is larger than line 9, subtract line 9 from line 8. This is your **refund.**   10

11 If line 9 is larger than line 8, subtract line 8 from line 9. This is the **amount you owe.** See page 20 for details on how to pay and what to write on your payment.   11

Sign your return

Keep a copy of this form for your records.

I have read this return. Under penalties of perjury, I declare that to the best of my knowledge and belief, the return is true, correct, and accurately lists all amounts and sources of income I received during the tax year.

Your signature

Spouse's signature if joint return

Date Your occupation

Date Spouse's occupation

For IRS Use Only -- Please do not write in boxes below.

For Privacy Act and Paperwork Reduction Act Notice, see instructions.

H807

Form **1040EZ** (1995)

Chart 21   Use This Form to File Your Income Tax Return Before April 15

Self-Employment Tax (Schedule SE)

When you work for an employer, the employer pays into your Social Security fund 7.65 percent of whatever your income is. When you retire or are disabled and can no longer work, your employers' contributions to your Social Security fund allow you to receive an amount each month.

The federal government takes another 7.65 percent out of your earnings, as your contribution to your own Social Security fund. Between your contributions and those of your employer, your Social Security fund is paid 15.3 percent of your income each year.

If you are self-employed—running your own business, for instance—there is no employer to make Social Security contributions. You must make up the difference by paying self-employment tax. If you have net income from self-employment of over $400 a year, you are required to pay 15.3 percent of your business income to Social Security as self-employment tax. The tax form, shown in Chart 22, is called Schedule SE.

Profit or Loss from Business (Schedule C)

In addition to self-employment tax, you will pay income tax on your entrepreneurship income. You will file that income using Schedule C, Profit or Loss from Business. The form is shown in Chart 23.

THE IRS CAN HELP

The tax code is very complex. The IRS offers booklets and telephone service to help answer questions. Help with the Form 1040 is available from 1-800-424-1040. You can also go to the IRS office in your town and meet with an IRS agent who will guide you through the forms for free. You must obtain new forms and booklets each year. Rules, rates, and forms change from one year to the next.

HELP YOURSELF BY KEEPING GOOD RECORDS

You can make filing your taxes easier by keeping good records throughout the year. You will have to determine your net income. If you ha

SCHEDULE SE (Form 1040) Department of the Treasury Internal Revenue Service	**Self–Employment Tax** ▶ See Instructions for Schedule SE (Form 1040). ▶ Attach to Form 1040.	OMB No. 1545-0074 **1995** Attachment Sequence No. **17**
Name of person with **self-employment** income (as shown on Form 1040)		Social security number of person with **self-employment** income ▶

Who Must File Schedule SE

You must file Schedule SE if:

- You had net earnings from self-employment from other than church employee income (line 4 of Short Schedule SE or line 4c of Long Schedule SE) of $400 or more, **OR**
- You had church employee income of $108.28 or more. Income from services you performed as a minister or a member of a religious order is not church employee income. See page SE-1.

Note: Even if you have a loss or a small amount of income from self-employment, it may be to your benefit to file Schedule SE and use either "optional method" in Part II of Long Schedule SE. See page SE-2.

Exception. If your only self-employment income was from earnings as a minister, member of a religious order, or Christian Science practitioner, **and** you filed Form 4361 and received IRS approval not to be taxed on those earnings, **do not** file Schedule SE. Instead, write "Exempt-Form 4361" on Form 1040, line 47.

May I Use Short Schedule SE or MUST I Use Long Schedule SE?

Section A--Short Schedule SE. Caution: Read above to see if you can use Short Schedule SE.

1	Net farm profit or (loss) from Schedule F, line 36, and farm partnerships, Schedule K-1 (Form 1065), line 15a	**1**
2	Net profit or (loss) from Schedule C, line 31; Schedule C-EZ, line 3; and Schedule K-1 (Form 1065), line 15a (other than farming). Ministers and members of religious orders see page SE-1 for amounts to report on this line. See page SE-2 for other income to report	**2**
3	Combine lines 1 and 2.	**3**
4	**Net earnings from self-employment.** Multiply line 3 by 92.35% (.9235). If less than $400, **do not** file this schedule; you do not owe self-employment tax . . . . ▶	**4**
5	**Self-employment tax.** If the amount on line 4 is:	
	• $60,600 or less, multiply line 4 by 15.3% (.153). Enter the result here and on **Form 1040, line 47.**	
	• More than $60,600, multiply line 4 by 2.9% (.029). Then, add $7,514.40 to the result. Enter the total here and on **Form 1040, line 47.**	**5**
6	**Deduction for one-half of self-employment tax.** Multiply line 5 by 50% (.5). Enter the result here and on **Form 1040, line 25.** **6**	

For Paperwork Reduction Act Notice, see Form 1040 instructions.

H807

Schedule SE (Form 1040) 1995

Chart 22   As a Self-Employed Entrepreneur, You File
Your Social Security Tax on Schedule SE

Schedule SE (Form 1040) 1995   Attachment Sequence No. **17**   Page **2**

Name of person with **self-employment** income (as shown on Form 1040)	Social security number of person with **self-employment income** ▶

Section B—Long Schedule SE

Part I Self-Employment Tax

Note: If your only income subject to self-employment tax is church employee income, skip lines 1 through 4b. Enter -0- on line 4c and go to line 5a. Income from services you performed as a minister or a member of a religious order is **not** church employee income. See page SE-1.

A If you are a minister, member of a religious order, or Christian Science practitioner **and** you filed Form 4361, but you had $400 or more of **other** net earnings from self-employment, check here and continue with Part I . . . . ▶ ☐

1 Net farm profit or (loss) from Schedule F, line 36, and farm partnerships, Schedule K-1 (Form 1065), line 15a. **Note:** Skip this line if you use the farm optional method. See page SE-3 . . . . **1**

2 Net profit or (loss) from Schedule C, line 31; Schedule C-EZ, line 3; and Schedule K-1 (Form 1065), line 15a (other than farming). Ministers and members of religious orders see page SE-1 for amounts to report on this line. See page SE-2 for other income to report. **Note:** Skip this line if you use the nonfarm optional method. See page SE-3 . . . . **2**

3 Combine lines 1 and 2 . . . . **3**

4a If line 3 is more than zero, multiply line 3 by 92.35% (.9235). Otherwise, enter amount from line 3 . . . . **4a**

  b If you elected one or both of the optional methods, enter the total of lines 15 and 17 here **4b**

  c Combine lines 4a and 4b. If less than $400, **do not** file this schedule; you do not owe self-employment tax. **Exception.** If less than $400 and you had church employee income, enter -0- and continue . . . . . . ▶ **4c**

5a Enter your church employee income from Form W-2. **Caution:** See page SE-1 for definition of church employee income **5a**

  b Multiply line 5a by 92.35% (.9235). If less than $100, enter -0- **5b**

6 **Net earnings from self-employment.** Add lines 4c and 5b **6**

7 Maximum amount of combined wages and self-employment earnings subject to social security tax or the 6.2% portion of the 7.65% railroad retirement (tier 1) tax for 1994 . . . . **7**   60,600.00

8a Total social security wages and tips (total of boxes 3 and 7 on Form(s) W-2) and railroad retirement (tier 1) compensation **8a**

  b Unreported tips subject to social security tax (from Form 4137, line 9) **8b**

  c Add lines 8a and 8b **8c**

9 Subtract line 8c from line 7. If zero or less, enter -0- here and on line 10 and go to line 11 . . . . ▶ **9**

10 Multiply the **smaller** of line 6 or line 9 by 12.4% (.124) **10**

11 Multiply line 6 by 2.9% (.029) **11**

12 **Self-employment tax.** Add lines 10 and 11. Enter here and on Form 1040, line 47 . . . . **12**

13 **Deduction for one-half of self-employment tax.** Multiply line 12 by 50% (.5). Enter the result here and on **Form 1040, line 25** **13**

Part II Optional Methods To Figure Net Earnings (See page SE-2.)

Farm Optional Method. You may use this method **only** if:
- Your gross farm income[1] was not more than $2,400, **or**
- Your gross farm income[1] was more than $2,400 and your net farm profits[2] were less than $1,733.

14 Maximum income for optional methods **14**   1,600.00

15 Enter the **smaller** of: two-thirds (2/3) of gross farm income (not less than zero) **or** $1,600. Also, include this amount on line 4b above **15**

Nonfarm Optional Method. You may use this method **only** if:
- Your net nonfarm profits[3] were less than $1,733 and also less than 72.189% of your gross nonfarm income,[4] **and**
- You had net earnings from self-employment of at least $400 in 2 of the prior 3 years.

Caution: You may use this method no more than five times.

16 Subtract line 15 from line 14 . . . . **16**

17 Enter the **smaller** of: two-thirds (2/3) of gross nonfarm income (not less than zero) **or** the amount on line 16. Also include this amount on line 4b above **17**

[1] From Schedule F, line 11, and Schedule K-1 (Form 1065), line 15b.   [3] From Schedule C, line 31; Schedule C-EZ, line 3; and Schedule K-1 (Form 1065), line 15a.

[2] From Schedule F, line 36, and Schedule K-1 (Form 1065), line 15a.   [4] From Schedule C, line 7; Schedule C-EZ, line 1; and Schedule K-1 (Form 1065), line 15c.

Chart 22   Continued

SCHEDULE C (Form 1040) Department of the Treasury Internal Revenue Service	**Profit or Loss From Business** (Sole Proprietorship) ▶ Partnerships, joint ventures, etc., must file Form 1065. ▶ Attach to Form 1040 or Form 1041. ▶ See Instructions for Schedule C (Form 1040).	OMB No. 1545-0074 **1995** Attachment Sequence No. **09**

Name of proprietor		Social security number (SSN)

A	Principal business or profession, including product or service (see instructions)	**B** Enter principal business code (see instr.) ▶

C	Business name. If no separate business name, leave blank.	**D** Employer ID number (EIN), if any

E Business address (including suite or room no.) ▶ _____
City, town or post office, state, and ZIP code

F Accounting method: **(1)** ☐ Cash **(2)** ☐ Accrual **(3)** ☐ Other (specify) ▶ _____

G Method(s) used to
value closing inventory: **(1)** ☐ Cost **(2)** ☐ Lower of cost or market **(3)** ☐ Other (attach explanation) **(4)** ☐ Does not apply (if checked, skip line H)   Yes | No

H Was there any change in determining quantities, costs, or valuations between opening and closing inventory? If "Yes," attach explanation

I Did you "materially participate" in the operation of this business during 1995? If "No," see instructions for limitations on losses.

J If you started or acquired this business during 1995, check here . . . . ▶ ☐

Part I Income

1	Gross receipts or sales. **Caution:** If this income was reported to you on Form W-2 and the "Statutory employee" box on that form was checked, see instructions and check here . . . . ▶ ☐	**1**	
2	Returns and allowances	**2**	
3	Subtract line 2 from line 1	**3**	
4	Cost of goods sold (from line 40 on page 2)	**4**	
5	Gross profit. Subtract line 4 from line 3	**5**	
6	Other income, including Federal and state gasoline or fuel tax credit or refund (see instructions)	**6**	
7	Gross income. Add lines 5 and 6 . . . . ▶	**7**	

Part II Expenses. Enter expenses for business use of your home only on line 30.

8	Advertising	**8**		19	Pension and profit-sharing plans .	**19**	
9	Bad debts from sales or services (see instructions)	**9**		20	Rent or lease (see instructions): a Vehicles, machinery, and equip. .	**20a**	
10	Car and truck expenses (see instructions)	**10**		b	Other business property	**20b**	
11	Commissions and fees	**11**		21	Repairs and maintenance	**21**	
12	Depletion	**12**		22	Supplies (not included in Part III) .	**22**	
13	Depreciation and section 179 expense deduction (not included in Part III) (see instructions) . . .	**13**		23	Taxes and licenses	**23**	
				24	Travel, meals, and entertainment:		
				a	Travel	**24a**	
14	Employee benefit programs (other than on line 19)	**14**		b	Meals and entertainment . .		
15	Insurance (other than health) . .	**15**		c	Enter 50% of line 24b subject to limitations (see C-4)		
16	Interest:						
a	Mortgage (paid to banks, etc.) .	**16a**		d	Subtract line 24c from line 24b . .	**24d**	
b	Other	**16b**		25	Utilities	**25**	
17	Legal and professional services	**17**		26	Wages (less employment credits) .	**26**	
18	Office expense	**18**		27	Other expenses (from line 46 on page 2)	**27**	

28	Total expenses before expenses for business use of home. Add lines 8 through 27 in columns . . . . . . ▶	**28**	
29	Tentative profit (loss). Subtract line 28 from line 7	**29**	
30	Expenses for business use of your home. Attach **Form 8829**	**30**	
31	Net profit or (loss). Subtract line 30 from line 29. ● If a profit, enter on **Form 1040, line 12,** and ALSO on **Schedule SE, line 2** (statutory employees, see instructions). Estates and trusts, enter on Form 1041, line 3. ● If a loss, you MUST go on to line 32.	**31**	
32	If you have a loss, check the box that describes your investment in this activity (see instructions). ● If you checked 32a, enter the loss on **Form 1040, line 12,** and ALSO on **Schedule SE, line 2** (statutory employees, see instructions). Estates and trusts, enter on Form 1041, line 3. ● If you checked 32b, you MUST attach **Form 6198.**	**32a** ☐ All investment is at risk. **32b** ☐ Some investment is not at risk.	

For Paperwork Reduction Act Notice, see Form 1040 instructions.   Schedule C (Form 1040) 1995

H807

**Chart 23 Your Profit or Loss from Your Single-Owner Business Is Recorded on
Schedule C and Filed with Your Tax Return**

Schedule C (Form 1040) 1995   Page **2**

Part III   Cost of Goods Sold (See instructions)

33	Inventory at beginning of year. If different from last year's closing inventory, attach explanation	33
34	Purchases less cost of items withdrawn for personal use	34
35	Cost of labor. Do not include salary paid to yourself	35
36	Materials and supplies	36
37	Other costs	37
38	Add lines 33 through 37	38
39	Inventory at end of year	39
40	**Cost of goods sold.** Subtract line 39 from line 38. Enter the result here and on page 1, line 4	40

Part IV   Information on Your Vehicle. Complete this part ONLY if you are claiming car or truck expenses on line 10 and are not required to file Form 4562 for this business. See the instructions for line 13 to find out if you must file.

41 When did you place your vehicle in service for business purposes? (month, day, year) ▶ _ _ _ _ _ _ _ _ _ _ _ _ _ _ .

42 Of the total number of miles you drove your vehicle during 1994, enter the number of miles you used your vehicle for:

a Business _ _ _ _ _ _ _ _ _ _ _ _ _ _ b Commuting _ _ _ _ _ _ _ _ _ _ _ _ c Other _ _ _ _ _ _ _ _ _ _ _ _ _ _

43 Do you (or your spouse) have another vehicle available for personal use? . . . . ☐ Yes ☐ No

44 Was your vehicle available for use during off-duty hours? . . . . ☐ Yes ☐ No

45 a Do you have evidence to support your deduction? . . . . ☐ Yes ☐ No
   b If "Yes," is the evidence written? . . . . ☐ Yes ☐ No

Part V   Other Expenses. List below business expenses not included on lines 8-26 or line 30.

------------------------------	
46 Total other expenses. Enter here and on page 1, line 27	46

Chart 23   Continued

kept your ledger of income and expenses up to date, this should not be too difficult.

When in doubt, call the IRS or visit an accountant or tax preparation office, such as H&R Block. Mistakes on your tax return could cause the IRS to **audit** you. That means the IRS will send an agent to your business to examine your ledgers, receipts, and invoices and to make sure your taxes were filed correctly.

Always fully comply with the IRS by keeping good records and filing your return and paying your taxes on time. Audits are nerve-wracking and time-consuming.

EVALUATING TAXES

Tax forms and laws are confusing and change frequently. People do not agree on who should pay taxes and what government programs and services taxes should support. As a taxpayer, you have the right to ask these questions:

- Where are my tax dollars going?
- Are my tax dollars supporting services that will benefit me and my community?
- Am I paying taxes to support services that could be better supplied by private industry than by the government?
- Are the tax rates fair?

Taxpayers demand answers to these questions from the politicians who represent them in city councils, state legislatures, and the U.S. Congress. One of the most important jobs politicians do each year is figure government budgets and then determine how much to tax people to finance them. They also pass laws to change the tax code.

ARGUMENTS FOR LOWER TAXES AND SIMPLIFYING THE TAX CODE

Many Americans believe taxes are too high and tax rates are unfair. They are putting pressure on politicians to respond to these concerns.

Many business owners argue that the tax laws are so complicated and the rates are so high that people are afraid to start new businesses.

The U.S. tax code now runs to 38,000 pages. The tax code also changes all the time, making it difficult for small business owners to handle their taxes without the expensive aid of accountants. This is one of my pet peeves, too. I believe the complexity of the tax code, combined with high tax rates, discourages low- to mid-income people from starting new businesses. It encourages others to start businesses, but keep them underground. I recently testified before the National Commission on Economic Growth and Tax Reform, headed by Jack Kemp and Ted Forstmann, on this subject. I told the Commission that both the complexity of the tax code and high rates of taxation do more to prevent people from rising out of poverty through entrepreneurship than almost anything else.

Some business owners argue that many of the services that various levels of government provide—such as the U.S. Postal Service, or garbage collection—could be supplied more efficiently by private industry. This transfer would lower taxes. Business owners also argue that the government should make the tax code easier to understand and should make it easier for would-be entrepreneurs to license their businesses and pay their taxes.

CASE STUDY: SPORTING GOODS STORE

Business for the Young Entrepreneur

"Before I opened my store, I registered my business, set up my files and record-keeping system, and got my taxes together," Frank says. "Today, I'm up on every tax, and I pay my taxes quarterly."

Frank says he learned how to do these things during a NFTE course. He took the course when he was eighteen at the first Boys Club that was ever established, on Manhattan's Lower East Side. Before he took the entrepreneurship class, Frank had wanted to be a physical education teacher.

The first business he had was making custom uniforms for local teams. Next, Frank managed to rent a storefront on a busy street not far from the Boys Club. At the time, Frank was attending college, and working part-time at the Boys Club. "I started the business with under $10,000, so I slept four hours a night for about six months because I had no capital to renovate the store. I did all the fixing and remodeling myself," he says.

Today, Frank's store, East Side Sports, is a neighborhood fixture. He runs an ad in The Yellow Pages, but says his most valuable promotion is community service. "I work with local teams and I give good deals to neighborhood people," he says.

Frank is currently running the store without credit. Although he has good relationships with his wholesalers, they want to see him in business for two years before they will extend him credit. "I'm almost at that two-year mark, so I should be able to get credit soon. Doing all my business without it gets really hectic, because I do some big orders," he says. Frank marks up the sporting goods he purchases from the wholesalers by 80 to 100 percent.

Once he gets his credit lined up, Frank wants to build a custom workshop in the store. "I do a lot of custom work, and if I had a shop in the store I could deliver my custom orders much more quickly."

Tips

- **Location, location, location!** Frank says he knew his business would succeed because he's located on a busy street in a neighborhood full of kids and teenagers.

- Establishing credit can be difficult for a young entrepreneur. To establish positive personal credit, apply for a charge card from a local department store. Buy a few items on the charge card and pay them off on time. Many college students are offered credit cards. If you apply for a credit card and are accepted, use it to establish a good credit record. Again, buy a few items with your card and pay them off on time. Having a record of responsible personal credit use can help you establish credit for your business.

21

REPLICATING YOUR
BUSINESS IDEA

Nothing in the world can take the place of persistence. Talent
will not; nothing is more common than unsuccessful men with
talent. Genius will not; the world is full of educated derelicts.
Persistence and determination alone are omnipotent.

—Ray Kroc (1902–1984)
Founder of McDonald's

FRANCHISING

As an entrepreneur, you might develop a business that could be reproduced or replicated. In that event, you could franchise your business
and reap the rewards of all your hard work. A **franchise** is a business
that markets a product or service in the manner prescribed by the person who developed the business.

McDonald's restaurants are examples of franchises. McDonald's
was developed by Ray Kroc, who had persuaded the McDonald brothers to let him become the franchising agent for their highly successful
hamburger restaurant in San Bernardino, California. Kroc's great insight was to realize that the **franchisees**—the people who bought Mc-
Donald's franchises—needed extensive training and support in order
to make the food taste just like the food from the original restaurant.
Kroc timed everything. McDonald's franchisees are taught exactly how
many minutes to fry potatoes and when to turn a burger. They are also
taught precisely how to greet customers and handle orders.

A McDonald's franchisee owns the restaurant, but agrees to market
the food, under the McDonald's name and trademark, in the exact fashion developed by Kroc. This is spelled out in the franchise agreement. In

return, the franchisee knows he or she is investing in a proven, successful business concept. The franchisee also benefits from use of the McDonald's trademark, and from McDonald's management training, marketing, national advertising, and promotional assistance. McDonald's receives a franchise fee and royalties. A **royalty** is a percentage of the revenue generated by the sale of each unit.

Here are some sample fees, start-up costs, and royalty fees for some popular franchises:

Franchise	Franchise Fee	Start-Up Costs	Royalty Fee
McDonald's	$22,000	various	4%
Arby's Inc.	$25,000–$37,500	$550,000–$887,500	4%
General Nutrition Franchising, Inc.	$17,500	$58,700–$137,500	5%
Hardee's	$15,000	$699,900–$1.7 million	4%

The Franchise Boom

Although franchising has been around since the Singer Sewing Machine Company first used it in the 1850s, its popularity has exploded in recent years. Many different kinds of businesses have been franchised—fast-food restaurants, auto repair shops, motels, health clubs, and hair salons.

Women and minorities have been especially drawn to franchises as a low-capital way to become entrepreneurs. Recognizing this, Burger King, Pizza Hut, Taco Bell, Kentucky Fried Chicken (KFC), and Baskin-Robbins all offer special financing and other incentives to recruit minority franchise owners. Other franchise programs have focused, with great success, on recruiting women.

Through franchising, Ray Kroc turned a simple idea—the fast production of inexpensive hamburgers—into an internationally recognized symbol of American enterprise. Today, franchising accounts for more than $800 billion in annual sales in a wide variety of industries.

A Word of Caution

Before you get involved in either franchising your business or becoming a franchisee, consult with a franchise attorney and do extensive research. Some eager franchisees have had bad experiences with franchisors who open too many franchises in an area or fail to honor the franchise contract. Before investing in a franchise, talk to other franchisees of the company you are researching. Ask questions such as: Are they happy with their sales? Are they satisfied with the level of support, training, and advertising provided by the franchisor? Get the answers to all your questions before you agree to become a franchisee.

LICENSING

Another way for an entrepreneur to profit from a business idea is through licensing. The difference between **licensing** and franchising is one of control. The franchisor controls every aspect of how the franchisee runs the franchise. It's all spelled out in the franchise agreement.

In contrast, the **licensor** grants the **licensee** the right to use the licensor's name on a product or service but has less control of how the licensee does business. The licensee simply pays a fee for the license and pays royalties to the licensor.

Licensing is only effective when the licensor is confident that his or her company name won't be tarnished by how the licensee uses it. When Coca-Cola licenses its name to a T-shirt maker, there's not much the T-shirt maker can do to tarnish the reputation of Coca-Cola. Coca-Cola gets free advertising, as well as royalties.

Coca-Cola would not license its name to a soft-drink manufacturer, however, because the licensing agreement would not guarantee that the manufacturer would make a product of the same quality as Coca-Cola's. If Coca-Cola wanted to expand in this fashion, it would be better served by a franchising agreement.

Fashion designers and celebrities have made millions by licensing their famous names for use on perfumes, athletic shoes, and other products. Licensing is subject to fewer government regulations than franchising.

CASE STUDY: ARTIST MANAGEMENT

Business for the Young Entrepreneur

Licensing is an important aspect of business for UP JAM Entertainment, a music management and production company that works primarily with hip-hop, rap, and R&B artists. UP JAM has secured product endorsement deals for its artists with NY, Lugz, Converse Sneakers, Oakley, Reebok, and Fox Racing.

UP JAM was founded in Philadelphia in 1989 by Jimmy Mac, 22. As a youngster, Jimmy excelled at bicycle racing and running. His success in these sports led to endorsement contracts with many top sporting goods companies. After high school, Jimmy began to pursue sports marketing and management as a career. His love of music, however, led him to realize that he could apply what he'd learned about sports marketing and management to management of artists.

Before he could do that, though, he knew he needed to learn more about starting and operating a business. He enrolled in the Young Entrepreneurs Program taught by NFTE at the Wharton School of Business. After achieving moderate success working with Philadelphia musicians, Jimmy decided to take his sharpened business skills to New York City. There, Jimmy began teaching and mentoring for NFTE.

While volunteering as a mentor/teacher with New York's Fresh Air Fund, he became friends with a fellow counselor. Joel, 23, had left IBM to pursue a career as a music industry executive. He was working his way up through the ranks at HUSH Productions, one of the top five African-American entertainment firms in the country.

Joel and Jimmy formed a partnership and quickly began landing freelance work with HUSH. Soon, HUSH offered UP JAM its present subsidiary status. Under the deal, Jimmy and Joel not only oversee HUSH's rap and R&B divisions, they also have the freedom to sign and develop acts independently under the umbrella of their own company, which they have renamed Bulldog Entertainment. Their tremendous success illustrates some of the key concepts I have tried to get across in this book: Do what you love, educate yourself about entrepreneurship, and give back to your community through volunteering, teaching, or philanthropy. You never know whom you might meet!

RESOURCES

Books

The most complete reference book on franchising is the *Franchise Opportunities Handbook,* a U.S. government publication. It costs $15 and can be ordered by calling or writing:

Superintendent of Documents
U.S. Government Printing Office
710 North Capital St., N.W.
Washington, DC 20402-9325
(202) 783-3238

Information Press publishes a directory of around 3,000 franchises. Contact:

Information Press
728 Center Street
P.O. Box 550
Lewiston, NY 14092
(716) 754-4669

NFTE's legal counsel, Andrew Sherman, happens to be an expert in the field of franchising and licensing. His well-known book, *Franchising and Licensing: Two Ways to Build Your Business* (New York: AMACOM, 1991), is an important resource.

Magazines

Entrepreneur magazine publishes an annual "Franchising Directory." Contact:

Entrepreneur
2311 Pontius Avenue
Los Angeles, CA 90064
(213) 477-1011

How to Raise Capital for Your Business

22

If you would like to know the value of money, go and try to borrow some.

Benjamin Franklin (1706–1790)
American statesman and writer

There are many sources for raising capital to start your business. Family, friends, colleagues, and acquaintances might be interested in investing in your business or making a loan to you. There are also investors and investment companies whose specialty is financing new, high-potential entrepreneurial companies. Because they often provide the initial equity investment to start up a business, they are called venture capitalists.

Venture capital is the money given to a new venture by an investor. Venture capitalists are looking for a high rate of return. They typically expect to earn back, over a five-year period, six times the amount invested. That works out to about a 45 percent return on investment. Professional venture capitalists won't usually invest in a company unless its business plan shows it is likely to generate sales of at least $25 million within five years.

VENTURE CAPITALISTS WANT EQUITY

Venture capitalists want **equity** or some share of ownership, in return for their capital. They are willing to take the higher risk of losing their capital for a chance to profit from the business's success. Henry Ford turned to venture capitalists to finance the Ford Motor Company. He gave up 75 percent of the business for $28,000 of badly needed capital.

It took Ford many years to regain control of his company. Still, many small business owners have turned to venture capital when they wanted to start or grow a business and couldn't convince banks to lend them money.

Anita Roddick, the owner of The Body Shop skin care and cosmetics stores, opened her first store in 1976 in England. Within a few months, she was eager to open a second store because the first one was doing so well, but no bank would lend her money. A friend named Ian McGlinn gave her the money she needed, in exchange for an equity share of half of her business. Although Roddick made McGlinn a millionaire, without his venture capital she might never have become one herself.

HOW VENTURE CAPITALISTS GET THEIR ROI

Venture capitalists typically reap the return on their investment (ROI) in one of two ways:

1. The venture capitalist sells his or her percentage of the business to another investor.
2. The venture capitalist waits until the company "goes public" (starts selling stock) and sells his or her stock in the business on the stock market.

A BUSINESS PLAN IS NECESSARY TO RAISE CAPITAL

No matter whom you approach to raise money for your business, you'll need a business plan. Venture capitalists and bankers will refuse to see an entrepreneur who doesn't have a business plan. You may have a brilliant business idea, but if it is not set forth in a well-written business plan, no potential investor will be interested.

A well-written business plan shows potential investors that the business owner has carefully thought through the business. All investors—bankers, friends, neighbors, or venture capitalists—crave information. The more information you offer investors about how their money will be used, the more willing they will be to invest in your business. Your plan should be so thoughtful and thorough that the only question it raises in an investor's mind is: "How much can I invest?" Chapter 23 provides more detailed information on how to write a business plan.

Nearly all the young entrepreneurs profiled in this book succeeded in part because they wrote a business plan before they made a single sale. A well-written plan not only helps you raise money, it also guides you as you develop your business.

A sample business plan drawn from a real business run by a young entrepreneur is included on pages 273–283. Following the sample are worksheets that will take you step-by-step through writing a business plan for *your* business. As you write the plan, problems you might not have thought of before will be uncovered. Working them out on paper will save you time and money. Before you serve your first customer, you will have answered every question that you might be asked. How much are you charging for your product or service? What exactly *is* your product or service? What is one unit? What are your costs? How are you going to market your product or service? How do you plan to sell it?

Questions like these can quickly overwhelm you if you start a business without a plan. By using the worksheets in the appendix, you will have both the answers you need *and* a rough draft of a business plan for your own business.

RESOURCES

Books

Many books are available on how to write a business plan. One of the classics is Joseph Mancuso's *How to Write a Winning Business Plan* (Englewood Cliffs, NJ: Prentice-Hall, 1985).

The Ernst & Young Guide to Raising Capital (New York: John Wiley & Sons, Inc., 1994) explores a wide variety of options for the entrepreneur.

Finding Money: The Small Business Guide to Financing by Kate Lister and Tom Harnish (New York: John Wiley & Sons, Inc., 1995).

Other Resources

The National Venture Capital Association is committed to stimulating the flow of capital to young companies. Contact:

National Venture Capital Association
1655 North Fort Meyer Drive, Suite 700
Arlington, VA 22209
(202) 528-4370
Fax (703) 525-8841

The National Association of Small Business Investment Companies publishes an annual directory called *Venture Capital: Where to Find It.* Contact:

National Association of Small Business Investment Companies
1199 North Fairfax Street, Room 200
Alexandria, VA 22314
(703) 683-1601

WRITING A BUSINESS PLAN FOR YOUR BUSINESS

23

DEFINING YOUR BUSINESS IDEA

On the first worksheet, describe your business idea clearly and concisely. What is your product or service? Who will want to buy it? Where will you sell it? Explain your competitive advantage—what you can do better than another businessperson with a similar business, and why. What gives you an advantage over your competitors?

THE ECONOMICS OF ONE UNIT

Your first decision is what kind of business you are planning to run. Is it a retail, wholesale, manufacturing, or service business? Once you decide, turn to the appropriate worksheet for calculating the economics of one unit.

You'll need to define one unit of your business before you can determine costs and profit. If you are selling just one product—ties, for example—one unit is one tie. The unit price would be the price of one tie. The cost of goods sold would be the cost of producing one tie. If you are selling a variety of products, define your unit as the average sale per customer. McDonald's, for example, defines its unit of sale as a $5 sale, which is roughly the cost of one sandwich, fries, and a soda.

If you are selling a service, the economic unit is usually one hour of service. Or, you could define your unit as the completion of one job.

Base your unit selling price on your cost of goods sold. It's a good idea for the selling price to "keystone," or be double the cost of producing one unit. To determine gross profit per unit, subtract your unit cost from your unit selling price. The worksheet will take you through this process.

MARKET RESEARCH

It is crucial that you research your market before developing a product or service. The worksheets offer good questions to ask your market. Check out your competitors, too. How are they serving your market? What price are they charging? What are their costs?

For a review of market research, see Chapter 13.

YOUR CUSTOMER

Close your eyes and picture your ideal customer. Is it a man or a woman? How old is the customer? Where does he or she live? Work? What does he or she eat for breakfast? Try to follow this person mentally through an entire day. You'll get all kinds of ideas for how to reach your customer.

List your promotional and advertising ideas. Posters, flyers, and business cards are inexpensive, yet effective promotions.

Take the time to write a sales pitch to your target customer. Write down some potential wholesalers or suppliers you could contact.

To review promotion and advertising, please see Chapter 12. For more on sales, see Chapter 11.

YOUR MARKETING PLAN

Use the marketing plan chart to plot the strategy that will most successfully market your product or service.

LEGAL STRUCTURE

Most small businesses start as sole proprietorships or partnerships. Before registering your business, research fees, permits, and licensing requirements.

If you form a partnership, be sure to write out a formal agreement with your partner. State each partner's financial and work obligations toward the business. As soon as you can afford to spend $500 to incorporate, you should consider doing so to protect your personal assets from any debts incurred by the business. A small business with fewer than thirty-five employees can incorporate as a Subchapter S corporation.

When incorporating or forming a partnership, see a lawyer for advice. Some lawyers are willing to work with a young person for free, or for a reduced fee.

Please see Chapter 15 for more information on business legal structures.

FINANCING AND BUDGETING YOUR BUSINESS

Your first concern is your start-up costs—the costs of items you need to purchase in order to make your first sale. Talk to a friend or mentor. He or she may think of some costs you didn't anticipate.

List where you plan to obtain the money to cover your start-up costs. List the amount you expect to get from personal savings, relatives, friends, investors, or other sources. Put a check mark ($\checkmark$) in the appropriate column to indicate whether the financing is equity, debt, or a gift. How much ownership are you willing to give up in exchange for equity financing? If you go with debt, what's the highest interest rate you are willing to pay?

Next, calculate your operating costs, both fixed and variable. Fixed costs are costs that do not change over a range of sales your business may make. Rent is a fixed cost; you pay the same rent whether you sell five units or fifty.

Variable costs change with the amount of sales your business makes. Sales commission is an example of a variable cost. The amount of sales commission the business owner pays rises when sales rise and falls when sales fall.

Typically, young entrepreneurs' businesses have only fixed costs, but you should have a friend or mentor look at your list of costs. You may have missed some operating costs.

At this point, you are ready to prepare your monthly budget. The goal of the monthly budget is to guess accurately how many units you can sell at the selling price you've designated. You'll need to estimate the following amounts and enter them into your calculations.

1. Total Sales

- Units Sold: How many units do you expect to sell each month? Enter your estimates for each month in the top row of the monthly budget chart. Remember: "Row" means across the chart, "column" means down.

- Unit Selling Price: For what price do you plan to sell one unit? Enter that *same* price for each month across the second row of the chart.

- Total Sales: Multiply Units Sold by Unit Selling Price to get Total Sales for each month:

$$\text{Total Sales} = \text{Units Sold} \times \text{Unit Selling Price}$$

Because Units Sold will probably differ for each month, do this calculation for every month and enter the results in the Total Sales row.

2. Total Cost of Goods (or Services) Sold

- Cost of Goods (or Services) Sold: Enter your Cost of Goods (or Services) Sold per Unit across this row. (You figured out this cost earlier.)

- Total Cost of Goods (or Services) Sold: Multiply Cost of Goods (or Services) Sold per Unit by Units Sold for each month.

$$\text{Total Cost of Goods (or Services) Sold} = \text{Units Sold} \times \text{Cost of Goods (or Services) Sold per Unit}$$

Do this calculation for each month. Enter the results in the Total Cost of Goods (or Services) row.

3. Gross Profit

To calculate Gross Profit, subtract Total Cost of Goods (or Services) Sold from Total Sales. Do this calculation for each month. Enter the results in the Gross Profit row.

$$\text{Gross Profit} = \text{Total Sales} - \text{Total Cost of Goods (or Services) Sold}$$

4. Operating Costs

- Monthly Fixed Costs: Enter your estimate of monthly Fixed Costs from your Operating Costs worksheet.
- Monthly Variable Costs: Enter your estimate of monthly Variable Costs from your Operating Costs worksheet.

To calculate Operating Costs, add Monthly Fixed Costs to Monthly Variable Costs.

Operating Costs = Monthly Fixed Costs + Monthly Variable Costs

5. Profit/(Loss) Before Taxes

To calculate Profit/(Loss), subtract Operating Costs from Gross Profit.

Profit/(Loss) = Gross Profit − Operating Costs

6. Total

To fill in the Total column for most of the entries, simply add together the numbers across a row. For example, if your Units Sold row contains twelve numbers, indicating sales in all twelve months, you get the total by adding up all twelve numbers. Your arithmetic might be: (40 + 35 + 60 + 75 + 80 + 85 + 90 + 90 + 85 + 100 + 75 + 90), or 905. You would then write 905 in the Total column at the end of the Units Sold row. Repeat this addition process to fill in the totals for all of the other rows **except** the Unit Selling Price and Cost of Goods Sold rows. *Do not add together the numbers in these rows!* Simply enter the same number all the way across *and* in the Total column.

7. Net Profit

If your total in the Profit/(Loss) row is positive, your business is showing a projected profit before taxes. To calculate Net Profit, you will have to subtract taxes. For our purposes, let's assume that taxes will be 25 percent of Profit. (Your actual taxes could be higher or lower.)

To calculate taxes, multiply Profit by .25.

Taxes = Profit × .25

Profit minus taxes gives you Net Profit.

$$\text{Net Profit} = \text{Profit} - \text{Taxes}$$

YOUR YEARLY INCOME STATEMENT

A yearly income statement will fall neatly out of the monthly projected income statement you have just created. Look at the last ("Total") column of the monthly statement. There you will find the numbers to plug into your yearly income statement.

SAMPLE
BUSINESS PLAN

The sample business plan that follows will show you, step by step, how to prepare a business plan for a small business. Be sure you understand each step before you go on to the next one. You can then use the Business Plan Workbook, in the next section, for the business plan that will launch your own venture.

Good luck, and have fun!

Your Business Idea

· ·

Describe your business idea:

My business idea is to clean and maintain home aquariums. I would clean each aquarium in a person's home twice a month.

What is the name of your business?

Fred's Aquarium Cleaners

What is the competitive advantage of your business?

The price for my service will be lower than my competitors' price.

Name Fred Marshall	**Business** Fred's Aquarium Cleaners	**Date** 1/4/95

Marketing

. . . .

Type of business you are in (please circle)

Manufacturer	Wholesaler	Retailer	Service Retailer
Sells to	Sells to	Sells to	Sells to
↓	↓	↓	↓
Wholesaler	Retailer	Consumer	Consumer

Consumer Description

Describe your target consumer <u>a home aquarium owner who is too busy to care for it,</u>
<u>or someone who would buy an aquarium if there were a service to care for it</u>

Expected age of consumer <u>any age</u>   Expected gender of consumer <u>M or F</u>

What need or want will your product fulfill? <u>save time</u>

Financial status of consumer <u>making enough money to afford an aquarium</u>

Promotion/Advertising

How will you reach this consumer? <u>Flyers</u>

What is the slogan for your business? <u>A clean fish is a happy fish.</u>

Will you make sales calls? ☑ Yes ☐ No When I start expanding to offices and
restaurants.

Write a four-sentence sales presentation:

<u>For only $30 a month my professional cleaning service will keep your fish healthy and</u>
<u>happy and your aquarium sparkling. You won't have to buy or store cleaning supplies. My</u>
<u>service saves you time and money. You can feel confident that the very latest techniques</u>
<u>and supplies are being used to care for your fish.</u>

| **Name** _Fred Marshall_ | **Business** _Fred's Aquarium Cleaners_ | **Date** _1/4/95_ |

Economics of One Unit:
Service Company

∙∙∙

Fill this out if you have a service business.

Economics of One Unit

Note: A service unit is typically defined as one hour of service or one job.

Define your unit: _One month of cleaning service for one aquarium._

_____

_____

Selling price per unit $_____30.00_____ **A**

Cost of services sold per unit

(Cost of services sold per unit must include both your labor and supplies.)

Labor

What value are you placing on your entrepreneurial time per hour?

$_____6.00_____ **B**

How long does it take to perform your service (in hours)?

_____2 hours_____ **C**

Labor cost per unit = B × C $_____12.00_____ **D**

Supplies

What is the supply cost per customer? $_____5.00_____ **E**

Cost of services sold per unit = D + E $_____17.00_____ **F**

Gross profit per unit = A − F $_____13.00_____ **G**

| **Selling Price per Unit** | **−** | **Cost of Services Sold per Unit** | **=** | **Gross Profit per Unit** |
| A | − | F | = | G |

Market Research

∙∙

Competition

Ask two people these questions about your business and write their answers in the space provided:

Do you like the name of my business?

#1 _Yes_

#2 _Yes_

What do you think of my logo?

#1 _like it_

#2 _a little confusing_

Where would you want to go to buy my product?

#1 _I like that you come to the home._

#2 _I wouldn't want a stranger in my home._

Do you think my product/service has value?

#1 _Yes_

#2 _Yes_

How much would you pay for my product?

#1 _$25 a month_

#2 _$35 a month_

How would you improve my business idea?

#1 _offer fish food, supplies_

#2 _service office, restaurant aquariums_

Who is my closest competitor(s)?

#1 _don't know any_

#2 _Manhattan Cleaning Services_

Do you think my product/service is better or worse than that offered by my competitor(s)?

#1 _don't know_

#2 _better, less expensive_

Why is your product/service going to beat the competition?

My service is cheaper and I will try to develop a good personal relationship with each customer.

Below is a sample strategy for a business selling handmade jewelry. Can you add other locations or methods of selling?

MARKETING PLAN LOCATIONS (WHERE TO SELL)

SELLING METHODS	Door to Door	Flea Markets	School/ Church Functions	Street (Street Vendors)	Through Local Stores	Your Own Home	Other
Business Cards	no	no	yes	no	yes	no	no
Posters	no	no	yes	yes	yes	no	no
Flyers	no	no	yes	yes	yes	yes	no
Phone	no	no	no	yes	yes	yes	no
Sales Calls	no	no	no	yes	yes	yes	no
Brochure	no	no	yes	yes	yes	yes	no
Mailings	no	no	no	yes	yes	yes	no
Other	no	no	no	yes	yes	yes	no

Legal Structure

....

Is your business a sole proprietorship, a partnership, a regular corporation, a subchapter S corporation, or a not-for-profit corporation?

sole proprietorship

Explain your decision:

I am the only employee and the owner.

How much will you be paying for legal fees?

Explain: _$33 to register as a sole proprietorship._

What permits and/or licenses will you need for your business?

I will need a sales tax identification number and a business certificate. I will look into any other permits.

What are the names, addresses, and phone numbers of the local official(s) in charge of the permits and licensing you need?

Name	Address	Phone
Business Permits Office	State Office Building, Albany, NY	800-342-3464
Tax Forms Office	State Office Building, Albany, NY	800-462-8100

| Name | Fred Marshall | Business | Fred's Aquarium Cleaners | Date | 1/4/95 |

Start-Up Costs (These are the items you need to earn your first dollar of sales.)

. . . .

What are your estimated start-up costs? Itemize:

Item	Where Will You Buy This?	Cost
Cleaning Equipment	Petland	$150
Medicine (Water Treatment)	Hertz	$ 61
Tools	Hunter Hardware	$ 25
Cart	Hunter Hardware	$ 42
Business cards	Kinko's	$ 20

Estimated Total Start-up Costs $298

List your sources of financing below. Indicate with a check mark whether each source is offering equity, debt, or a gift.

	Amount	Equity (Investment)	Debt (Loan)	Gift
Personal Savings:	$150	✓		
Relatives:	$100		✓	
Friends:	$48		✓	
Investors:				
Grant:				
Other:				
Total:	$298			

If you receive equity financing, what percentage of ownership will you give up? 20%

If you receive debt financing, what is the maximum interest rate you will pay? 10%

Operating Costs (Fixed & Variable)

. . . .

Monthly Fixed Costs

Monthly Operating Costs include USAIIR: utilities, salaries, advertising, interest, insurance, and rent. In a small business, many operating costs are usually fixed, although a few may be variable, depending on your business.

Type of Fixed Costs	Monthly Fixed Cost
Advertising (Flyers and Posters)	$26
Monthly Fixed Costs	$26

Variable Costs

(Estimate those operating costs (USAIIR) that fluctuate with sales and cannot be directly assigned to a unit of sale. Example: utilities = 1% of sales.)

Type of Variable Costs	Estimated Variable Cost as a % of Sales
	$0
Estimated Variable Costs as a % of sales	_____ %

Remember . . . to get total monthly variable costs you must multiply variable cost as a percentage of sales by total monthly sales. Note: you may set variable costs equal to zero.

Name Fred Marshall   **Business** Fred's Aquarium Cleaners   **Date** 1/4/95

Monthly Budget: Projected Income Statement for a Service Company

	Jan	Feb	Mar	Apr	May	Jun	Jul	Aug	Sep	Oct	Nov	Dec	Total
Units Sold	2	4	6	8	8	16	18	20	8	8	8	6	112
Unit Selling Price	30	30	30	30	30	30	30	30	30	30	30	30	30
Total Sales	60	120	180	240	240	480	540	600	240	240	240	180	3,360
Cost of Services Sold per Unit	17	17	17	17	17	17	17	17	17	17	17	17	17
Total Cost of Services Sold	34	68	102	136	136	272	306	340	136	136	136	102	1,904
Gross Profit	26	52	78	104	104	208	234	260	104	104	104	78	1,456
Fixed Costs	26	26	26	26	26	26	26	26	26	26	26	26	312
Variable Costs	0	0	0	0	0	0	0	0	0	0	0	0	0
Total Operating Costs	26	26	26	26	26	26	26	26	26	26	26	26	312
Profit/(Loss) before Taxes	0	26	52	78	78	182	208	234	78	78	78	52	1,144

Less Taxes (25%, Estimated)   286

Net Profit   858

Total Sales = Units Sold × Unit Selling Price
Total Cost of Services Sold = Units Sold × Cost of Services Sold per Unit
Gross Profit = Total Sales − Total Cost of Services Sold
Variable Costs = Multiply Variable Costs as a % of Sales by Sales
Operating Costs = Fixed Costs + Variable Costs
Profit/(Loss) = Gross Profit − Operating Costs
Taxes = Profit × .25

Budgeted Yearly Income Statement for a Service Business

Sales	Amount	
Units Sold	112	
Unit Selling Price	$30	
Total Sales	$3,360	Total Sales = Units Sold × Unit Selling Price

Costs	Amount	
Cost of Services Sold per Unit	$17	
Total Cost of Services Sold	$1,904	Total Cost of Goods or Services Sold = Units Sold × Cost of Goods or Services Sold per Unit
Gross Profit	$1,456	Gross Profit = Total Sales − Total Cost of Goods or Services Sold
Fixed Expenses	$312	
Variable Costs	0	Variable Costs = Variable Costs as a % of Sales × Sales
Operating Costs	$312	Operating Costs = Fixed Costs + Variable Costs

Profit	Amount	
Profit/(Loss) before Taxes	$1,144	Profit/(Loss) = Gross Profit − Operating Expenses
Less Taxes (25%, Estimated)	$286	Taxes = Profit × .25
Net Profit	$858	Net Profit = Profit − Taxes
Net Profit per Unit	$7.66	Net Profit per Unit = $\dfrac{\text{Net Profit}}{\text{Units Sold}}$

BUSINESS PLAN
WORKBOOK

Your Business Idea

....

Describe your business idea:

_____
_____
_____
_____
_____
_____
_____
_____
_____
_____
_____

What is the name of your business?

_____
_____

What is the competitive advantage of your business?

_____
_____
_____
_____
_____
_____

Marketing

....

Type of business you are in (please circle)

Manufacturer	Wholesaler	Retailer	Service Retailer
Sells to	Sells to	Sells to	Sells to
↓	↓	↓	↓
Wholesaler	Retailer	Consumer	Consumer

Consumer Description

Describe your target consumer _____

_____

_____

Expected age of consumer _____   Expected gender of consumer _____

What need or want will your product fulfill? _____

Financial status of consumer _____

Promotion/Advertising

How will you reach this consumer? _____

What is the slogan for your business?_____

Will you make sales calls? ☐ Yes ☐ No

Write a four-sentence sales presentation:

_____

_____

_____

_____

Economics of One Unit:
Manufacturing Company

....

Fill this out if you have a manufacturing business.

Economics of One Unit

Define your unit: _____

_____

_____

Selling price per unit $_____ **A**

Cost of goods sold per unit

(Cost of producing one additional unit must include both your labor and supplies.)

Labor

What value are you placing on your
entrepreneurial time per hour? $_____ **B**

How long does it take to make your product
or perform your service (in hours)? $_____ **C**

Labor cost of goods sold per unit = B × C $_____ **D**

Raw materials

What is the raw material cost of goods sold
per unit? $_____ **E**

Cost of goods sold per unit = D + E $_____ **F**

Gross profit = A − F $_____ **G**

Selling Price	**−**	**Cost of Goods Sold per Unit**	**=**	**Gross Profit per Unit**
A	**−**	**F**	**=**	**G**

Economics of One Unit:
Wholesale Company

....

Fill this out if you have a wholesale business.

Economics of One Unit

Note: A wholesale unit is typically measured in dozens, because wholesale items are sold in bulk.

Define your unit: _____

_____

_____

_____

_____

_____

_____

Selling price per unit $_____ A

(Price at which you plan to sell one unit.)

Cost of goods sold per unit $_____ B

(Cost to you of producing one unit.)

Gross profit per unit (A − B) $_____ C

(Gross profit of one unit.)

Selling Price per Unit	−	Cost of Goods Sold per Unit	=	Gross Profit per Unit
A	−	B	=	C

Economics of One Unit:
Retail Company

....

Fill this out if you have a retail business.

Economics of One Unit

Define your unit: _____

_____

_____

_____

_____

_____

_____

_____

_____

Selling price per unit $_____ A

(Price at which you plan to sell one unit.)

Cost of goods sold per unit $_____ B

(Cost to you of producing one unit.)

Gross profit per unit (A − B) $_____ C

(Gross profit of one unit.)

Selling Price per Unit	−	Cost of Goods Sold per Unit	=	Gross Profit per Unit
A	−	B	=	C

Economics of One Unit:
Service Company

....

Fill this out if you have a service business.

Economics of One Unit

Note: A service unit is typically defined as one hour of service or one job.

Define your unit: _____

_____

_____

Selling price per unit $_____ **A**

Cost of services sold per unit

(Cost of producing one additional unit must include both your labor and supplies.)

Labor

What value are you placing on your
entrepreneurial time per hour? $_____ **B**

How long does it take to perform your service
(in hours)? $_____ **C**

Labor cost per unit = B × C $_____ **D**

Supplies

What is the supply cost per customer? $_____ **E**

Cost of services sold per unit = D + E $_____ **F**

Gross profit per unit = A − F $_____ **G**

Selling Price per Unit	−	Cost of Services Sold per Unit	=	Gross Profit per Unit
A	−	F	=	G

Name_____ Business_____ Date_____

Market Research

....

Competition

Ask two people these questions about your business and write their answers in the space provided:

Do you like the name of my business?

#1 _____

#2 _____

What do you think of my logo?

#1 _____

#2 _____

Where would you want to go to buy my product?

#1 _____

#2 _____

Do you think my product/service has value?

#1 _____

#2 _____

How much would you pay for my product?

#1 _____

#2 _____

How would you improve my business idea?

#1 _____

#2 _____

Who is my closest competitor(s)?

#1 _____

#2 _____

Do you think my product/service is better or worse than that offered by my competitor(s)?

#1 _____

#2 _____

Why is your product/service going to beat the competition?

_____

_____

_____

_____

_____

_____

Below is a sample strategy for a manufacturing, wholesale, retail, or service company. Can you add other locations or methods of selling?

MARKETING PLAN LOCATIONS (WHERE TO SELL)

S E L L I N G M E T H O D S		Door to Door	Flea Markets	School/ Church Functions	Street (Street Vendors)	Through Local Stores	Your Own Home	Other
	Business Cards							
	Posters							
	Flyers							
	Phone							
	Sales Calls							
	Brochure							
	Mailings							
	Other							

Legal Structure

....

Is your business a sole proprietorship, a partnership, a regular corporation, a subchapter S corporation, or a not-for-profit corporation?

_____

_____

Explain your decision:

_____

_____

How much will you be paying for legal fees?

Explain: _____

_____

_____

What permits and/or licenses will you need for your business?

_____

_____

_____

What are the names, addresses, and phone numbers of the local official(s) in charge of the permits and licensing you need?

Name	Address	Phone

Name_____ **Business**_____ **Date**_____

Start-Up Costs   (These are the items you need to earn your first dollar of sales.)
....

What are your estimated start-up costs? Itemize:

Item	Where Will You Buy This?	Cost
_____	_____	_____
_____	_____	_____
_____	_____	_____
_____	_____	_____
_____	_____	_____
_____	_____	_____

Estimated Total Start-up Costs   _____

List your sources of financing below. Indicate with a check mark whether each source is offering equity, debt, or a gift.

	Amount	Equity (Investment)	Debt (Loan)	Gift
Personal Savings:	_____	_____	_____	_____
Relatives:	_____	_____	_____	_____
Friends:	_____	_____	_____	_____
Investors:	_____	_____	_____	_____
Grant:	_____	_____	_____	_____
Other:	_____	_____	_____	_____
Total:	_____	_____	_____	_____

If you receive equity financing, what percentage of ownership will you give up? _____

If you receive debt financing, what is the maximum interest rate you will pay? _____

Operating Costs (Fixed & Variable)

Monthly Fixed Costs

Monthly Operating Costs include USAIIR: utilities, salaries, advertising, interest, insurance, and rent. In a small business, many operating costs are usually fixed, although a few may be variable, depending on your business.

Type of Fixed Costs	Monthly Fixed Cost
_____	_____
_____	_____
_____	_____
Monthly Fixed Costs	_____

Variable Costs

(Estimate those operating costs (USAIIR) that fluctuate with sales and cannot be directly assigned to a unit of sale. Example: utilities = 1% of sales.)

Type of Variable Costs	Estimated Variable Cost as a % of Sales
_____	_____
_____	_____
_____	_____
Estimated Variable Costs as a % of sales	_____%

Remember . . . to get total monthly variable costs you must multiply variable cost as a percentage of sales by total monthly sales. Note: you may set variable costs equal to zero.

Monthly Budget: Projected Income Statement for a Manufacturing, Wholesale, Retail, or Service Company

	Jan	Feb	Mar	Apr	May	Jun	Jul	Aug	Sep	Oct	Nov	Dec	Total
Units Sold													
Unit Selling Price													
Total Sales													
Cost of Goods or Services Sold per Unit													
Total Cost of Goods or Services Sold													
Gross Profit													
Fixed Costs													
Variable Costs													
Total Operating Costs													
Profit/(Loss) before Taxes													

Less Taxes (25%, Estimated) _____

Net Profit _____

Total Sales = Units Sold × Unit Selling Price

Total Cost of Goods or Services Sold = Units Sold × Cost of Goods or Services Sold per Unit

Gross Profit = Total Sales − Total Cost of Goods or Services Sold

Variable Costs = Multiply Variable Costs as a % of Sales by Sales

Operating Costs = Fixed Costs + Variable Costs

Profit/(Loss) = Gross Profit − Operating Costs

Taxes = Profit × .25

Name_____ Business_____ Date_____

Budgeted Yearly Income Statement for a Manufacturing, Wholesale, Retail, or Service Business

Sales	Amount	
Units Sold	_____	
Unit Selling Price	_____	
Total Sales	_____	Total Sales = Units Sold × Unit Selling Price

Costs	Amount	
Cost of Goods or Services Sold per Unit	_____	
Total Cost of Goods or Services Sold	_____	Total Cost of Goods or Services Sold = Units Sold × Cost of Goods or Services Sold per Unit
Gross Profit	_____	Gross Profit = Total Sales − Total Cost of Goods or Services Sold
Fixed Expenses	_____	
Variable Costs	_____	Variable Costs = Variable Costs as a % of Sales × Sales
Operating Costs	_____	Operating Costs = Fixed Costs + Variable Costs

Profit	Amount	
Profit/(Loss) before Taxes	_____	Profit/(Loss) = Gross Profit − Operating Expenses
Less Taxes (25%, Estimated)	_____	Taxes = Profit × .25
Net Profit	_____	Net Profit = Profit − Taxes
Net Profit per Unit	_____	Net Profit per Unit = $\dfrac{\text{Net Profit}}{\text{Units Sold}}$

EPILOGUE

I hope this book will help you to understand and apply the simple concepts of entrepreneurship to your life. It has been a great joy for me to teach entrepreneurship. I have watched my students succeed in business and develop mental strength and self-esteem.

I've always encouraged my students to memorize the poem "Invictus" by William Ernest Henley. It expresses, better than I ever could, my belief that knowing how to start and operate a small business will make you master of your own fate.

Invictus

Out of the night that covers me,
Black as the pit from pole to pole,
I thank whatever gods may be
For my unconquerable soul.

In the fell clutch of circumstance
I have not winced nor cried aloud:
Under the bludgeonings of chance
My head is bloody, but unbowed.

Beyond this place of wrath and tears
Looms but the Horror of the shade,
And yet the menace of the years
Finds and shall find me unafraid.

It matters not how strait the gate,
How charged with punishments the scroll,
I am the master of my fate:
I am the captain of my soul.

William Ernest Henley

GLOSSARY

asset   any item of value owned by a business. Cash, inventory, furniture, and machinery are examples of assets. **Ch. 1**

audit   a formal study of accounts conducted by the Internal Revenue Service to determine whether the taxpayer being investigated is paying appropriate taxes. **Ch. 20**

balance   1. the difference between the credit and the debit side of a ledger; also, the difference between the assets and liabilities sides of a financial statement. 2. to calculate such differences; to settle an account by paying debts; to keep books properly so credit and debit sides of an account equal each other. **Ch. 6**

bankrupt   the condition of a business that is unable to pay its bills. A business declared legally bankrupt may have its property confiscated by the courts and divided up among its creditors. **Ch. 1**

business   the buying and selling of goods and services in order to make a profit. **Ch. 1**

capital   money or property owned or used in business. **Ch. 1**

cash flow   cash receipts less cash disbursements over a period of time. Cash flow is represented by the cash balance in an accounting journal or ledger. **Ch. 6**

checking account   a bank account against which the account holder can write checks. Some banks pay interest on checking accounts that maintain a minimum balance. **Ch. 19**

compromise   a settlement in which each side has given in on some demands. **Ch. 5**

consumer   a person or business that buys goods and services for its own needs, not for resale or to use to produce goods and services for resale. **Ch. 2**

copyright   exclusive right to a literary, dramatic, musical, or artistic work or to the use of a commercial print or label, as granted by law. **Ch. 14**

corporation   a legal "person" or entity" that is composed of stockholders, is granted the right to buy, sell, and inherit possessions, and is legally liable for the entity's actions. **Ch. 15**

Ch. = Chapter (chapter numbers show where glossary word first appears).

cost   an expense; the amount of money, time, or energy spent on something. **Ch. 7**

cost of goods sold   the cost of selling one additional unit. **Ch. 7**

credit   in bookkeeping, a recording of income. **Ch. 6**

creditor   a person who extends credit or to whom money is owed. **Ch. 1**

customer service   the maintenance and servicing of a product once it has been sold; the act of keeping customers happy and loyal to one's business. **Ch. 15**

debit   in bookkeeping, a recording of an expense. **Ch. 6**

debt   an obligation or liability to pay back a loan. **Ch. 17**

debt ratio   the ratio of debt to assets. **Ch. 17**

debt-to-equity ratio   a financial ratio that expresses the financial strategy of a company by showing how much of the company is financed by debt and how much by equity. **Ch. 17**

deduction   expenses incurred during the course of doing business. A business owner may subtract deductible amounts from income when figuring income tax due. **Ch. 6**

demand   the desire for a commodity together with the ability to pay for it; the amount consumers are ready and able to buy at all the prices in the market. **Ch. 3**

demographics   population statistics. **Ch. 13**

Dow Jones Averages   three averages of stock market prices that represent how well the stock market (and, therefore, the economy) is performing. The three averages comprise: (1) thirty industrial stocks, (2) twenty transportation stocks, (3) fifteen utility stocks. **Ch. 10**

employee   a person hired by a business to work for wages or salary. **Ch. 1**

endorsement   signature on the back of a check that renders it payable. **Ch. 19**

entrepreneur   a person who organizes and manages a business, assuming the risk for the sake of the potential return. **Ch. 1**

equity   ownership in a company received in exchange for money invested in the company. In accounting, equity is equal to assets minus liabilities. **Ch. 15, 17**

expense   cost of doing business. **Ch. 6**

file   when referring to taxes: to fulfill one's legal obligation by mailing a tax return, and any taxes due, to the Internal Revenue Service or state or local tax authority. **Ch. 20**

finance   to raise money for a business. **Ch. 17**

fixed costs business expenses that must be paid whether or not any sales are being generated; USAIIR: utilities, salaries, advertising, insurance, interest, and rent. **Ch. 7**

franchise a business that markets a product or service developed by the franchisor, in the manner specified by the franchisor. **Ch. 21**

franchisee owner of a franchise unit or units. **Ch. 21**

franchisor person who develops a franchise or a company that sells franchises. **Ch. 21**

free enterprise system economic system in which businesses are privately owned and operate relatively free of government interference. **Ch. 3**

gross total or entire amount before deductions, as opposed to net. **Ch. 7**

gross profit total sales revenue minus total cost of goods sold. **Ch. 7**

immigrant a person who settles in a new country or region, having left his or her country or region of birth. **Ch. 4**

incentive something that motivates a person to take action—to work, start a business, or study harder, for example. **Ch. 20**

income money received from the sale of products or services, from a job or gift, or from a deferred payment fund such as a trust, annuity, or pension. **Ch. 6**

income statement a financial statement that summarizes income and expense activity over a specified period and shows net profit or less. **Ch. 8**

infringe to violate a copyright, trademark, or patent. **Ch. 14**

insolvent the condition of a business that is unable to pay its bills. **Ch. 1**

interest payment for using someone else's money; payment you receive for lending someone your money. **Ch. 9**

interest rate money paid for the use of money, expressed as a percentage per unit of time. **Ch. 9**

Internal Revenue Service the federal government bureau in charge of taxation. **Ch. 20**

investment something into which one puts money, time, or energy with the hope of gaining profit or satisfaction, in spite of any risk involved. **Ch. 9**

investor person who purchases securities or puts money into a business venture in hopes of earning a satisfactory return. **Ch. 9**

invoice an itemized list of goods delivered or services rendered and the amount due; a bill. **Ch. 6**

keystone to buy an item wholesale and sell it for twice the wholesale price; to double one's money. **Ch. 1**

leveraged financed with debt, not equity. **Ch. 17**

liable   responsible for any lawsuits that arise from accidents, unpaid bills, faulty merchandise, or other business problems. **Ch. 15**

license   (1) authorization by law to do some specified thing (2) to grant the right to use the licensor's name on a product or service. **Ch. 21**

licensee   person granted the right to use the licensor's name on a product or service sold by the licensee. **Ch. 21**

licensor   person who sells the right to use his or her name or company name to a licensee; unlike the franchisor, the licensor does not attempt to dictate exactly how the licensee does business. **Ch. 21**

liquidity   the ease with which an investment can be converted into cash. **Ch. 9**

management   the art of planning and organizing a business so it can meet its goals. **Ch. 15**

manufacturing   the activity of a business that makes or produces a tangible product. **Ch. 15**

market   a group of people interested in buying a product or service; any situation or designated location where trade occurs. **Ch. 1**

market clearing price   the price at which the amount of a product or service demanded equals the amount the supplier is willing to supply at that price; the price at which the supply and demand curves cross. Also called "equilibrium price." **Ch. 3**

middleman   descriptive often substituted for "wholesaler"; a trader who buys commodities from the producer or wholesaler and sells them to the retailer. **Ch. 15**

monopoly   a market with only one producer; the control of the pricing and distribution of a product or service in a given market as a result of lack of competition. **Ch. 3**

negotiation   discussing or bargaining in an effort to reach agreement between parties with differing goals. **Ch. 5**

net   final result; in business, the profit or loss remaining after all costs have been subtracted. **Ch. 8**

notary public   person authorized to witness and certify the signing of documents. **Ch. 16**

operating cost   each cost necessary to operate a business, not including cost of goods sold. Operating costs can almost always be divided into USAIIR: utilities, salaries, advertising, insurance, interest, and rent. Operating costs are also called "overhead." **Ch. 7**

optimist   a person who consistently looks on the bright side of situations or outcomes. **Ch. 4**

overhead the continuing fixed costs of running a business; the costs a business has to pay just to have a place from which to operate. **Ch. 7**

partnership an association of two or more partners in a business enterprise. **Ch. 15**

patent an exclusive right to produce, use, and sell an invention or process. **Ch. 14**

percentage literally, "a given part of every hundred" or "out of one hundred"; a number expressed as part of a whole, with the whole represented as 100 percent. **Ch. 9**

perseverance the ability to keep trying, even when that effort is difficult. **Ch. 4**

principal the amount of a debt or loan before interest is added. **Ch. 17**

privatization the transfer of ownership of a government-owned business to a private owner. **Ch. 3**

product something that is made by nature, human industry, or art and is sold on the market. **Ch. 2**

profit the sum remaining after all costs are deducted from the income of a business. **Ch. 1**

profit and loss statement an income statement, showing the gain and loss from business transactions and summarizing the net profit or loss. **Ch. 8**

profit per unit the selling price minus the cost of goods sold of an item. **Ch. 7**

promissory note a written promise to pay a certain sum of money on or before a specified date. **Ch. 17**

prototype a model or pattern that serves as an example of how a product would look and operate if it were manufactured. **Ch. 14**

public domain free of copyright or patent restrictions. **Ch. 14**

rate of return the return on an investment, expressed as a percentage of the amount invested. **Ch. 9**

receipt a written acknowledgment that goods or services have been received; includes the date and amount of purchase. **Ch. 6**

resource something that can be used to make something else or to fill a need. **Ch. 1**

retail (1) to buy from a wholesaler or manufacturer and sell directly to the consumer; (2) the goods sold to a consumer by a retailer. **Ch. 1**

return on investment profit on an investment, expressed as a percentage of the investment. **Ch. 9**

revenue money earned by a business from sales of products or services. **Ch. 2**

risk   the chance of loss. **Ch. 9**

royalty   a share of the proceeds of the sale of a product paid to a person who owns a copyright; also refers to fee paid to a franchisor or licensor. **Ch. 21**

sales tax   tax levied on items that are sold by businesses to consumers. States raise revenue through sales tax. **Ch. 20**

savings account   a bank account in which money is deposited and on which the bank pays interest to the depositor. **Ch. 19**

service   intangible work providing time, skills, or expertise in exchange for money. **Ch. 2**

share   a single unit of stock in a corporation. **Ch. 9**

sole proprietorship   a business owned by one person. The owner receives all profits and is legally liable for all debts or lawsuits arising from the business. **Ch. 15**

start-up costs   the expenses involved in getting a business started; also called the original investment. **Ch. 8**

statistics   facts collected and presented in a numerical fashion. **Ch. 13**

stock   an individual's share in the ownership of a corporation, based on how much he or she has invested in the corporation. **Ch. 9**

stock market   market where shares of stock are traded. **Ch. 9**

supply   the amount of a product or service made available by sellers. **Ch. 3**

tax   a percentage of a business's gross profit or an individual's income taken by the government to support public services. **Ch. 20**

tax evasion   deliberate avoidance of the obligation to pay taxes; may lead to penalties or even jail. **Ch. 20**

tax-exempt   the condition of an entity that is allowed to produce income sheltered from taxation. **Ch. 15**

test the market   to offer a product or service to a very limited, yet representative, segment of consumers in order to receive customer feedback and improve the product or service as necessary, before attempting to sell it in a larger market. **Ch. 14**

trademark   any word, name, symbol, or device used by a manufacturer or merchant to distinguish a product from a competitor's. **Ch. 12**

tradeoff   an exchange in which one benefit or advantage is given up in order to gain another. **Ch. 1**

variable cost   any cost that changes based on the volume of units sold; sometimes used instead of "cost of goods sold." **Ch. 7**

venture   a business enterprise in which there is a danger of loss as well as a chance for profit. **Ch. 1**

venture capital   funds invested in a potentially profitable business enterprise despite risk of loss. **Ch. 22**

venture capitalist   investor who provides venture capital for a business; typically expects a high rate of return and equity in exchange for capital investment. **Ch. 22**

wholesaler   a business that purchases goods in bulk from the manufacturer and sells smaller quantities to retailers. **Ch. 1**

NOTES

Chapter 1

1 *Individualism and Economic Order* by Friedrich A. Hayek (Chicago: The University of Chicago Press, 1948).
2 Sources: Small Business Administration, 1990; U.S. Census, 1990.
3 With thanks to The National Federation of Independent Business, *The Entrepreneurs Series,* 1983.

Chapter 2

1 Adapted from the *Master Curriculum Guide: Economics and Entrepreneurship,* edited by John Clow et al. (New York: Joint Council on Economic Education, 1991).

Chapter 3

1 The Jane Hirsh story came from *Enterprising Women: Lessons from 100 of the Greatest Entrepreneurs of Our Day* by A. David Silver (New York: American Management Association, 1994).
2 See *Master Curriculum Guide: Economics and Entrepreneurship,* edited by John Clow et al. (New York: Joint Council on Economic Education, 1991), for an excellent discussion of supply and demand.
3 The MCI story is told in *Entrepreneurial Megabucks: The 100 Greatest Entrepreneurs of the Last Twenty-Five Years* by A. David Silver (New York: John Wiley & Sons, Inc., 1985).
4 *Capitalism, Socialism and Democracy* by Joseph Schumpeter (New York: Harper & Row, 1942).
5 For the story of James Sharp and other young entrepreneurs, see *Fast Cash for Kids,* 2nd Edition, by Bonnie and Noel Drew (Hawthorne, NJ: Career Press, 1995).

Chapter 4

1 From *Dave's Way* by David Thomas (New York: G.P. Putnam's Sons, 1991).
2 With thanks to Joseph Mancuso, founder of the Center for Entrepreneurial Management.

3 Adapted from The National Federation of Independent Business, *The Entrepreneurs Series,* 1983.

Chapter 5

1 Details of the Microsoft–IBM negotiations are taken from *Gates* by Stephen Manes and Paul Andrews (New York: Touchstone Press, 1994), and *Hard Drive: Bill Gates and the Making of the Microsoft Empire* by James Wallace and Jim Erickson (New York: HarperBusiness, 1993).

2 With thanks to Joseph Mancuso.

Chapter 7

1 The story of Jacoby & Meyers was drawn from *Enterprising Women: Lessons from 100 of the Greatest Entrepreneurs of Our Day* by A. David Silver (New York: American Management Association, 1994).

Chapter 8

1 For the story of Charles Schwab and others, see *Entrepreneurial Megabucks: The 100 Greatest Entrepreneurs of the Last Twenty-Five Years* by A. David Silver (New York: John Wiley & Sons, Inc., 1985).

Chapter 9

1 With thanks to NFTE teacher Frank Kennedy.

2 Adapted by NFTE teacher Jack Hemphill from *Common Sense: A Simple Plan for Financial Independence* (10th revision) by Art Williams (Minneapolis: Park Lane Publishers, Inc., 1991).

Chapter 10

1 Adapted from materials prepared by *The Wall Street Journal* and Dow-Jones Co.

Chapter 11

1 Special thanks to Bart Breighner, president of Artistic Impressions, and to NFTE teacher Glenn Swanson for this acronym.

Chapter 12

1 From *Have You Got What It Takes?: How to Tell If You Should Start Your Own Business* by Joseph Mancuso (Englewood Cliffs, NJ: Prentice-Hall, 1982).

Chapter 14

1 Special thanks to Sylvia Stein, co-founder of Consumer Eyes, Inc., for the ideas in this chapter.

Chapter 16

1 From an article by Rita Ciolli in *New York Newsday,* July 6, 1995.

Chapter 17

1 *Forbes* magazine, May 1989.

Chapter 18

1 The Sue Scott story is from *Enterprising Women: Lessons from 100 of the Greatest Entrepreneurs of Our Day* by David Silver (New York: American Management Association, 1994).

Chapter 19

1 See *How to Get a Business Loan Without Signing Your Life Away* by Joseph Mancuso (Englewood Cliffs: Prentice-Hall, 1990) for more helpful hints on how to develop a great relationship with a banker.

ABOUT THE NATIONAL FOUNDATION FOR TEACHING ENTREPRENEURSHIP

The National Foundation for Teaching Entrepreneurship, Inc. (NFTE) is a nonprofit organization founded in 1987. Its mission is to introduce young people—including at-risk youth, the physically challenged, and those in detention—to the world of business and entrepreneurship. In partnership with academic partners such as the University Community Outreach Program, Babson College, Columbia University, The Wharton School at the University of Pennsylvania, and corporate partners such as Koch Industries and Artistic Impressions, NFTE (pronounced "nifty") presently conducts entrepreneurship programs in fourteen American cities. Through licensing agreements, NFTE is also developing entrepreneurship programs in other countries.

NFTE teaches young people, through hands-on experience, to start and operate their own small businesses. We believe that many young people have extraordinary potential for business success and possess many of the characteristics of successful entrepreneurs, such as mental toughness, the willingness to take risks, resiliency, and sales ability. We also believe that each young person has unique knowledge about his or her market that can be a competitive advantage. These beliefs have been proven correct many times over by the enthusiasm and success of NFTE's young entrepreneurs.

By teaching business through demystifying, hands-on experience, NFTE seeks to encourage the economic participation of young people in their local communities as well as in society at large. Through their entrepreneurial initiatives, they can begin to make changes in their lives and their neighborhoods.

NFTE's "product" is a business-literate young entrepreneur who has experienced buying and selling in the marketplace and keeping accurate financial records. The larger goal, however, is to help renew the spirit of enterprise in America's inner cities through cutting-edge youth training, teacher training, curriculum research and development, and public education forums.

NFTE Products

As an educational nonprofit foundation, NFTE produces a variety of products for young entrepreneurs. All proceeds from the sale of the products described below go to support its programs.

The NFTE "Core" Curriculum: *How to Start and Operate a Small Business: A Guide for the Young Entrepreneur* by Steve Mariotti and Tony Towle. This three-module, fifty-chapter course in entrepreneurship for classroom use is the foundation of NFTE's programs. It provides a thorough guide to entrepreneurship complete with exercises and the NFTE business plan workbook, and is widely viewed as the standard in high school entrepreneurship education.

Entrepreneurs in Profile by Steve Mariotti and Jenny Rosenbaum is a collection of fascinating profiles of outstanding entrepreneurs from a wide variety of backgrounds. Included are current favorites among young people such as Spike Lee, Russell Simmons, and Anita Roddick, as well as historically important entrepreneurs such as King C. Gillette and Henry Ford.

The NFTE BizBag™ is a great asset for any young entrepreneur. This attractive black canvas shoulder bag contains the NFTE "Core" Curriculum, *Entrepreneurs in Profile,* a calculator, memo pad, receipt book, watch, record-keeping book, and deluxe datebook.

NFTE Programs

NFTE runs entrepreneurship educational programs in partnership with schools and youth-service organizations. The programs range from weekly after-school seminars, to intensive in-school classes, to summer BizCamps™. We train teachers and youth-service workers in the NFTE curriculum and offer a wide variety of participation options, including organization and city-wide licenses. For more information on any of its products, to inquire about making a tax-deductible contribution, or bringing the NFTE to your community, please contact the national headquarters at:

The National Foundation for Teaching Entrepreneurship, Inc.
120 Wall Street, 29th Floor
New York, NY 10005
(212) 232-3333.
Fax (212) 232-2244

ACKNOWLEDGMENTS

I would like to thank my writing partners, Tony Towle, who from NFTE's very beginning helped me organize my thoughts and experiences, and Debra DeSalvo, without whose gift for organization and rewriting, this book would never have been possible. I am also grateful to literary agent Jeff Herman, for introducing me to our editor at Random House, John Mahaney, and his assistant, Eleanor Wickland, who have helped us take this book to another level. I would also like to acknowledge the large contribution by New York Metro director Chris Meenan and NFTE Northern California director Duane Moyer, who, along with NFTE teachers Juan Casimiro and Kevin Wortham, provided invaluable field testing of NFTE's curriculum as it developed. NFTE divisional directors Cindy Kelley, Julie Silard, Kevin Greaney, and Kari Davis have also had a profound impact on this book via their helpful suggestions and work in the field.

In addition, I want to thank my brother, Jack, the best CPA I know, and my father, John, for financing much of NFTE's early work and for their continuing love and guidance. I'd also like to acknowledge my colleague on NFTE's Executive Committee, Mike Caslin, for bringing organization and discipline to the field of entrepreneurship education and for invaluable counsel in building our organization and helping me learn the finer points of vision and leadership. I also look forward to continuing to work with Maximo Blake, who is helping to fulfill NFTE's dream of building student business incubators. Thanks are due, also, to Alaire Mitchell for her educational expertise; to Peter Eisen for helping me get the accounting sections "right"; and to all the other teachers, students, experts, and friends who were kind enough to review this book and help me improve it.

I'd also like to thank Jenny Rosenbaum for helping me write many of the profiles of entrepreneurs that are included in this book (and are adapted from our book *Entrepreneurs in Profile*). Thanks, also, to Howard Stevenson, Jeff Timmons, and Bill Bygraves for their academic and business expertise; my first three students—Vincent Wilkins, Josephine Reneau, and Howard Stubbs; and Lisa Hoffstein, executive director of the University Community Outreach Program, who gave us our first contract and has been instrumental in NFTE's development. The efforts of Richard Fink of Koch Industries, Michie Slaughter of the Marion Kauffman Foundation, Verne Harnish of the Young Entrepreneur's Organization, and Jean Thorne, Mike Hennessy, and John Hughes of the Coleman Foundation, Inc. have also been crucial to NFTE's development. I also greatly appreciate the efforts of Jim Holden, Al Abney, Joe Dolan, Andrew Sherman, Bella Frankel, and Jack Stack from NFTE's national board, and the guidance provided by our national advisory board's executive committee: William Crerend, Ted Forstmann, Bernie Goldhirsh, Jack Kemp, Elizabeth Koch, Alan Patricof, Ray Chambers, and Jeff Raikes.

I also want to thank visionary entrepreneurial philanthropists including: Vicky and Max Kennedy, The Scaife Family Foundation, The Heinz Endowments, James H. Herbert, Jr. and The First Republic Bancorp, The W. H. Donner Foundation, The W. K. Kellogg Foundation, The R. K. Mellon Foundation, The Clark Foundation, The New York Community Trust, The J. M. Kaplan Fund, and a number of anonymous donors.

Finally, I want to thank my mother, Nancy, a wonderful special-education teacher who taught me that one great teacher affects eternity; my friends and mentors, Ray Chambers, John Whitehead, and Marilyn Kourilsky; Gloria Appel, for funding NFTE teacher training and being a good friend; Julian Robertson, Tref Wolcott, and John Griffin of the Tiger Foundation for funding NFTE's research project; and Clara Del Villar, Laurel Skurko, Ken Dillard, Cynthia Miree, Peter Janssen, Elizabeth Wright, Andrea Leavitt, Christine Chambers, Janet McKinstry Cort, and Dilia Wood who provided so many insights into how to encourage children to become business-literate.

Steve Mariotti

INDEX